The Rhetoric of Renaissance Poetry
From Wyatt to Milton

The Annunciation
By the Master of the Retable of the Reyes Católicos
(Spanish, School of Valladolid, active 15th century).
See Chapter 10.

The Rhetoric
of
Renaissance Poetry

From Wyatt to Milton

Edited by

THOMAS O. SLOAN

and

RAYMOND B. WADDINGTON

UNIVERSITY OF CALIFORNIA PRESS

Berkeley · Los Angeles · London

University of California Press, Berkeley and Los Angeles, California
University of California Press, Ltd., London, England
Copyright © 1974, by The Regents of the University of California
ISBN 0–520–02501–6
Library of Congress Catalog Card Number: 73–80824
Printed in the United States of America
Designed by Dave Comstock

Contents

Acknowledgments

T HE EDITORS gratefully acknowledge the assistance of Mrs. Wanda Schultz, E. David Cronon, Charles T. Scott, Andrew R. Weiner, Eric Skjei, and Kent Kessinger. The editors also wish to thank the Fine Arts Museum of San Francisco for permission to reprint "The Annunciation" and M. Knoedler & Co., Inc., for permission to reprint "Rhetorica" and "Poesia"; and Edizioni D'Arte il Fiorino di A. & R. Senatori for permission to reprint "Rhetorica" from the *Tomb of Pope Sixtus, IV*.

Introduction

> For when God shakes a kingdom with strong and heartful commotions to a general reforming, it is not untrue that many sectaries and false teachers are then busiest in seducing; yet more true it is that God then raises to his own work men of rare abilities and more than common industry, not only to look back and revise what hath been taught heretofore, but to gain further and go on some new enlightened steps in the discovery of truth. (*Areopagitica*)

MILTON'S PROPOSITION that the abundance of sects and schisms signifies a condition of strength not weakness may legitimately apply to lesser skirmishes in the wars of Truth than the one he had in mind. Doubtless most academic disciplines undergo a standard evolutionary process—first primary exploration, then consolidation and refinement, and finally reaction, reform, and exploration of new directions. In the past thirty years the study of rhetoric in relation to Renaissance English poetry has undergone just such a process. And the essays in this book suggest that we are beyond the period of consolidation and well into the "commotions" of reform.

The general importance of rhetorical study to this poetry now seems thoroughly accepted. By compiling the essays in this volume the editors hope to represent the kind of work actively being done by younger scholars and to forecast by example some of the directions which this work will take in years to come. To this end the editors decided to include no essay which had been published previously in any form and to assign no topics to their contributors, maintaining instead a general consistency with the methodology and with the chronological scope from Wyatt to Milton. This editorial decision has resulted in certain imbalances and omissions (e.g., there should be more attention devoted to narrative and philosophical poetry; no essays on Jonson and on Marvell are included). But the vigor and intellectual engagement of the collection appear to justify the decision and to more than offset the omissions.

The tone of the collection is a contentious one, sometimes bordering on the outright polemical. The authors challenge received opinion, champion causes in distress, chide their elders and fellows for errors of commission and omission. Indeed, the reader may notice with a certain amount of amusement that, amid all this healthy disagreement, the inevitable occurs: several contributors discussing the same question will arrive at several different answers. This should surprise no one, least of all the authors represented in these pages. If they arrive at different answers to common questions, they are united in their belief that the understanding of Renaissance poetry requires painstaking attention to intellectual and literary traditions. And they are equally united in the conviction that the awareness of such contexts must not be permitted to substitute for critical sensitivity to the poems per se.

A number of common concerns emerge from the volume. One overriding concern, perhaps surprisingly, is with what could be termed the limits of rhetorical criticism. There is a distinct feeling that too much rhetorical criticism has been of an external and rather mechanical nature, contenting itself with glossing figures and tropes from the rhetorical handbooks or merely labeling the divisions of a poem with the parts of an oration. The present writers choose to emphasize that, however closely Renaissance poets followed rhetorical theory or the precepts of the rhetorical handbooks, they never forgot the difference between poems and orations. Nor should their critics. Consequently there are efforts to define and respect the necessary areas of interpretation beyond the directly rhetorical. Others in the group would have us recognize that rhetorical theory, like world communism, is not a monolithic entity. Classical rhetoric, therefore, will often be inadequate or misleading for understanding the rhetorical strategems of Renaissance poetry. Indeed, in the century under scrutiny Renaissance rhetorical theory undergoes a number of significant changes, impelling the need for more precise critical discriminations and even recognition that frustrated poets sometimes turned away from rhetoric for theoretical justification. Still other writers wish us to see that too much existing rhetorical analysis has focused narrowly, often simply on the epideictic genres, ignoring other kinds of poetry and other modes which are less self-evidently rhetorical.

Several essays dealing with sixteenth-century poets share a common interest of trying to isolate the particular identity of the Renaissance lyric—what differentiates it from its medieval predecessors, what are its characteristic structures, preoccupations, modes. Other essays direct themselves to describing and explaining the phenomenon, emerging in the late sixteenth century, of the poetic strategy which places the poem's real audience in an overheard relationship to its discourse, the private voice of direct thought captured. While one finds here the predictable—and necessary—attention to organizational principles, to style and word-play, to imagery, metaphor, and allegory, the editors find it significant that these matters are not ends, but means to such broader issues as the projected speaker-audience relationship, the "rhetorical situation." As a consequence, our writers direct themselves to the description of speaker's voice; to the definition of audience, both fictive and real; and, capitalizing upon the recent critical concern with "reader's response," to the way in which the rhetoric of these poems directly involves the reader in the formulation of their meanings.

Finally, we might note that rhetoric is not treated as an end, but consistently related to such humane and philosophic concerns as ethics and morality, epistemology and ontology. However, as we implied earlier, there is a sense in which rhetorical criticism itself is our subject. During recent years when rhetorical criticism has become absorbed into the mainstream of literary studies, it has become increasingly unnecessary for the rhetorical critic to distinguish his work narrowly from other approaches. His uniqueness now is not simply acknowledged but accepted. He is thus free to employ a critical approach that is properly syncretic, which allows labels to be assigned according to emphasis and attitude rather than relying heavily on one analytic technique. That earlier narrow view which demanded that the rhetorical critic examine only the public features of a strongly didactic work has been superseded by a view that permits the rhetorical critic to examine even the more or less private relation of a poet to his poem. Of course such an examination might begin and end with the means whereby that relation becomes publicly accessible through the use of conventions and expectations in the poet's audience. But this public accessibility remains only a single and simple distinguishing mark of rhetorical criticism. More to our purpose, we invite the reader who seeks to learn something about rhetorical criticism to look about him, for the rhetorician's emphasis, attitude, and methods are everywhere to be found in these essays.

The essays are presented in a chronological order determined by the dates of the authors and poems to which they are devoted. The two exceptions to this pattern are the first and last essays, which range over the entire period, thus providing a larger perspective within which the particular issues raised by the more specialized essays may be considered. While undoubtedly some few readers will perceive this collection of authors as seductive "false teachers," the editors firmly believe that they have found "men of rare abilities and more than common industry," who not only "revise what hath been taught heretofore" but gain "some new enlightened steps." We hope the majority of our readers will agree.

1. The Poet as Orator:
One Phase of His Judicial Pose

JOHN T. SHAWCROSS

CITY UNIVERSITY OF NEW YORK, STATEN ISLAND

1

WHILE HISTORICAL scholarship has recognized the importance of rhetoric to literature during the English Renaissance, it has insufficiently understood the significance of a poet's employment of rhetorical stance. The rhetor assumes a stance to achieve the aims of his oratory (or writing), and stance implies not the frequent modern blunder that literature is identical to the spontaneous, highly emotive, and directly candid personal experiences which have given rise to that literary expression, but instead it indicates that the orator has chosen a point of view, a strategy, a set of techniques or devices, perhaps specific language to enhance his chances for success. What such a statement predicates is a literature that is contrived, the result of the author's manipulation of theme, form, and writing techniques. Literature is cerebral, despite its emotionalism; it consists of artifacts, not pieces taken out of a rap session or a verbatim reaction to some stimulus. The boredom of Andy Warhol's film "Sleep" with its eight hours of film of a man sleeping is certainly a case in point. It is not art. The Renaissance saw the question as a dichotomy between nature and art. For me, the answer is not that nature is God's art and thus the highest art possible; rather the more viable answer is Richard Crashaw's in "Music's Duel": nature has limitations (the nightingale) but the art of man may achieve superiority over nature since the musician has the advantage of being able to employ nature to raise it to art.

The stances of the rhetor are three according to Aristotle in *De Rhetorica* (I, III.1–52; trans. W. Rhys Roberts): deliberative, forensic, and epideictic. The deliberative orator aimed at exhorting or dissuading his auditor to or from some course of action or thought (a futural context) by pointing out expediency or harmfulness. The forensic orator aimed at defending or accusing someone's course of action or thought (a preteritive context) by pointing out its justifiability or its unjustness. The epideictic orator aimed at praising or blaming someone or his actions or thought (a present context) by pointing out his honorableness or disgracefulness or such qualities in his actions or thought. All other points in any argument are "merely accessory" (I.i.1354a) or "subsidiary and relative to" (I.iii.1358b) the basic aim of the orator. Further, "persuasion must in every case be effected either (1) by working on the emotions of the judges themselves, (2) by giving them the right impression of the Speaker's character, or (3) by proving the truth of the statements made" (III.i.1403b).

The forensic mode therefore has these characteristics: it is based on past action or thought; such action is either justified or unjustified; the aim is not to get the auditor to do something, nor is it to praise or blame him or his action; its aim is to have the auditor agree that the past action is justified or unjustified; and this may be effected by working on the emotions of the auditor or by assuring the auditor of the orator's worthy character or by demonstrating the truth of an enthymeme (or syllogistic reasoning). The forensic orator, as in a court of law, may be appealing to a third party who is the judge of the action of the second party. Here the judge (or jury) is the auditor; he represents, as it were, public opinion of the action in question on the basis of the oration which the writer offers as persuasive evidence. The judgment, whether of a second or third party, will exonerate or condemn the action of either the first or the second party. In either case the context is public; it is not a matter kept exclusively between the orator and his auditor. The decision, it is hoped, will be that desired by the orator (cf. II.xviii.1391b). In addition Aristotle noted (III.xiii.1414a) that " 'narration' surely is part of a forensic speech only."

Apparently since it is so appropriate to a court of law, and usually considered only in such debating contexts, the forensic mode has—erroneously—been overlooked as significant for Renaissance poetry. Through a specific technique employed by the forensic orator (it does not appear in the deliberative or epideictic situation) I hope in this paper to demonstrate (1) that this technique, employed in various poems of the period, offers another approach to rhetorical analysis of literature, (2) that the forensic mode is employable in "creative" literature,

(3) that the poems employing this technique must be read differently from the way they usually are, and (4) that recognition of this mode of persuasion in poetry of the English Renaissance reinforces the view of the poet as maker, not poet as philosopher or poet as emotionalist. Awareness of the forensic pose of the poet will be, I believe, unavoidable, and this awareness in turn goes a long way in separating the lyric from the epic, from dramatic poetry, and from didactic poetry (like Thomas Tusser's, for example), and what is more important, from other kinds of poems which are often categorized under the catch-all word "lyric."

The forensic technique I shall examine is that of *distributio-recapitulatio*;[1] that is, the citing of a series of specific facts or arguments followed by a summing up or restating of these same facts or arguments in brief form. The lawyer in court often employs this technique: the specifics he cites derive from past actions on record or they are arguments of refutation of such past actions; he then reminds his audience of all these things which he has previously pointed out by restating them in brief form; the recital is a narration of those specifics which the lawyer wishes the judge or jury to consider in exonerating his client or in condemning the defendant. He will be persuasive if the elements of the narration strike the chords of the audience's emotions and if the summary appears to be a valid view of the situation. Almost certainly he must also assure his audience of his truthfulness and sincerity through delivery. The lawyer's address is fairly obviously selective of many specifics he might cite, and his arrangement of these specifics or their juxtaposition should lead to inferences on the part of his audience (whether valid or invalid). Such inferences complete the enthymeme which the orator has created. Selection and manipulation of audience seem evident when one watches a television lawyer operate, but for some reason the poet's selection and manipulation seem often to escape notice. The lawyer employs *distributio-recapitulatio* most prominently in his summing up of a case, and Aristotle's remarks on epi-

---

1. In "A Rhetorical Pattern in Renaissance and Baroque Poetry," *SRen* 3 (1956): 23–48, Joseph G. Fucilla discusses the *disseminative-recapitulative* poem. His concern is linguistic, and he therefore considers Sidney's sonnet beginning, "In wonted walks" (and a few other English authors and poems) because Sidney cites "rocks," "woods," "hills," "caves," "dales," "meads," and "brooks," and then repeats the seven items in lines 12–13. But this technique is not forensic, since it does not cite facts or arguments of past action on the part of the pleader or on the part of one acting against him. It is a linguistic device of words only. Fucilla does not mention any of the poems considered in this essay.

logues are therefore appropriate (III.xix.1419b): "You must (1) make the audience well-disposed towards yourself and ill-disposed towards your opponent, (2) magnify or minimize the leading facts, (3) excite the required state of emotion in your hearers, and (4) refresh their memories." One way to achieve these goals is "by following the natural order of the arguments as spoken" (III.xix.1420a). "For the conclusion," he adds, "the disconnected style of language is appropriate" (III.xix. 1420b).

A clear literary example using this rhetorical technique is Sir Thomas Wyatt's "Disdain me not":

> Disdain me not without desert,
> Nor leave me not so suddenly,
> Since well ye wot that in my heart
> I mean ye not but honestly.
>   Refuse me not without cause why,
> Nor think me not to be unjust,
> Since that by lot of fantasy
> This careful knot needs knit I must.
>   Mistrust me not, though some there be
> That fain would spot my steadfastness;
> Believe them not since that ye see
> The proof is not as they express.
>   Forsake me not till I deserve,
> Nor hate me not till I offend.
> Destroy me not till that I swerve.
> But since ye know what I intend,
>   Disdain me not that am your own;
> Refuse me not that am so true;
> Mistrust me not till all be known;
> Forsake me not ne for no new.[2]

Distributed through the first four stanzas are the arguments "Disdain me not" since I love you, "Refuse me not" since I give you no cause, "Mistrust me not" on the basis of others' reports, and "Forsake me not" until I give you cause. Recapitulated in stanza five are these same

---

2. Throughout this paper I have used standard texts of authors, when available, or sometimes original editions, and I have modernized as well as possible, since nothing is served here by "old-spelling" texts. However, versions of some poems do differ in various editions; for example, "Disdain me not" is often printed with a half line, repeating the opening imperative, added to each of the five stanzas. It does not really change my remarks, except that the addition of "Disdain me not" to the fifth stanza breaks a pattern of change within the poem, as pointed out later.

arguments in brief. The stance taken by the poet is certainly not epideictic, but neither is it deliberative, for no expediency or harmfulness
are advanced as evidence for exhorting or dissuading. The stance is
that of the forensic orator defending his course of action in the past
by pointing out the justifiability of his relations with the auditor or the
unjustness of the things that have been said against him. Like a lawyer pleading a case he cites "evidence" positive to himself ("Since well
ye wot that in my heart / I mean ye not but honestly," "Since that
by lot of fantasy / This careful knot needs knit I must"), but stresses
the rebuttal of evidence negative to himself. This rebuttal takes two
forms: it gives reasons why judgment on the part of the auditor should
not be negative toward him ("without desert," "without cause why,"
"till I deserve," "till I offend," "till that I swerve," "that am your own,"
"that am so true," "till all be known") and it points out the unreliability
of contrary evidence ("though some there be / That fain would spot my
steadfastness," "The proof is not as they express"). The poet selects
arguments which he hopes will manipulate his auditor to reach the
judgment he desires: "Forsake me not ne for no new."

The arguments are enthymemes; for example, "Disdain me not
without desert" really says:

A. If I am not honest with you, disdain me.

B. There is no evidence that I am not honest with you.

Therefore, C. Do not disdain me.

Or, "Mistrust me not, though some there be / That fain would spot
my steadfastness":

A. If I am not steadfast, mistrust me.

B. Some people have accused me of not being steadfast, but these people may not be trustworthy.

Therefore, C. Do not mistrust me since my lack of steadfastness
has not been proved.

The arguments, however, do not verify anything. They suggest and
raise questions and try to rebut, but the poet gives no hard evidence.
The plea is a manipulation of the auditor by words only; her emotions
are worked on, the validity of the opposing view is questioned, and,
most important, the poet presents himself as a maligned person—
neither groveling in repentance, nor condemnatory of others. The
character presented is the winning one of the unjustly accused, who
seeks the truth and implies that the truth will exonerate him. The plea
is basically, Don't trust what you've heard, for why should you distrust

me any more than you should distrust gossip? He becomes the falsely accused, but he is not arrogant and he does not fall into name-calling or the like. Whether there is desert or spots on his steadfastness, we know that the auditor is not—at this time at least—going to investigate further.

The poem really narrates what has occurred: stories have circulated about the poet's having fooled around with someone else and his lover has accused him to his face and has threatened to terminate their relationship. The poet's aim is to defend himself against these accusations, to justify himself and to point out the unjustness against him should the girl terminate their relationship. The narrative of the poem is totally preteritive. The auditor is the judge of whether he has refuted the case against himself. The substance of the poem is public: the poet talks of nothing which is personally private between the girl and him.

Wyatt is not necessarily reciting a "true" experience; he is not, surely, composing a poem that he expected to send to achieve his aims; and he is not merely giving an immediate ("sincere") reaction to a love problem. The arrangement of parts is chronological, and the refreshing of the auditor's memory (in stanza five) follows this order. The *recapitulatio* is effective because each of its parts is a single, unenjambed line (that is, "disconnected"), presented succinctly (thus magnifying what is stated and minimizing what is left out), allowing each part to sink into the auditor's mind more strikingly. There is a natural arrangement of the parts of the *distributio*: from the mere breaking of sympathetic relationship (disdain) to actual refusal of intercourse (the point, of course, in talking of "This careful knot")—these both implying briefer periods of nonrelationship—to general mistrust of all past (and, implied, present and future) action, to actual severing of their relationship—both a longer-lasting and then more final nonrelationship. The structure of the poem therefore also moves from more specific to more general, from ephemeral to final. The poem is not—as I suspect it most often has been read—exhortatory, and it evidences that the forensic mode is employable in poetry. What particularly is gained by such recognition is that we see the action of the poem as being in the past and it defines the tone of the orator as well as his aims in the poem. I thus read the poem quite differently from the way I first did some years ago. Of most note is the realization that the poem is not really asking the auditor to take a course of action but is rather presenting a case to be judged. Even though the verbs are given in the imperative, they do not exhort a specific futural action any more than the lawyer's summarizing statement, "Free this man, unjustly accused of these dastardly crimes; free this man and give the lie to the envious, the greedy, and the desecrators of truth in this world."

Perhaps it would be wise to compare a seemingly similar poem, but one which instead is built on the deliberative mode. I choose Wyatt's "Forget not yet":

> Forget not yet the tried intent
> Of such a truth as I have meant;
> My great travail so gladly spent
>   Forget not yet!
>
> Forget not yet when first began
> The weary life ye know, since whan
> The suit, the service, none tell can;
>   Forget not yet!
>
> Forget not yet the great assays,
> The cruel wrong, the scornful ways,
> The painful patience in denays,
>   Forget not yet!
>
> Forget not yet, forget not this,
> How long ago hath been, and is,
> The mind that never meant amiss,
>   Forget not yet!
>
> Forget not then thine own approved,
> The which so long hath thee so loved,
> Whose steadfast faith yet never moved;
>   Forget not this!

The poet is using the argument that in the past he has been true and loving and has done much for his lover. She should not forget these things, and if she does not forget these things, she will not forsake him. The aim is to persuade her future action as he desires it. He exhorts by using evidence of the past. The enthymeme is:

> A. I have shown my love and faith in these ways in the past.
>
> B. One owes the lover who is faithful continued love and faith.

Therefore, C. Do not alter our relationship.

The poet stresses by implication the harmfulness to him of breaking their relationship; he is not concerned with justifying his past actions. The tone of this orator is pleading; he throws himself on the mercy of his auditor. What is important for the poem is what will happen next.

The imperatives here are designed to influence the behavior of the auditor. They are always the same since that stresses the main argument: he has been loving and faithful in the past and those things should be rewarded in the future. They are examples of anaphora, not of a *distributio-recapitulatio* construction. There is no natural arrangement within the poem of the various elements which constitute the argument; they are simply a recitation of things of the past, drawn randomly from the abyss of the past. The deliberative orator is selective, but less manipulative than is the forensic orator. He tries to persuade by precept; if the precept (premise B above) is valid and cogently expressed, the chances are he will be successful in his aim. This is not necessarily so with the forensic orator who must overcome the fact or seeming fact of the past—and there it is much less the precept that is important than the angle of vision by which any precept may be viewed. It may be a wise precept that judgment should never entail capital punishment; but the precept alone is not going to control the decision in most criminal courts even today.

These two Wyatt poems illustrate subtle differences in meaning, tone, and the stance of the author. And recognition of the forensic mode, as here, more firmly asserts that the important matter in the study of literature is the poet's craft. His "intention" in doing any writing whatsoever, is, at the most basic level, to produce "art."

2

I have attempted to examine the poetry of most of the important poets of the English Renaissance to determine which poems of the period employ the rhetorical technique of *distributio-recapitulatio* and thus evidence a forensic mode. Both use and nonuse are significant in deducing the themes and generic forms which have an affinity for this technique. The technique undergoes some variation or simplification as we shall see. Among the earlier (sixteenth-century) Renaissance authors reviewed were Thomas Churchyard (c. 1520–1604), Barnaby Googe (1540–94), Nicholas Grimald (1519–62), Henry Howard, Earl of Surrey (c. 1516–47), George Turberville (c. 1540–c. 1610), and Thomas, Lord Vaux (1510–56), who do not evidence use of this technique, and George Gascoigne (c. 1527–77) and Sir Thomas Wyatt (c. 1503–42), who do.

Gascoigne's "The Constancy of a Lover Hath Thus Sometimes Been Briefly Declared" employs the technique in conjunction with anatomic structuring:

> That self-same tongue which first did thee entreat
> To link thy liking with my lucky love,
> That trusty tongue must now these words repeat,
> *I love thee still,* my fancy cannot move.
> That dreadless heart, which durst attempt the thought
> To win thy will with mine for to consent,
> Maintains that vow which love in me first wrought,
> *I love thee still,* and never shall repent.
> That happy hand, which hardely did touch
> Thy tender body to my deep delight,
> Shall serve with sword to prove my passion such
> *As loves thee still,* much more than it can write.
> Thus love I still with tongue, hand, heart and all,
> And when I change, let vengeance on me fall.

The arrangement is *tongue* to *heart* to *hand;* the *recapitulatio* rearranges this to *tongue, hand, heart.* The parallelism among the three distributions, each in a quatrain, is emphasized by the repetition of "I love thee still" / "As loves thee still," and the *recapitulatio,* in a contrasting couplet, likewise repeats the phrase as "Thus love I still." Gascoigne paid attention to structure, we easily see, and built the poem by the anatomic contrasts, by parallelism, and by contrasting variation in order and metric unit. But he has also enhanced the structure by assuming the pose of the forensic orator, who distributes his argument (proof) and then briefly recalls those arguments for greater persuasion. The poet recites his past love and the evidence for it which he says is the same now as then. He is obviously not exhorting his auditor or dissuading her from a course of action, nor is he concerned with praising her. The enthymeme which the poem creates is:

> A. I have shown my love in these ways in the past.
> B. I am, in this poem, exhibiting my love in these same ways.

Therefore, C. I love you still.

The situation provoking the poem would seem, thus, to be doubt on the auditor's part that the poet still loves her. The poem is evidence that his tongue, which has said the words of the poem, repeats his love of the past; his hand, which has written down these words, serves to prove his passion; and his heart, which has informed these words, maintains his vow of love. The poem itself is the perfect expression of his love, the clearest illustration of the evidence of his love. The poet is defending himself as constant lover through reminding his lover of the evidence of the past; his continued and current love is attested by the poem she is reading. Through past action and present illustration he expects her to judge him constant and to reject any opposing hint that might arise. The last line suggests that such a hint has indeed arisen.

The poet's aim here is to justify himself to his lover. She acts as a judge, using the poem as evidence, of the truth of his assertions. What we the readers may infer about the circumstances giving rise to the poem and about the poet's intent is due largely to recognition of its forensic mode. Gascoigne has his poet move from tongue to heart to insure the sincerity of the poet's word to the auditor; he then introduces the hand to lead the auditor to realize that these lines she is reading are the heartfelt words of the tongue. But Gascoigne then transposes "hand" and "heart" to give heart a more prominent position in the *racapitulatio*, thus stressing sincerity in the poem. (In addition, "heart and all" would allow more proper abstract meanings for "all" than the more bodily suggestions of "hand and all.")

There is a second poem by Wyatt which employs this rhetorical technique:

> Patience, though I have not
>   The thing that I require,
> I must of force, god wot,
>   Forbear my most desire;
> For no ways can I find
> To sail against the wind.
>
> Patience, do what they will
>   To work me woe or spite,
> I shall content me still
>   To think both day and night,
> To think and hold my peace,
> Since there is no redress.

Patience, withouten blame
   For I offended naught;
I know they know the same,
   Though they have changed their thought.
Was ever thought so moved
To hate that it hath loved?

Patience of all my harm,
   For fortune is my foe;
Patience must be the charm
   To heal me of my woe:
Patience without offence
Is a painful patience.

The presence of this rhetorical stance in this poem is less obvious than in "Disdain me not," but it is accordingly of more significance in reading the poem "correctly." While the poet seems to address a personified Patience, it is clear that he is counselling himself. But that counsel is only a part of a pose to make the poet appear a deliberative orator while he himself is also the audience. Stanza one addresses Patience and remarks that the poet has not obtained what he desired, for things of nature militate against his achieving it. The *recapitulatio* of stanza four restates the "harm" he has experienced and the opposition of his lot. Stanza two also addresses Patience and remarks his woe and the counteraction which only patience will afford. The *recapitulatio* restates that patience "must be the charm / To heal me of my woe." Stanza three again addresses Patience and remarks that he has given no cause for the plight in which he finds himself now. The *recapitulatio* restates the idea of "Patience without offence" and draws the conclusion to which each stanza has moved: Patience is painful when there is no reason for the opposition of the "wind," when there is "woe or spite" and "no redress," and when he has "offended naught." The narrative behind the poem concerns the poet's actions in the past to achieve, perhaps, position at court, but his actions and desires have been thwarted, although they have not hurt anyone else. There are those who have worked to harm and thwart him, although they too know that he has been without blame in his actions. Those who have opposed have been friendly with him in the past, but now (out of jealousy? out of fears of their own displacement?) they hate him, and so he sees no way to alter what they have wrought against him. He has concluded before writing the poem that only time (and thus patience) will perhaps alter the present state of things. But the forensic aim is not to counsel himself to be patient; rather he defends himself to his reader as one not deserving the treatment he has received or the lack of preferment which he has had to endure. Again the recognition of the forensic mode behind the poem alters our reading of it.

The orator of the poem is, of course, defending his past action, pointing out its justifiability (that is, its lack of offense) and the unjustness of treatment which "they" have rendered against him. The auditor is rhetorically Patience, who will thus judge whether his argument presents the correct angle of vision or not, thereby exonerating him of any criticism of his former acts. Actually, of course, Patience is succeeding generations who will have a time perspective behind them to determine the validity of his case. No one is being exhorted, and the character of the orator is perhaps the most important issue broached in his argument. The poet offers no "proof," really; he is rather arguing with words only, words which suggest an honest man, confused by unjust opposition shown by former friends, and which imply a nonaggressiveness on his part (the major counter to what his former friends' opposition implies). He—probably the biographical Wyatt—has thrown himself on the court of the public to judge his case. His strategy is not to plead with that public, nor is it to demand of them a decision. Rather he uses the effective ploy of intimating that the future will find him guiltless and so the public, to reach a decision which will eventually prove valid, must likewise judge him guiltless, honest, and true. The poem was not written for the orator himself, as if some kind of meditation—though I suspect that this is the way others have viewed it.

In the poetry of the later sixteenth-century Renaissance poets and their seventeenth-century heirs there are further examples of the use of this technique, often in variation. I do not find it employed by Richard Barnfield (1574–1627), William Browne (1591–c. 1643), Thomas Campion (c. 1566–1619), John Davies of Hereford (c. 1565–1618), Sir John Davies (1569–1626), Michael Drayton (1563–1631), Sir Edward Dyer (d. 1607), Giles Fletcher (c. 1584–1623), Phineas Fletcher (1582–1650), John Milton (1608–74), Sir Walter Ralegh (c. 1552–1618), Sir Philip Sidney (1554–86), Robert Southwell (c. 1561–96), or George Wither (1583–1667). It is employed by Samuel Daniel (1562–1619), William Drummond (1585–1649), Fulke Greville, Lord Brooke (1554–1628), and Edmund Spenser (c. 1552–99).

Daniel's Sonnet XI from *Delia* appears to be an exhortation to his cruel mistress to win her through the repeated triad of tears, vows, and prayers:

> Tears, vows, and prayers win the hardest heart,
> Tears, vows, and prayers have I spent in vain;
> Tears cannot soften flint, nor vows convart,
> Prayers prevail not with a quaint disdain.
>
> I lose my tears where I have lost my love,
> I vow my faith where faith is not regarded;
> I pray in vain, a merciless to move:
> So rare a faith might better be rewarded.
>
> Yet, though I cannot win her will with tears,
> Though my soul's idol scorneth all my vows;
> Though all my prayers be to so deaf ears,
> No favor though, the cruel fair allows,
> Yet will I weep, vow pray to cruel she:
> Flint, frost, disdain, wears, melts, and yields we see.

These tears, vows, and prayers have been spent already, and they have not persuaded his loved one to be his. The first twelve lines are all decidedly preteritive; the final couplet states what will continue in the present and future and what should be the result of such continued action. The mistress, we should note, is not addressed; the poem is spoken to an uncertain public (the reader). The *distributio* has been consistently joined with the *recapitulatio* throughout the poem. The poet thus attempts to achieve what, he expresses in the last line, will be the result of repetition of past action. He tries to influence his auditor by repetitions: there are ten citations of tears, vows, prayers. While these have not worn down the flint which is his mistress's heart, or melted her coldness toward him, or yielded her disdain of him, yet their continuance should. That is, they will if their tenfold use in this poem has caused the auditor to judge well of him, to conclude that his actions have been worthy of reward (line 8). The meaning of "we see" in line 14 is: You the reader have been won over to my cause, haven't you? Well, so will she be eventually. The poet is not exhorting his mistress; he is rather asking for a positive judgment by the reader of his past actions as he has narrated them and a negative judgment of the mistress's cruel treatment of him.

The stance the poet takes in this poem from the sonnet sequence complicates our reading of that sequence. First, he is not simply writing love poems to the addressee, Delia; second, he implies that at times his audience is conceived of as other than Delia; third, the poem implies that the sequence represents a *past* situation despite the importance for the present and perhaps the future; and fourth, the anagram which Delia is, "Ideal," indicates that Daniel is concerned in the poem (and the sequence) with achievement in writing. His mistress is not some real or feigned love mistress, but his Muse. The poem's structure alone underscores Daniel's concern with writing, but the forensic mode of this particular sonnet (meaningfully assigned the number of regeneration or resurrection?) implies that he hopes to achieve a "better reward" through his continued attention to the craft of poetry. The case before the court involves judgment of his poetic abilities.

William Drummond's rather long poem "For the King" consists of a number of poems on "Seeing," "Hearing," "Tasting," "Smelling," "Feeling," and an "Epilogue," which recapitulates the prior materials:

> And now, great God, I humbly pray
> That thou may take the self away
> That keeps my sovereign's eyes from wooing
> The thing that may be his undoing
> And let him hear, good God, the sounds
> As well of men as of his hounds.
> Give him a taste, and truly too
> Of what his subjects undergo.
> Give him all feeling of their woes,
> Will quickly smell these rascals forth,
> Whose black deeds have eclipsed his worth;
>   Then found syne scourged for their offences,
>   Heavens bless my sovereign and his senses.[3]

Drummond writes as if his king were on trial, and in a very "literary" manner, through the use of an obvious structural principle, offers his view of the king's past actions and their defense. Should, of course, the judge decide that the past failures due to the natural inclination of the five senses are exonerable, the person of the king will be saved. In the epilogue Drummond prays that God will lead the king to recognize his follies and thus renounce them; hopefully this will come through a reversal of the means of his failures in the past. The *recapitulatio* repeats the charges laid forth before but now points the way to reverse

3. In L. E. Kastner's edition (1913), II, 296–99. A line is missing from the section quoted here: "Then soon no doubt this royal nose" (l. 76).

them: for example, the king has heard only the yelping of the hounds when he so frequently rode on the hunt, enjoying himself, but he should hear also the cries of men, his subjects, who are oppressed and ill looked after. The aim is ultimately deliberative, but the stance and structure are forensic. For what poet could address the king in the deliberative mode? The orator of this poem both accuses and defends (or rather excuses), for he would have no hope of success if his charges of dereliction of duty were chalked up to the king as a total and single culprit. His strategy is to address God in the epilogue, since James I was a king by "divine right," and to praise the king by placing blame elsewhere: "These rascals . . . / Whose black deeds have eclipsed his worth." Still there is a final jab ("Heavens bless my sovereign and his senses") that only when he comes to his senses (uses common sense, that is) will the king show his worth. The auditor and judge is God, or the wide public, rather, although the real addressee and thus judge is James himself. The combination of advice and praise, while remaining within the forensic mode, make this poem one of the more interesting examples employing a variation of the rhetorical technique.

Sonnet XVI from Greville's *Caelica* can be viewed as a lyric apostrophizing love and giving solace to the poet that, though his mistress seems to be cold toward him, their love will shine forth brightly again in time:

> Fie, foolish Earth, think you that heaven wants glory,
> Because your shadows do yourself benight?
> *All's dark unto the blind*: let them be sorry,
> The heavens in themselves are ever bright.
>
> Fie, fond desire, think you that Love wants glory,
> Because your shadows do yourself benight?
> The hopes and fears of lust may make men sorry,
> But *love still in herself finds her delight.*
>
> The Earth stand fast; the sky that you benight
> Will turn again, and so restore your glory;
> Desire be steady; hope is your delight,
> An orb wherein no creature can be sorry;
>   Love being placed above these *middle* regions,
>   Where every passion wars itself with legions.

The poet is not assuming a deliberative or even an epideictic stance; he is not concerned with influencing his turned-off mistress to accept the rationalization of the poem, and though there is perhaps unstated praise of her, his goal is not to express either praise or blame of her actions. Nonetheless, the forensic stance may not at first seem to apply either, but note the narrative that lies behind the poem. Something has occurred in the lovers' relationship (particularly discernible when the sonnet is read in sequence) which has caused the poet to see that relationship as bleak and broken. It would appear that a false show of "glory" has been expected (or demanded) by the poet's mistress. The poet argues that such glory is not necessary, is only a mundane fallacy, for love exists above and behind such crassness. The difficulties that their relationship has seemed to provoke are part of the "middle region," which is that section of the air in which clouds, winds, rains, snow, thunder, and storms are generated. Love—true love—lies above this region and does not partake of such warring passions.

In a sense, perhaps, the poet is trying to persuade himself that this precept is valid. He is not addressing his mistress, however, to try to persuade her. Essentially his pose is that of the forensic orator marshalling his brief against the prevailing accusation that has been levelled in the past. Myra (the poet's mistress) has apparently judged him unloving or their relationship not to be love because he has not evidenced sufficiently the proper "glory," and so has turned cold toward him. He argues by analogues that love is above such want of glory; ultimately it is love, almost in the words of a latter-day sentimentalizer, that is seen as "An orb wherein no creature can be sorry." The poet as forensic orator is defending the action that has occurred between the lovers in the past, pointing out that it has been misinterpreted and been made falsely relevant and arguing that a new judgment be given to correct the unjustness of past decision. If his analogies stand, then his precept will be judged valid and the past decision should be reversed. Although the brief may be directed toward Myra, it is not rhetorically; although it may have most effect for his "hope," he is not the auditor. Instead there is some public—the reader —who is asked to judge, and that judgment does not concern only this one poem but the sequence (or that part of the sequence) in which the sonnet appears.

The reduced technique of *distributio-recapitulatio* points directly to the forensic mode: the earth (lines 1–4), desire (lines 5–8); the earth (lines 9–10) + desire (lines 11–12) = the conclusion to be approved. Strategic reduction is also seen in the use of the same rhyme words in the first three quatrains, and by the similarity of expression in these three quatrains, including the same line for 2 and 6. Love, we may conclude, is simpler, less "glorified" than is usually thought—simpler and less "glorified" than a number of other sonnets in the sequence might lead one to believe. Greville's sonnet, when read in this way, casts another level of light on the art of the sonnet sequence, one suggesting a greater organicity than has sometimes been allowed for the *poem* which the sequence constitutes.

The first of Spenser's *Amoretti* is structured on the principle of *distributio-recapitulatio* and thus indicates the forensic stance which at times underlies this sonnet sequence. The sonnet works through "leaves," "lines," and "rimes," each being given a quatrain, to move to summary in the concluding couplet. The sonnet throws the whole sequence into relief as a fact accomplished and offers that sequence as evidence for the public to judge his sincerity in love:

> Happy ye leaves when as those lily hands
>   Which hold my life in their dead doing might
>   Shall handle you and hold in love's soft bands,
>   Like captives trembling at the victor's sight.
> And happy lines, on which with starry light,
>   Those lamping eyes will deign sometimes to look
>   And read the sorrows of my dying spright,
>   Written with tears in heart's close bleeding book.
> And happy rimes bath'd in the sacred brook
>   Of *Helicon* whence she derived is,
>   When ye behold that Angel's blessed look,
>   My soul's long lacked food, my heaven's bliss.
> Leaves, lines, and rimes, seek her to please alone,
>   Whom, if ye please, I care for other none.

The poet's loved one is expected to be pleased by these "Leaves, lines, and rimes," and he protests that he cares for no one else's opinion. But addressing his "evidence" makes clear that the sonnet—and thus really the total literary artifact constituted by each of the sonnets in it—is offered up to a public court for judgment (the reader). The sequence becomes the defense of his love, and if indeed he achieves what he says he does (note that the context is really preterite), then his mistress should be pleased. If not—and there are love difficulties later on in the sequence—then at least the public will recognize that she has wrongly appraised his love. Spenser's strategy is to prepare his reader from the beginning to be judge of this affair by employing a technique which sets up a forensic situation. He should be exonerated from fault by his judges since they thus will understand his intent.

Those generally classified as seventeenth-century poets of a non-Spenserian school who do not exhibit this rhetorical technique are Sir William Alexander (c. 1567–1640), William Cartwright (1611–43), George Chapman (c. 1559–1634), John Cleveland (1613–58), Richard Corbett (1582–1635), Abraham Cowley (1618–67), Richard Crashaw (c. 1612–49), Sir John Davenant (1606–68), Sir John Denham (1615–69), Sidney Godolphin (1610–43), William Habington (1605–54), George Herbert (1593–1633), Robert Herrick (1591–1674), Ben Jonson (c. 1573–1637), Henry King (1592–1669), Andrew Marvell (1621–78), Thomas Randolph (1605–35), Sir John Suckling (1609–42), Thomas Traherne (1637–74), Henry Vaughan (c. 1622–95), and Edmund Waller (1606–87). But examples of the technique which expose the stance will be found in certain poems by Thomas Carew (c. 1595–c. 1639), John Donne (c. 1572–1631), Edward, Lord Herbert of Cherbury (1553–1648), and Richard Lovelace (1618–58).

"The Complement" by Thomas Carew is organized as a blazon: eyes, hair, cheeks, mouth (lips), neck, breasts, abdomen (belly), thighs, limbs, and wit and charm are described in as many stanzas and then summarized in the final stanza thus:

> I love not for those eyes, nor hair,
> Nor cheeks, nor lips, nor teeth so rare;
> Nor for thy speech, thy neck, nor breast,
> Nor for thy belly, nor the rest,
> Nor for thy hand nor foot so small:
> But, wouldst thou know, dear sweet, for all.

This final stanza indicates that the preceding stanzas are all viewed with retrospect and that the anatomizing of the physical elements of love does not fully equate the whole of love. (The whole is not equal to the sum of its parts.) Note the spelling of the punning title; the emphasis is upon the "all." Rather than narrative we have description; rather than action we have attitude; rather than a seeming need to justify we have an explanation. But this does not any the less remove the poem from being a variant of the forensic stance. While such description praises and lies within an historical present, the final stanza of recapitulation and conclusion ("But, wouldst thou know, dear sweet, for all") implies a defense of that conclusion—explanation, yes, but an anatomy of as much evidence as possible to answer the question, "Why?" (that is, "Why do you love me?"). It doesn't quite explain his attitude, but it comes as close as he can. The attitude exists and has existed. The judge is the woman herself, and the basic aim of the poet is to present himself in such light as to win her approval. "All these physical things are marvelous, but this is not why I love you—it is all of these and more." The lover is revealed as more than voyeur or sexist, while such traits do have their significant effect; he is not enamored only of the outward being of his love, though he appreciates that surface well. He is somewhat like the mistress sought in Donne's "The Blossome" (in reverse, of course, because of the sexual reversal): "As glad to have [her] *mind*, as [her] *body*."

The difference between this poem and Carew's "In Praise of His Mistress" is the difference between the forensic mode and the epideictic:

> You that will a wonder know,
>   Go with me;
> Two suns in a heaven of snow
>   Both burning be:
> All they fire, that but eye them,
> Yet the snow's unmelted by them.
>
> Leaves of crimson tulips met
>   Guide the way
> Where two pearly rows be set,
>   As white as day:
> When they part themselves asunder,
> She breathes oracles of wonder.
>
> Hills of milk with azure mixed
>   Swell beneath,
> Waving sweetly, yet still fixed,
>   While she doth breathe:
> From those hills descends a valley,
> Where all fall, that dare to dally.
>
> As fair pillars under stand
>   Statues two;

Whiter than the silver swan
    That swims in Po:
If at any time they move her,
Every step begets a lover.

All this but the casket is,
    Which contains
Such a jewel, as the miss
    Breeds endless pains;
That's her mind, and they that know it
May admire, but cannot show it.

Also a blazon, this poem is addressed to some unidentified "You" (the reader) with the single purpose of describing (praising) his loved one. There is no *recapitulatio*; the poem is not thrown into relief; the poet is in no way explaining his love in order to defend it. The reading of the two poems must be different, and that difference lies in the stances of the two orators.

Two of Donne's poems partake of the simplified structure we have seen in Greville's sonnet: two items in two stanzas, combined in summation in a third. "The Message" images eyes ("Send home my long strayed eyes to me"), then heart ("Send home my harmless heart again"), then both in reverse ("Yet send me back my heart and eyes"). Recognizing the technique for what it is, we understand that the poet is discussing past action (the eyes and heart have been enthralled by the false mistress before the poem begins), which he finds unjust. To correct that unjustness he first requests return of the stolen property, only immediately to realize that their return would have little worth. But, as if thinking on his feet and offering his train of thought as evidence of his own artlessness, he reverses that realization to request their return again, whereby he will become more sensible to the crime of which his loved one stands accused. The prosecuting attorney in iambic! What is seemingly being argued here is the loved one's falseness and the poet's love and faith. The enthymeme on which the poem is built is:

    A. I have lost my eyes and heart to you.

    B. You have shown only false passions and broken vows.

Therefore, C. You should return those things taken under false pretenses.

But the poem continues with a further set of premises:

  A. I should get something out of this for my loss.

  B. On the one hand, my heart and eyes may be useless to me, and on the other, maybe they will make me discern her treachery better.

Therefore, C. Send back my heart and eyes since they may furnish means ["may laugh and joy"] for me to be avenged.

Donne is subtly giving us the portrait of a poor loser, one who feels martyred and who finds solace only in a kind of "just wait until the shoe's on the other foot" revenge. The poet is certainly not asking the addressee for a judgment; instead it is Donne who is setting up a situation in which the reader will judge the worthiness of the lover's plaint—and I for one am not going to take the side of the whiner.

The other poem, "The Prohibition,"[4] has the same structure ("Take heed of loving me," "Take heed of hating me," "Yet love and hate me too"), being on the surface a deliberative stance of offering two courses of action, each the opposite of the other and "compromising" to unite the two. The poet does point out the expediency or harmfulness involved in his request. But the expediency and harmfulness accrue to him, not the doer of the action. As the structure of the poem suggests, behind it is the debater suggesting a course of a judgment on the part of the auditor. He ranges over all possibilities by suggesting diametric opposites and then cleverly combining the two opposites so that any judgment partakes of both. He is attempting to persuade to a course of action as in the deliberative form, yet his stance is that of the forensic orator who hopes to achieve his ends by justifying the action he recommends. Implied is a narrative of the loved one's having exhibited both love and hate in the past; the poet seems to be trying to rationalize the continuance of the action. The tone has some forensic feeling to it, and the structure accords with that mode, but the thrust is deliberative and thus illustrates the way in which stances may be combined and aims be confounded.

Neither of Donne's poems—as one really should have expected—

---

4. The third stanza has been dismissed from the Donne canon by some commentators, although the point does not alter my remarks here about the present literary artifact. The third stanza is omitted in Group II MSS (e.g., that at Trinity College, Dublin) and the Dobell MS (at Harvard), which shows some affinities at times with Group II MSS, and which is classified in Group III. But it does appear in Group I MSS (i.e., H49, D, and SP), in the O'Flaherty MS (at Harvard), a Group III MS, and in others in which the poem is found. The scribe of the antecedent of the Group II MSS seems simply to have made an error of omission.

is unrelentingly in any single mode or easily categorized. Donne took traditions and turned them on their ear—witness "Twicknam Garden" and Petrarchanism or the epithalamic genre and his Lincoln's Inn excursion. Indeed, I do not find the seemingly epideictic verse letter to Lucy, Countess of Bedford, starting "Reason is our Soul's left hand, Faith her right," so singularly classified: the paraenectic intent is much stronger in the poem, when it is read carefully.

The poems written by Edward Herbert are similar in structure to the foregoing poems by his friend Donne. The first works on the Petrarchan imagery of tears (water) and heart (fire):

> Tears, flow no more; or if you needs must flow,
>   Fall yet more slow,
>   Do not the world invade;
> From smaller springs than yours rivers have grown,
>   And they again a sea have made,
> Brackish like you, and which like you hath flown.
>
> Ebb to my heart, and on the burning fires
>   Of my desires
>   O let your torrents fall;
> From smaller heat than theirs such sparks arise
>   As into flame converting all,
> This world might be but my love's sacrifice.
>
> Yet if the tempests of my sighs so blow,
>   You both must flow
>   And my desires still burn;
> Since that in vain all help my love requires,
>   Why may not yet their rages turn
> To dry those tears, and to blow out those fires?

The tense of the poem is basically past with the conclusion seeming to move into the future as the two images combine to nullify each other. The loved one is not addressed, and the auditor seems to be (nonexplicitly) the reader. The intent of the poem thus is to communicate the effects which his love creates: tears (with accompanying sighs) and burning passion. Certainly no one and nothing is being exhorted, surely not the tears and heart. The unwritten conclusion of the enthymeme of the poem is: thus you (reader) may judge how much in love I am; for its premises are: My tears and passion show my love;

one has not cancelled the other, but both continue. The seeming exhortation for tears to quench fire, and fire to dry up tears is fully a pose assumed to assure the reader that this has not happened and will not. (Of course, the way in which this will happen is in coition when male fire is quenched by female water, and female water desiccated by male fire.) The poem is forensic, not deliberative; the aim is approval of the lover's sense of plight.

"To her Hair" first talks of the relationship of Lady Cecil's hair to her eyes, then to her forehead and temples; next it remarks that her hair blinds us with its glories; and finally it contrasts the black hair with the whiteness of her face and then with all other colors. The distribution is two stanzas, one stanza, and two stanzas. These are followed by a recapitulatory stanza:

> Tell us, when on her front in curls you lie,
>> So diapered from that black eye
> That your reflected forms may make us know
> That shining light in darkness all would find,
>> Were they not upward blind
> With the sunbeams below.

The front and eyes are explicit; the blindness is reprised as "your reflected forms" and "shining light in darkness"; and the contrast of hair and face and colors is hidden in "upward blind" and "sunbeams" (with their spectrum of color). While the poem is epideictic, it is so structured that one suspects something more than only praise is involved. And this seems to be so. What I suggest is involved is the subject matter of the poem (and the others of the group from which this comes). The poet as poet has chosen a subject which is not usual for poetry—black hair; his treatment vies with the more usual apostrophes to a woman's face (from which here one's sight recoils); it rather becomes the center of our sight; and the heavenly implication in the upward blindness (of the sun, as it were) with the sunbeams below (in her face) raise the subject to a much more exalted level. The treatment is one of mockery of the standard, the hackneyed, the expected. And I suggest, therefore, that Herbert chose his rhetorical technique to let us understand that rather than primarily being driven by epideictic concerns he was defending such writing as his own and asking us, the readers, to judge his success or failure in this attempt to wrest poetry back to something not merely imitative and variant. If the suggestion is valid, we have an excellent example of the artifice of poetry and another example of how rhetorical analysis can cause us to see the poem differently—as literary artifact and not so much as a rather routine verse of praise.

The poem is one of a group which have been viewed in philosophic terms (largely, I suppose, because Herbert was a philosopher and wrote two—for me, rather undistinguished and philosophically fuzzy —poems on "Platonic Love"). The sequence examines the aesthetic nature of Beauty, moving from particular to general and from material to ideal. In this regard, "To her Hair" illustrates, through the forensic technique involved, the relationship between the aesthetics of physical beauty and the aesthetics of poetry: beauty may be seen in the separate and specific, but moved to the plane of a composite whole in which of necessity the details become less distinct through merger, the aesthetic becomes ironically deeper and more clearly a reality. It is not the components of the poem but the fully realized poem which makes it an aesthetic experience. Herbert's defense and aesthetic is the superiority of the whole.

As this essay makes apparent, I classify poetry as the creation of artifacts with aesthetic appeal. It is "contrived" in all the positive and pejorative meanings of that word. Thus, while Herbert's aim may be to argue for and to demonstrate a philosophic concept of aesthetics in the Lady Cecil poems, I believe that critical thrust should be on the poems as literature, not as philosophy. At best the Platonic concept which these poems demonstrate was commonplace; whatever achievement lies in the poems is seen in the techniques and strategies which make that concept functional. And one of these techniques is *distributio-recapitulatio*, the recognition of which negates praise as Herbert's main intent within this one poem, and by inference within the sequence.

In the poetry of Richard Lovelace, influenced by Donne in theme and treatment of theme, we have further examples of the forensic pose and the rhetorical *distributio-recapitulatio*, though less variant in usage than in Donne or Herbert. One of Lovelace's poems presents an argument that leads to an expected judgment of "What punishment do we mete out?" for the accusations seem valid. But the poem then goes on to supply a judgment, which is what the poet really wants the reader to pass judgment on. However, Lovelace is never simple, and the judgment on his judgment really involves the reader's deciding

28

whether the poet has properly presented his evidence, whether the accused has acted as she has out of good cause (this is basically dependent upon our view of the poet-lover), and whether his judgment is not unduly tinged with vengefulness. Here is the poem, "To Lucasta. Ode Lyric":

> Ah, Lucasta, why so bright,
> Spread with early streaked light!
> If still veiled from our sight,
> What is't but eternal night?
>
> Ah, Lucasta, why so chaste!
> With that vigor, ripeness graced!
> Not to be by man embraced
> Makes that royal coin embased,
> And this golden orchard waste.
>
> Ah, Lucasta, why so great
> That thy crammed coffers sweat!
> Yet not owner of a seat
> May shelter you from Nature's heat,
> And your earthly joys complete.
>
> Ah, Lucasta, why so good,
> Blest with an unstained flood
> Flowing both through soul and blood!
> If it be not understood,
> 'Tis a diamond in mud.
>
> Lucasta, stay! why dost thou fly?
> Thou art not bright, but to the eye,
> Nor chaste, but in the marriage-tie,
> Nor great, but in this treasury,
> Nor good, but in that sanctity.
>
> Harder than the orient stone,
> Like an apparition,
> Or as a pale shadow gone,
> Dumb and deaf she hence is flown.
>
> Then receive this equal doom:
> Virgins strow no tear or bloom,
> No one dig the Parian womb;
> Raise her marble heart i' th' room,
> And 'tis both her corse and tomb.

The first four stanzas are geared to win over the furtive loved one, but these failing, the poet-lover in the fifth stanza recapitulates them and denies she is really any of these things. One suspects that sexual disunion has been with him only. Maybe stanza five is telling it like it is: maybe she isn't chaste. Or maybe he just wants to insult, sour-grapes fashion. To this point the seeming seduction poem has been reversed, and the praise is reversed to scorn. To this point the addressee is po-etically Lucasta, who through praise is being wooed to a course of action. But she turns down such action (nullifying the deliberative mode). In fact we have quite a narrative going for us even so far in the poem. But the two added stanzas (the first of which is a quatrain like the first stanza of the poem, the second of which is a cinquain like stanzas 2–5) make clear that the real auditor is not Lucasta but the reader (note "she" and "her"). The first part of the poem, therefore, must be forensic in asking the reader to judge what should be the penalty on one who is so unloving or so discriminatory as Lucasta. It backfires on the poet-lover (as Lovelace makes it do), so that one ques-tions his truthfulness, his motives, and his appraisal of the whole matter. The judgment I would give is, "Wise girl, Lucasta! it's good you got away when you could."

And the final two stanzas confirm this judgment. The orator loses whatever advantage his forensic may have achieved for him, for since his judgment is that no virgin should strew her tomb with tears or flowers, then she herself was no virgin, and since his judgment in-cludes no further sexual love for her, then he shows himself vindictive. Let no monument be erected for her (as of one martyred in the re-ligion of love) with maidens honoring it, he says, for her hard heart is sufficient monument and at the same time her tomb (with a pun on death as sexual intercourse). Lovelace has given us not a picture of himself, thwarted in love for his Lucasta (whoever one wants to as-sign that role from his biography), but a picture of man rejected and cursing his poor luck. After all, she may be rejecting him—and our judgment goes along with this possibility—because he's a creep.

The other well-known Lovelace poem is "Gratiana Dancing and Singing":

> See! with what constant motion,
> Even and glorious as the sun,
>   Gratiana steers that noble frame,
> Soft as her breast, sweet as her voice

That gave each winding law and poise,
    And swifter than the wings of Fame.

She beat the happy pavement
By such a star made firmament,
    Which now no more the roof envies,
But swells up high with Atlas ev'n,
Bearing the brighter, nobler heav'n,
    And, in her, all the deities.

Each step trod out a lover's thought
And the ambitious hopes he brought,
    Chained to her brave feet with such arts,
Such sweet command and gentle awe,
As when she ceased, we sighing saw
    The floor lay paved with broken hearts.

So did she move; so did she sing
Like the harmonious spheres that bring
    Unto their rounds their music's aid;
Which she performed such a way,
As all th' enamour'd world will say
    The Graces danced, and Apollo played.

The judgment of the reader is being asked to confirm the last line. If the poet has well represented Gratiana's dancing and singing, then it is a justified remark. But the poet is really concerned with whether *he* has represented them in such a way that this will be the conclusion rather than whether they should indeed be so epitomized. Each of the first three stanzas is divided between three lines concerned with dancing and three with singing. Stanza four pulls these arts together. (The divine nature of this dancing and singing, and particularly as it is associated with the Three Graces and Apollo, may have purposely been enhanced by the trinal arrangement.) The fourth stanza alternates between dancing and singing: line one has both; line two, dancing; line three, singing; line four, dancing; line five, singing; line six, both. The alternation suggests the duality of the two arts rendered in Lovelace's dancing and singing verse; the six lines may suggest the wedding of these two arts, and the four stanzas may suggest that the poem is of the world of man and his art. Lovelace is the master forensic orator offering the best proof possible that "The Graces danced, and Apollo played" in his verse.

3

The foregoing illustrates the employment of the forensic mode in English Renaissance poetry through the rhetorical technique of *distributio-recapitulatio*. This is but one technique and does not therefore define all the rhetorical figures through which the forensic mode may be invoked. The technique appears in only short lyrics, including sonnets. It would not appear in epideictic types like epithalamia, funeral elegies, odes, or satires of dispraise, nor in occasional poetry like verse epistles, most other kinds of satire, or political verse, since these comment on present or future action. These poems, along with the epigram, self-evidently dismiss the use of a stance to defend or accuse past action in order to influence judgment, the aim of the forensic stance. Some few shorter lyrics cast as verse epistles and perhaps a verse satire or two will partake of the forensic mode, but not of the technique discussed in this essay.

The affinity of this mode and this particular technique would therefore seem to be with what has been defined as "private" rather than "public"; yet the public setting of the forensic mode argues against the label "private." Earl Miner has most specifically set down the differences between these terms. Of them he writes, "The primary bases of distinction involve esthetic distance and assumptions about the poet's (or his speaker's) relation to other men and women. . . . The convenient symptoms of the private mode are speech approaching dialogue or monologue, with use of the singular first and second person pronouns; the symptoms of the public mode are allusion and public detail, with use of the plural first, second, and third person pronouns."[5] The poet of the "private" poem, therefore, is removed from the world of the reader and moves close to the world observed and portrayed in the poem; in contrast, the poet of the "public" poem is one with his audience and removed from the situation observed. The distinction seems broadly to separate, for example, a poem like Milton's Sonnet 21, "*Cyriack, whose Grandsire on the Royal Bench*" (private) from his Sonnet 18, "*Avenge O Lord thy slaughter'd Saints*" (public). But ultimately in terms of Milton the poet rather than their externals these poems should be labelled in reverse. Recognition of the forensic mode in the poems treated in this paper argues against these labels, for the

5. Earl Miner, *The Metaphysical Mode from Donne to Cowley* (Princeton, 1969), pp. 4–5.

poems have all the earmarks of the "private" mode according to Miner's definition until we consider poetic techniques, strategy, stance, and authorial involvement. What I am arguing is that a poem like Wyatt's "Disdain me not" as it is usually read falls into the category of "private" mode but that this poem is misread because the forensic mode has not previously been recognized and, accordingly, it should be called "public." The problem with the terms, it seems to me, is that they will apply for only the most obvious examples or for only superficial readings of a poem.

That other forensic techniques may be employed in poetry, however, should be noted very briefly. Not mentioned before was the epic because it incorporates many modes and is not essentially one "oration"; yet it too may have its forensic quality as in the Father's address to the Son in *Paradise Lost* III.80–134. Here the Father defends his course of action, accuses the real culprit, and lays the foundation for the parole which Man will be granted. The words almost sound like those from a court of law. God even alludes to the justifiability of his action: "nor can [they] justly accuse / Thir maker, or thir making, or thir Fate"; "in Mercy and Justice both, / Through Heaven and Earth, so shall my glorie excel." The Father achieves his intent of appearing just to the Son and the angelic host by working on the emotions of his auditors, by emphasizing his own favorable character (for example, he will not revoke his high decree though he could, for this would take away man's freedom), and by such syllogistic logic as:

A. Satan and his cohorts fell by their own suggestion.

B. Man falls deceived by Satan and his cohorts.

Therefore, C. Man will not meet the fate of the self-depraved and evil agents.

The technique is the straightforward one of presentation of past action and analysis of intent on the one hand (the law) and a statement of the breaking of that law and the requisite adjudication (disposition of the lawbreakers). In the background of the Father's speech is narration, as would be expected.

But the technique of *distributio-recapitulatio*, in its nature, is employable only in shorter pieces or at least briefer sections of larger poems, as in sonnet sequences we have looked at. As we have seen, it occurs in lyrics which are relatively short and which do not fall under such subgeneric forms as epithalamion, verse satire, etc. The definition of "lyric" still has to be devised; it has generally included all poetry which is not distinctively narrative or drama. But the word should be used not as a catch-all term, but for a poem of a specific nature. I firmly believe that distinctions should be attempted between "lyric" and other poetry today loosely classified as "lyric." The poems we have looked at in this paper through this forensic technique suggest first that the definition of "lyric" might describe the poet's aim (as determined by analysis of the literary artifact). The lyric would thus be a poem of a briefer nature whose author's *primary* aim is to create a poetic work. He may use a personal experience or emotion and may achieve a catharsis for himself, but the poem itself as end product is the first aim of his writing. The technique discussed here makes this point emphatic since it makes clear that the poet's prime intention is not something like catharsis. This separates the lyric from narrative and drama and didactic poetry most obviously, but it also separates "lyric" from other types like the epithalamion, the epigram, most verse satires (including such comic forms as parody and burlesque, even when the object of derision is a lyric), the funeral elegy, the hymn, most verse epistles, the praise, most topographical poetry. The term "lyric" has been employed indistinctly for all of these subgeneric forms. The fact that "hymn" implies music and singing does not make it "a lyric" though it is "lyrical"; the ode is a special case and, despite its origins, is dependent upon other elements. Indeed the term "ode" is extremely loose in any case, with a poem like Jonson's "To the Immortal Memory" best classified as nonlyric (though lyrical), and Milton's "Nativity Ode" as a lyric. (Of course, a lyric may be narrative or dramatic though not classifiable as narrative or dramatic poetry.)

Second, the definition of "lyric" might describe the poet's concept of his role as poet; it is obviously different among the three usual divisions. But the poet's relationship to the artifact produced also involves, besides his talents as poet, the form, the technique, the tropes, the strategy, and the language chosen to create the envisioned artifact. (Longer forms and perhaps certain of the shorter forms may also employ similar material and approaches for sections of the whole.) The emphasis here is on the means to achieve successfully the primary purpose of creating a poetic work. My discussion of the forensic technique in this paper indicates one of the kinds of means the poet may employ. Though Spenser's "Epithalamion" is built on specifically chosen lengths of verse paragraphs and lengths of lines, employs an appropriately varied last line in each verse paragraph, develops certain patterns of language and numerical composition, yet these involve emphasis upon Spenser's primary intention of celebrating his marriage and giving it mystical overtones of endlessness, of the significance of that marriage in a cosmic order. Not to be included under this definition is also the too-frequent modern (and usually inadequate) poem which offers a kind of ((supposedly) spontaneous set of words setting forth an emotional or mental reaction to some stimulus either in so-called "free verse" or in some kind of rhymed form. To me, this kind of poem is not what I want to call a lyric, and its differences from the poems taken up in this paper make the distinction mandatory. It may be some kind of poem, but it's not a lyric. It should be apparent, though, that I do not mean to exclude, for example, the poems of Allen Ginsberg's "Howl" from a classification of "lyric," for analysis of such very accomplished poetry will indicate that both of the foregoing criteria are eminently met.

Third, the definition of lyric might describe the poet's relationship to his subject and his audience, both functions of the two prior points. A lyric would thus imply a poem written with esthetic closeness but with ideological distance *as far as the writing of the poem is concerned*. Though the lyric may present matter of emotional and philosophical significance for its author, he is concerned with the creation of a literary artifact—not primarily the presentation of that emotion or that idea. He is offering a piece of creative work for esthetic evaluation by his readers; what concomitant effects there may be—catharsis, for example —are secondary. The examples examined in the paper certainly illustrate this point. The frequent question of the poet's "sincerity"—for example, Donne in "The Good-morrow" or "The Extasie"—is seen to be meaningless and beside the point when "lyric" is viewed in this way. This third point of definition stresses the execution of the writing, not the substance of the work.

In short the definition of lyric which the present study of the forensic mode and one of its techniques leads to is a shorter poem in which the author intends to produce a successful literary creation by specific, chosen techniques, devices, form, language, and the like, in a competive spirit (ultimately) for evaluation by his readers. "Lyric," I am thus urging, should be distinguished from the various poetic forms noted before, for the definition assumes the poet's function as rhetor and his recognition of that function. I believe it returns us to a closer relationship for "lyric" with its original development from "lyre." It takes us back, for instance, to *stasima* (choral odes) but not to Pindaric odes, which have this name because of the relationship of parts (the strophe, the antistrophe, and the epode) imitated from the dramatic *stasima*. While any poet employs rhetorical principles, he—the epic poet, say—is not necessarily the rhetorician of the lyric in the way we have seen him function in this paper. And my suggested definition adds fuel to the distinction between "lyric" and "discursive" poetry, for these distinctions depend on the three points noted above. By the term "discursive" I mean that poetry concerned primarily with the presentation of "ideas" (a broad word, unfortunately, to suggest emphasis upon subject matter rather than on execution) through a lengthier— and probably looser, more digressive—series of poetic lines. It is my belief that only awareness of the poet's position as rhetor will enable us to appreciate the achievement of the English Renaissance *lyric*.

2. The Humanism of
Sir Thomas Wyatt

THOMAS A. HANNEN

SAN JOSE STATE UNIVERSITY

FIFTEEN YEARS AGO H. A. Mason, in *Humanism and Poetry in the Early Tudor Period,* depreciated Wyatt's native courtly lyrics in favor of his translations. Two years later John Stevens, in *Music and Poetry at the Early Tudor Court,* agreed with Mason and asserted that Wyatt's lyrics are seldom interesting when considered apart from their social setting. Since then other scholars, notably Southall and Thomson, have argued that this judgment on the lyrics is extreme, although they agree that Mason is right in giving an important place to the psalms and satires. Recently Winifred Maynard has looked again at possible musical settings for the lyrics and has concluded that as many as fifty of these poems could have been intended as songs, while Robert Twombly, in a further study of Wyatt's adaptation of the penitential psalms, claims that "Wyatt's poem stands out as the most dramatic and least dogmatic, most original and least sectarian religious poem of its age."[1]

From this and other recent criticism we have been led to a higher estimate of all of Wyatt's work. He emerges as a poet with firm roots in the native Chaucerian tradition yet searching in the direction of humanism to find new forms of expression appropriate to the issues of his own day.[2] Mason's book set this trend, and, although its conclu-

1. H[arold] A[rthur] Mason, *Humanism and Poetry in the Early Tudor Period* (London, 1959), p. 178. John Stevens, *Music and Poetry in the Early Tudor Court* (Lincoln, Nebraska, 1961), chap. 10. Raymond Southall, *The Courtly Maker* (Oxford, 1964). Patricia Thomson, *Sir Thomas Wyatt and His Background* (London, 1964). Winifred Maynard, "The Lyrics of Wyatt: Poems or Songs?" *RES* NS 16 (1965): 1–13, 245–57. Robert G. Twombly, "Thomas Wyatt's Paraphrase of the Penitential Psalms of David," *TSLL* 12 (1970): 345–80; the quotation is from p. 346.

2. Even Kenneth Muir, who insists that the lyrics are Wyatt's greatest poems, grants that the translations are more important than he once thought. *Life and Letters of Sir Thomas Wyatt* (Liverpool, 1963), pp. 259–60. See also Maurice Evans,

sions have required extensive qualification, it remains, after Hallett Smith's classic article,[3] the most provocative point from which to begin a study of Wyatt's poetry. Yet there is a problem in Mason's work that lies not so much with his conclusions as with the presupposition that generates them. His purpose, to unify historical scholarship and literary criticism around Matthew Arnold's phrase: "a central, a truly human point of view," is in itself commendable but in this case it leads him to adopt a view of humanism that places too much emphasis on translation and limits too severely our view of what Wyatt was trying to do.[4]

According to Mason, the greater humanists are those who translate (in the Latin sense of "carry across") basic human values from one culture to another. They continually renew the tradition while lesser humanists never get beyond translating words. He discusses at length Wyatt's translation of Seneca:

> Stond who so list vpon the Slipper toppe
> Of courtes estates, and lett me heare reioyce;
> And vse me quyet without lett or stoppe,
> Vnknowen in courte, that hath such brakish ioyes.
> In hidden place, so lett my dayes forthe passe,
> That when my yeares be done, withouten noyse,
> I may dye aged after the common trace.
> For hym death greep'the right hard by the croppe
> That is moche knowen of other, and of him self alas,
> Doth dye unknowen, dazed with dreadfull face.
>
> (CXXL)[5]

This fine poem is certainly not just a translation of Seneca's words, nor is it a translation of the original values. It is an adaptation

---

English Poetry in the Sixteenth Century, 2d ed. rev. (London, 1967), and A. N. Brilliant, "The Style of Wyatt's 'The Quyete of Mynde,' " *E&S* NS 24, ed. Bernard Harris (London, 1971). There is a bibliography of Wyatt to about 1968 by Michael C. O'Neel in *Bulletin of Bibliography and Magazine Notes* 27 (1970): 76–79, 93–94.

3. Hallett Smith, "The Art of Sir Thomas Wyatt," *HLQ* 9 (1949): 323–56.

4. Mason, pp. 1–24.

5. Mason, pp. 181–86, 234–35. The text of Wyatt that I am using throughout this essay is *The Collected Poems of Sir Thomas Wyatt,* ed. Kenneth Muir and Patricia Thomson (Liverpool, 1969). Numbers at the ends of poems refer to the numbers in this edition which will henceforth be cited as "Muir-Thomson." Although I reprint Muir-Thomson's punctuation I have sometimes ignored it in my analyses. For further comment on this see: Joost Daadler, "Some Problems of Punctuation and Syntax in Egerton Ms. 2711 of Wyatt's Verse," *N&Q* 18 (June 1971): 214–16; and H. A. Mason "Editing Wyatt," *CQ* 5 (1971): 355–71. I have not seen Mason's more extensive pamphlet which is also entitled *Editing Wyatt.*

of what Seneca says to the problems of Wyatt's own circumstances. The vivid imagery of the last three lines focuses all our attention on the man "moche knowen of other"—the courtier—while Seneca's speaker has been reduced to a foil. Instead of a poem in praise of provincial life or Stoic self-knowledge, we have a poem about the difficulty of achieving self-knowledge while serving at court. Characteristically, Wyatt is delineating a problem rather than providing an answer, and it is his concern for this problem—how to bring to the public life the wisdom and stability usually found only in philosophy—rather than his interest in translation that, I would suggest, most effectively defines his humanism. In justification of this new emphasis let me turn to some of the work that has been done recently by intellectual historians.

At about the same time that Mason was writing, P. O. Kristeller called attention to the confusion in Renaissance scholarship that the lack of a common definition of humanism was causing, and he proposed that we use the term as it was understood in early fifteenth-century Italy to refer to the *studia humanitatis*: a scholarly curriculum based on the reading of Latin (and some Greek) authors of works on grammar, rhetoric, poetry, history and moral philosophy and excluding such other contemporary university studies as logic, natural philosophy, metaphysics, mathematics, astronomy, medicine and law.[6] This minimal definition allows him to go further and distinguish the humanist educational and cultural ideal from those of the Scholastics and Platonists. The latter two are mainly theologians and philosophers while the humanists are rhetoricians. This conclusion is close to what Mason dismisses as a merely historical estimate,[7] but it has been accepted as a starting point by many scholars. For example, according to Hanna Gray:

> The bond which united humanists, no matter how far separated in outlook or in time, was a conception of eloquence and its uses. Through it, they shared a common intellectual method and a broad agreement on the value of that method. Classical rhetoric—or classical rhetoric as interpreted and adapted in the Renaissance—constituted the main source for both. It provided the humanists with a body of precepts for

6. Paul Oskar Kristeller, *Renaissance Thought: The Classic, Scholastic and Humanist Strains* (New York, 1961), pp. 9–10, and several of Kristeller's other works.
7. Mason, p. 32.

the effective communication of ideas and, equally important, with a set of principles which asserted the central role of rhetorical skill and achievement in human affairs.[8]

Gray agrees with Kristeller's basic claim that rhetoric is at the center of humanism but she offers an important qualification. Kristeller had emphasized the stylistic concerns of the early humanists which grew out of their medieval professional concerns as *dictatores* and Mason had made a similar point when he dismissed most of the humanists as belle-lettrists. But Gray points out that although the humanists did not set another systematic philosophy against scholasticism, neither did they simply set verbal dexterity against truth. The humanist notion of eloquence was much more comprehensive than anything in medieval rhetoric. "They distinguished carefully between 'true eloquence' and 'sophistry' perceiving in the latter a perversion, not a consequence, of the former. True eloquence, according to the humanist, could arise only out of a harmonious union between wisdom and style; its aim was to guide men towards virtue and worthwhile goals, not to mislead them for vicious or trivial purposes."[9] This was in fact a return to the values of the classical sophistical tradition at its best, but the argument in the ancient world between Plato and Gorgias was transformed in the Renaissance to an argument between Aristotle and Isocrates.[10] In Isocrates, or in his Roman counterpart Cicero, the humanists found verbal ability coupled with high moral seriousness and political involvement which was very different from the essentially scientific stance they found in Aristotle as well as from the ornamentation that passed for eloquence among scholastic rhetoricians. In *De oratore*, true eloquence is contrasted with mere rhetoric when Cicero has Crassus say:

> If you take my advice you must treat with derision and contempt all those persons who suppose that the rules laid down by these rhetoricians, now so called, have enabled them to compass the whole range of oratorical power, but who have not so far suceeded in understanding what character they are appearing in or what it is that they profess.

8. Hanna H. Gray, "Renaissance Humanism: The Pursuit of Eloquence," *JHI* 24 (1963): 497–514; rpt. in *Renaissance Essays*, ed. Paul O. Kristeller and Philip P. Wiener (New York, 1969), p. 200.

9. Gray, p. 200.

10. For a brilliant survey of the sophistical tradition and its relationship to the Renaissance see Nancy S. Struever, *The Language of History in the Renaissance* (Princeton, 1970). The notes in this work will lead one to most of the other important sources.

For the genuine orator must have investigated and heard and read and discussed and handled and debated the whole of the contents of the life of mankind, inasmuch as that is the field of the orator's activity, the subject matter of his study. For eloquence is one of the supreme virtues . . . which, after compassing a knowledge of the facts, gives verbal expression to the thoughts and purposes of the mind in such a manner as to have the power of driving the hearers forward in any direction in which it has applied its weight; and the stronger this faculty is, the more necessary it is for it to be combined with integrity and supreme wisdom, and if we bestow fluency of speech on persons devoid of those virtues, we shall not have made orators of them but we shall have put weapons into the hands of madmen.[11]

Sir Thomas Elyot is alluding to this or a similar passage when in *The Boke Named the Governour* he notes: "Wherefore they be moche abused that suppose eloquence to be only in wordes or coulours of Rhetoricke, for, as Tulli saith, what is so furious or mad a thing as a vaine soune of wordes of the best sort and most ornate, contayning neither connynge nor sentence?"[12] Elyot, like Erasmus, thought that some of the minor humanists as well as those in the medieval philosophical and theological tradition were guilty of this sort of word play, whereas those in the tradition of the classical sophists could contribute significantly to the development of Christian virtue. Eusebius, a character in one of the colloquies of Erasmus—"The Godly Feast"—says in a well known passage: "I would rather let all of Scotus and others of this sort perish than the books of a single Cicero or Plutarch. Not that I condemn the former entirely but I perceive I am helped by reading the others, whereas I rise from the reading of these somehow less enthusiastic about true virtue but more disputatious."[13]

The goal, then, for the true humanist was an eloquence that would combine wisdom with rhetorical skill so as to produce virtuous action in both speaker and audience. Erasmus does not seem to have been bothered by limiting his own action to writing, but many others in this tradition have felt impelled to a more direct involvement in practical affairs. As soon as this happens the ideal of eloquence be-

11. Cicero, *De oratore*, trans. H. Rackham, Loeb Classical Library (London, 1942), III, xiv, 54–55.
12. Sir Thomas Elyot, *The Boke Named the Governour*, ed. from the first edition of 1531 by Henry Herbert Stephen Croft (1880; rpt. Research and Source Works Series, no. 165, New York, 1967), I, 116 (bk. I, ch. xiii). Croft cites *De Oratore* I, xii as the source of the quoted passage.
13. Craig R. Thompson, *Ten Colloquies of Erasmus* (New York, 1957), p. 155.

comes notoriously difficult to achieve. Debates about the active versus the contemplative life had gone on long before Plato attacked the sophists; and even when Cicero reduced wisdom to ethics and politics, as he was willing to do in some of his discussions of oratory, there was still a tension between theory and practice.[14] He found few orators who could come up to the standards he had established in *De oratore*.

The dilemma, which faces any man who must combine a devotion to high ethical standards with political service, is also set forth by Sir Thomas More in Book One of *Utopia*, and of course it became a central issue in his life. The retirement suggested by Seneca was always an attractive temptation for More, but, in contrast to his friend Erasmus, he thought it necessary to engage in politics in order to maintain the consistency of his ideas. For Wyatt, however, the temptation to retire was never as great. By inclination he seems to have preferred the courtly life in spite of what he says in "Stond who so list" and the three satires. The speaker in these poems is not struggling with the decision of whether or not to remain at court. The agony for Wyatt, who was just as sensitive to the humanist dilemma as More, appears when a persona must find a way to maintain his integrity while he continues to be fully involved in the ever changing patterns of court intrigue.

> What vaileth trouth? or, by it, to take payn?
> To stryve, by stedfastnes, for to attayne,
> To be iuste, and true: and fle from dowblenes:
> Sythens all alike, where rueleth craftines
> Rewarded is boeth fals, and plain.
> Sonest he spedeth, that moost can fain;
> True meaning hert is had in disdayn.
> Against deceipte and dowblenes
>   What vaileth trouth?
>
> Decyved is he by crafty trayn
> That meaneth no gile and doeth remayn
> Within the trapp, withoute redresse,
> But, for to love, lo, suche a maisteres,
> Whose crueltie nothing can refrayn,
>   What vaileth trouth?

(II)[15]

14. *De oratore*, I, xv, 68–69.
15. For the problems of punctuation in this poem, see Daalder (n. 5).

It is almost a surprise to find out three lines from the end that this is a love complaint. But the problems of courtly love are a microcosm of the larger problems at court, and Wyatt is often able to use the love conventions to raise more general questions about values. Although it is not known to be a translation, neither the subject matter nor the phrasing of this poem is original. What is new is the insistence with which Wyatt asks his question. A medieval poem on the same subject might have stopped when a description of the conditions had been related to a suitable *sententia*. If a question had been raised it would have been a rhetorical question. In Wyatt's poem the speaker really wants to know the worth of honesty in an environment dominated by treachery. The temptation for Wyatt is the opposite of that which faced More. It is the temptation to give up wisdom for sophistry and let the courtly ways take over. When the question of the poem is rewritten: "What is the advantage to be gained by honesty in a world where advantage determines behaviour?" we can see rather clearly the standards behind the speaker's position. Wyatt is not a saint reluctantly dealing with the world; he is an active courtier trying to remain a decent man, and a poet trying to find an honest and appropriate stance towards his experience.

In the rapidly changing Europe of the sixteenth century, the court of Henry VIII, like most of the continental courts, was a place of deadly serious intrigue where each faction plotted against every other for royal favor. Behind the artificial frivolity and the macabre mask of charm, every word or deed was weighed for the information it could yield, for courtiers had to be sure that they appeared to reflect the opinions of the King even when they intended to effect change. It was a company in which duplicity and secrecy were a necessity if one was to avoid the wrong move that often meant death.

Wyatt's work as an ambassador was a natural extension of the life he led as a courtier at home.[16] From his letters it is clear that, although his precise duties varied with each mission, he was usually charged with gathering intelligence, mainly by interpreting carefully everything he heard, and then with reporting the information or using

16. Wyatt had experience with the two main sorts of Renaissance diplomatic activity—resident embassies and special missions. He accompanied Cheney on a special mission to the French court of Francis I in 1526, and in 1527 he went to the Papal court in Italy with Sir John Russell. In 1537 he was appointed resident ambassador to the Imperial court in Spain where he served until June 1539. In November 1539 he was instructed to return to the Imperial court, now in France, on a special mission to sow discord between the Emperor and Francis I.

it to promote the King's policies. He was known for his wit. Henry Howard, Earl of Surrey, eulogised him as "A hand that taught what might be said in ryme / That reft Chaucer the glory of his wit,"[17] and Richard Tottel in his *Songes and Sonettes* spoke of "the depewitted sir Thomas Wyat,"[18] but it is unlikely that, while becoming neither a cipher nor a sycophant, he survived two imprisonments in the tower and succeeded as a diplomat by relying on his wit alone. Besides luck and friends he could also depend on a thorough practical knowledge of rhetorical technique. As Patricia Thompson has noted: "The fact that ambassadors were called 'orators' draws attention to a *sine qua non*."[19] He needed all the ability with language that he could possibly muster.

Although some occasions called for ceremonial oratory that could be prepared in advance, the more important diplomatic encounters were usually less formal. The real test of an ambassador's skill was the situation in which he had to understand and respond on the spur of the moment usually in a language other than English. We can imagine that an audience with the king (or Pope or Emperor) would sometimes allow only one or two vital sentences. He had to be quick and to the point; had to insinuate or persuade without commanding; and had to leave an ambiguous loophole through which to evade if the king preferred a different opinion. Whenever he spoke he had also to recognize that his words could be used against him not only by the government he was visiting, where at least he had diplomatic immunity, but, in addition, by his detractors at home. As Wyatt's experience with Bonner testifies, the potential of any utterance or written document as a basis for future calumny had always to be given as much consideration as

17. Henry Howard, Earl of Surrey, "W. resteth here, that quick could never rest," *Poems*, ed. Emrys Jones (Oxford, 1964).
18. *Tottel's Miscellany*, ed. Hyder Edward Rollins, rev. ed. (Cambridge, Mass., 1966), I, [2].
19. Thomson, p. 48. See also Garrett Mattingly, *Renaissance Diplomacy* (Baltimore, 1955), p. 26: "Throughout the Renaissance diplomatic agents, sometimes of the highest rank, were frequently referred to as 'orators.'" Cromwell wrote to Wyatt: "Your parte shalbe nowe like a good Oratour, both to set furthe the princely nature and inclynation of his highnes and all dexteritie, and soo to observe Themperours answers . . . as you may thereby fishe out the bottom of his stomake, and advertise his Maieste how he standethe disposed toward him," (10 October 1537, Merriman, No. 222) quoted by Thomson, p. 46. Wyatt signs the 1541 declaration of his innocence: "The King's true faythefull subiecte/ and servante and humble orator/ T. WIATT." (Muir, *Life and Letters*, no. 36, p. 184). Of course Wyatt's letters, and the speech he prepared for his defense in 1541, show his practical ability in *ars dictaminis* and formal oratory.

the immediate goal.[20] The very real danger attendant on courtly or diplomatic life always encouraged an interest in *le mot juste*.

Although there is no direct evidence that Wyatt actually read any of the contemporary rhetoric books, he could not have avoided the subject in his early schooling or at St. John's College, Cambridge. Poetry was often thought of as a subdivision of rhetoric and he must have spent some time in school or with a tutor writing Latin verse exercises. Some of the stanza forms that he was to use later may even have been borrowed from the Latin models which were available in medieval rhetorical and grammatical textbooks;[21] but by far the most useful of the techniques that he learned from this tradition was the use of commonplaces. Developed in the first place to facilitate extemporary speaking, they became the basis of many of Wyatt's poems. It is important, however, to make a distinction, which Mason and Stevens sometimes overlook, between those poems which use commonplaces and those which are nothing more than commonplaces. Many of the poems in the Devonshire manuscript are of the latter sort but they may not have been written by Wyatt.[22] In the better poems, on the other hand, the commonplaces often provide the shared experience between speaker and audience that is the necessary starting point of argument.

> Ys yt possyble
> That so hye debate,
> So sharpe, so sore, and off suche rate
> Shuld end so sone and was begone so late?
> Is it possible?
>
> Ys yt possyble
> So cruell intent,
> So hasty hete and so sone spent,
> Ffrom love to hate, and thens ffor to Relent?
> Is it possyble?

20. See Bonner's letter to Cromwell in Muir, *Life and Letters,* pp. 64–69.
21. John M. Berdan, *Early Tudor Poetry* (1920; rpt. New York, 1961), pp. 125–26.
22. Southall has studied the manuscripts and shows that there is no external evidence for believing that Wyatt wrote many of the poems usually attributed to him; but according to Winifred Maynard (pp. 246–47) the use of the first line of a stanza as the refrain line is almost peculiar to Wyatt and is relevant to attributing authorship. For lists of clichés see Southall, Thomson, and Mason. Leonard Nathan, in "Tradition and Newfangleness in Wyatt's 'They Fle From Me,' " *ELH* 32 (1956): 1–6, is also informative about the sources of some commonplaces.

Is it possyble
That eny may fynde
Within on hert so dyverse mynd,
To change or torne as wether and wynd?
Is it possyble?

Is it possyble
To spye yt in an Iye
That tornys as oft as chance on dy?
The trothe whereoff can eny try?
Is it possyble?

It is possyble
Ffor to torne so oft,
To bryng that lowyste that wasse most Alofft,
And to fall hyest yet to lyght sofft:
It is possyble.

All ys possyble,
Who so lyst beleve;
Trust therefore fyrst, and after preve;
As men wedd ladyes by lycence and leve,
All ys possyble.

(CLXXXIV)

Here Wyatt shows his control of technical rhetoric quite clearly as he plays with an argument of the sort practiced in school progymnasmata. Such exercises typically concentrated on one of the ingredients in the structure of a larger oration—topics such as praise or blame, possibility or probability, and so forth. They were not far removed from the exercises on paragraph development that we find in modern textbooks, but the classical practice was also designed to give an introduction to the larger problems of structure and so we usually find the progymnasmata straining to become little orations in themselves. The poem "Ys yt possyble" has an arrangement that can be seen as a variation of the standard formula of *propositio, narratio, refutatio, confirmatio,* and a *peroratio* that includes a call to action. The whole is a development of the topic of possibility. Stanza one presents the issue which is amplified in a *narratio*-like stanza two. In stanzas three and four, the other side, or the audience in general, is challenged to present its arguments. Stanza five is the speaker's conclusion, while stanza six gives his reason and issues a call to action. The stanza form reflects the progress of the "hye debate" which rises to a climax and then returns to its starting point.

Stanza one starts with what appears to be a rhetorical question, but the refrain line shows us that for the speaker the obvious answer "yes" is not adequate. Stanza two, the *narratio*, amplifies the proposition of stanza one by giving us further details of the "hye debate." The omission of the verb may suggest that the speaker is mulling over the question within his mind. Yet it would be a mistake to forget that, whether they were sung or spoken, Wyatt's poems were probably meant to be delivered orally. If the speaker is thinking, he is like a dramatic character thinking out loud on stage—a persona adopting a meditative stance.

The speaker's concern for the subject matter—the progress and conclusion of the high debate—is a further indication that for the first two stanzas he is adopting the stance of the thinker. As those of us who lecture are well aware however, the thinker on stage often finds his stance shifting to that of the orator. It is a fairly subtle shift that the speaker himself may not be aware of at first as he moves from his own thoughts on the subject to a concern for the response of others to the problem. This seems to be the shift that is indicated at the beginning of stanza three by the word "eny." The rhetoric intensifies here as the speaker makes a more direct appeal to his audience. If we think of the poem as a performance it would be appropriate for the speaker to look around the room at this point in hope of confirmation of his incredulity or for some sort of answer to his question. Can anyone present him with positive evidence that it is possible to find "within on hert so dyverse mynd"? The simile "as wether and wynd" gives some specificity to his appeal, but it is a commonplace and does not carry much conviction.

Stanza four continues the appeal for an argument that will answer his question. The simile here, while still a cliché, is more complex than that of the previous stanza. Along with its more general meanings it can refer to a courtly game in which dice were thrown for fortune-telling and so bring into the poem all the capriciousness of courtly life.[23] This is the first stanza in which the question is completed in the third line rather than the fourth, and it allows space for the additional

---

23. See Stevens p. 174 for a discussion of dice used for fortune-telling in matters of love.

question: "The trothe whereoff can eny try?" The appearance again of
the word "eny" which brackets stanzas three and four signals the end
of this more direct appeal to the audience, but as the speaker waits for
the answer he realizes that his stance has shifted from that of thinker
to that of orator and that if he reverts to his role as thinker he can answer the question for himself. He sees that the question of line nineteen ("The trothe whereoff can eny try?") can refer to either side of
the simile of the previous line. He might have scoffed at the truth of
fortune-telling, but the connection between the ever-changing eye and
the courtly game is a vivid enough image to create a new insight for
him when he thinks about it seriously. This convinces him in stanza
five, to our surprise, to affirm the position he has been questioning and
to see even further implications in it. The turning of an eye is transformed into the old medieval image of the turning wheel of fortune,
but in the fourth line there is an ambiguity that explains his own good
fortune. The line means to fall *from* the highest place and yet to land
softly, which in itself is a variation from the usual *de casibus* tragedy,
but here it also means to reach the highest position by sheer accident,
with the implication that it is a calamity to be in a high position. Yet
even there things can sometimes go well. He is now in a high position,
the recipient of good fortune, but he has no sooner made his affirmation
than the wheel spins round again, for he realizes that in the very act
of affirming that "it is possible" he has himself "relented" in precisely
the fashion of his mistress. He too, after carrying the debate to a
climax, has changed his mind. Looking back now, the "Iye" in stanza
four becomes a pun on "I." (The spelling of the Devonshire manuscript
is "yIe." Muir-Thomson has emended this to "Iye" but the original
spelling which both turns the word and centers the "I" may be inten-
tional to reinforce the pun.)

This revelation forces him, in the last stanza, to admit that all is
possible. As thinker, his reason for believing this is the insight he has
just experienced, but as orator, he has still given no reason to his audience for the conclusion "It is possyble." The sententia, "All ys
possyble, / who so lyst beleve," provides that reason. His advice, "Trust
therefore fyrst, and after preve" is the rhetorical call to action which
follows logically from the first two lines of the stanza while it wittily
mirrors his practice in putting the conclusion in stanza five before the
reason in stanza six. The sententia is enough, along with the old-
fashioned diction ("preve") and the inane simile which may even hint

of a hidden meaning—Henry's divorces or Wyatt's own marital difficulties—to be comfortably convincing to those who do not think too
deeply. Courtesy and danger demand this sort of pious resolution, and
on the oratorical level the overall structure of the poem, like the stanza
form, and the high debate itself, returns to the tranquility from which
it started. The courtly audience is pleasantly brought back by the
orator to the security of the world of Chaucer none the worse for its
experience. The argument has been just another courtly game. But this
is not the whole explanation.

Mason has noticed the discontinuity between the last stanza and
the rest of the poem. "I conjecture that if the rest of the poem was
written by Wyatt this stanza was an addition by another hand."[24]
My response must be "it is possible," but the poem is one of the few
specifically attributed to Wyatt in the Devonshire manuscript, and the
rhyme "preve" / "leve," which is the only evidence Mason gives for
rejecting the last stanza, seems to me to be justified by the rest of the
poem, even in the analysis I have made so far. If we look again, however, at the progression of tropes in the poem we can go further.

In stanza one, there are no tropes except the dead metonymies
"sharpe" and "sore" for we are still on the surface of what appears to
be a fairly simple question. Stanza two introduces a more complex
scheme, but again the only tropes are dead metonymies—"hete" and
"spent." The scheme is, however, important in indicating a little more
confusion on the part of the speaker. It may indicate a move towards
reflection and a resulting hesitancy which he tries to counteract in the
direct address of the following stanza. Here, in stanza three, the first
real trope appears—the bland simile "as wether and wynd." Its very
blandness keeps it from interrupting the flow of the poem, but it provides a suitable introduction to the more complex tropes to follow. It
has appeared in this stanza because here the speaker, now adopting a
more oratorical stance, wants to put on a little ornamental elegance.
In stanza four we have another cliché simile, "an Iye [yIe] / That
tornys as oft as chance on dy," introduced by the speaker for the same
ornamental effect. But this simile has a wider range of connotations
than its predecessor and is further brought to life by the question which
follows—a question which turns the cliché into a vivid metaphor for
the speaker as thinker. This forces a split for the rest of the poem between the meaning of the tropes for the courtly audience of the orator

24. Mason, p. 174.

49

and their meaning for those who are listening to the voice of the thinker. The oxymoron and irony of stanza five can be understood by the orator's audience as just another of the courtly clichés, but for the speaker as thinker the ambiguity in "to fall hyest yet to lyght sofft" intensifies the discovery he has made in the previous stanza and carries him forward to the conclusion in stanza six that "All ys possyble."

The courtly audience, responding to the stance of the orator, is carried along on the surface of the clichés, and for them the poem ends in the manner I have outlined above, but for the audience responding to the thinker the result is very different. The thinker is devastated by the realization that words (and by extension all human interaction) cannot be trusted. The sententia "All ys possyble, / Who so lyst beleve" is fine for those who do believe, but its positive meaning has an underside of chaos which the thinker recognizes only too easily. For him the resolution of his question came when some words took on a new meaning for him, and his demonstration for the rest of the poem that they can continue to shift their meanings would seem to indicate once and for all that wisdom and eloquence are irreconcilable. All he can say is "Trust therefore fyrst, and after preve," but the notion of proof in this context is now open to question since experience depends so much on words. He draws attention to this problem by using the slightly unusual word "preve." At the same time, however, he recognises that he has come to his conclusion about the limitations of language by using language. There is no rational way for him to solve this paradox and so he leaves his statement of faith couched in the most artificial rhetoric of the poem. He is contemptuous of the idea that "All ys possyble" but he does not know how to deny it—until, that is, he thinks of the simile of the last two lines.

In the Muir-Thomson edition there is a note: "This poem, with a varied refrain and lengthening lines, is not quite regular in form: in half the stanzas the fourth line has five stresses; in the others, four" (p. 416). I do not find this to be true. The fourth line of every stanza can be read with four stresses. The fourth line of the last stanza is, however, an exception since it can also be read with five stresses. The result is again an ambiguity which reflects the two conflicting stances of the speaker in the poem although this time the ambiguity is created by a different technique.

The four-stress reading which the courtly audience, not overly concerned with precision, expects from their orator is "As mén wedd ládyes by lýcence and léve." This preserves the cliché doublet "lycence and leve." The alternative stress is that of the thinker which might be adopted by the speaker if he was before an appropriate audience: "As mén wédd ládyes by lýcence [pause] and léve." This is a common device in oral poems and in songs. It is reminiscent of the end of line five of *Gawain and the Green Knight*, where a similar pause has led to incredible annotation by print-oriented scholars. This alternative stress pattern in Wyatt's poem once again gives an old cliché a new meaning. With four stresses the advice of the previous line is reinforced; but with five the advice is shown to be nonsense for it is an example of a situation in which blind trust leads to disaster. In Henry's court it was perfectly obvious that men could wed ladies and desert them whenever it was convenient.

There is more than this of course but I think I have gone far enough to show that the last stanza is an integral part of a poem that is about a subject that was always troubling for Wyatt—the relationship of words and rhetoric to thought and action. For him rhetoric could never have meant only the art of *belles-lettres* or a dusty subject for schoolbooks. It was a subject for deep moral concern and sometimes, at the dangerous court, the science of self-preservation. As G. K. Hunter remarks: "All the flexibility of mind that humanist training could impart was needed by those who came close to the centers of power."[25] It was a flexibility that Wyatt feared and hated even though he was well trained in its use himself.

> It may be good, like it who list,
> But I do dowbt: who can me blame?
> For oft assured yet have I myst,
> And now again I fere the same:
> The wyndy wordes, the Ies quaynt game,
> Of soden chaunge maketh me agast:
> For dred to fall I stond not fast.
>
> Alas! I tred an endles maze
> That seketh to accorde two contraries;
> And hope still, and nothing hase,
> Imprisoned in libertes,
> As oon unhard and still that cries;
> Alwaies thursty and yet nothing I tast:
> For dred to fall I stond not fast.

25. G. K. Hunter, *John Lyly: The Humanist as Courtier* (London, 1962), p. 26.

Assured, I dowbt I be not sure;
And should I trust to suche suretie
That oft hath put the prouff in vre
And never hath founde it trusty?
Nay, sir, In faith it were great foly.
And yet my liff thus I do wast:
For dred to fall I stond not fast.

(XXI)

The success of "It may be good" is the result of Wyatt's skillful
control over the interaction of rhythm and rhetorical texture and it
demonstrates again that his concern for eloquence was grounded in
rhetorical competence of a more technical sort. The poem seems to
start in the middle of a brisk discussion which is interrupted by the
reflections of the speaker as he moves from exclamation to contemplation. Only with the sudden "Nay, sir" near the end are we jerked back
to a realization that the discussion is still going on. It gives us a fairly
complete picture of the poet's dilemma, for the speaker is disgusted
and horrified by the sudden changes in the alignment of loyalties at
court, yet his fear forces him to play the same game himself. Although
it is probably a love poem, its concerns, as is usual with Wyatt, are
much wider.

As the poem begins, the speaker is commenting on some news
that has just been received. The separation of the opening phrases indicates his hesitancy. He is being careful and diplomatic yet seems
quite confident until he utters the rhetorical question "Who can me
blame?" Sensing that he has said just a little too much and has revealed a weakness, he begins to justify himself by explaining the
rhetorical question. The carefully controlled *synathroesmus* of lines
three through six mixes bitterness and fear with contempt.[26] There
is an iambic accent on "For oft assured," then a trochaic "yet" to
emphasize the antithesis. In line four the word "again" gets the heavi-
est stress, for the reader anticipates a caesura like that of the previous
lines. The alliteration of "wyndy words" slows the pace and adds
weight as the speaker moves into the final stage of his buildup. The
three strong stresses of "Ies quaynt game" lend importance to the
figure, while they also hold us back in anticipation of the increasing
speed in line six. The enjambment adds to the impetus, and the trochee

26. The names of rhetorical figures in this essay are taken from Richard A.
Lanham, *A Handlist of Rhetorical Terms*, (Berkeley and Los Angeles, 1969).

"maketh" in line six has the effect of an ellipse, a jump in the rhythm, which leaves three light syllables to reinforce the climactic accent on "agast."

In line seven the speaker presents us with the sudden change he had mentioned in line six, for when he says "For dred to fall I stond not fast," he is no longer talking to his opponent; he is talking to himself. The change is signalled by the change in rhythm for line six. It is a change that is as bewildering to the speaker as it is to the listener, for like the speaker in "Ys it Possyble," he is showing himself to be just as flexible and insecure as those he condemns.

After this shock of realization, which has been given prominence by the split it creates in the final couplet of the stanza, the speaker continues in the second stanza musing more quietly on his plight: "Alas! I tred an endles maze / That seketh to accorde two contraries." The rhythm has settled into a more regular pattern. The phrases are longer, lasting for the entire line, although possibly one is supposed to hear in line nine some wandering against an iambic norm. What follows is a parade of contraries, but, unlike most of the lines of the first stanza, these do not break sharply in the middle; they are antithetical but smooth. Not one of them has a stress immediately after the break in meaning at the center of the line. This, along with the confused syntax, is what creates the feeling that these contraries are simply flowing through the speaker's mind. Perhaps the syntactical problems of lines nine and ten are the result of carelessness or scribal error, but they can also be explained as the deliberate use of *alleotheta*. Certainly any reading of this poem must consider this passage rather carefully. It is not just a question of finding a rhyme, for the confusion of first and third person in "seketh" and "hope" in line nine must be explained along with "hase" in line ten. One possible explanation is that this is a purposeful attempt to mirror the speaker's lack of self-knowledge in his inability to distinguish between himself as first or as third person. The "I" of line eight is balanced by the "one" of line twelve. The "two contraries" then become the speaker in his role as thinker which is at odds with his public oratorical role. Wisdom and eloquence are inextricably linked yet impossible to harmonize.

The third stanza starts ironically with "Assured." Now the speaker is returning in his mind to the words he expressed aloud in the first stanza. A complex figure of repetition (*polyptoton*), "Assured, sure, suretie," combined with the long question, gives the impression that the speaker is sinking deeper and deeper into his thoughts. Unlike the rhetorical question of line two, this is a real question, for here the speaker is genuinely puzzled. Suddenly he remembers where he is and resumes the conversation of the first stanza with "Nay, sir, in faith it were great foly." While the exclamation of line nineteen answers the question of line eighteen, it also follows perfectly well on line six. The speaker's use of this line to get back into the conversation shows his hesitancy to use it to answer his own private question. As this idea occurs to him he reacts sharply. Now he is the one using "wyndy wordes" to evade, for he does not want to admit to himself that "suretie" is "great foly." As soon as he has made his exclamation however, he realizes its devastating truth and falls back into the reverie of the final couplet. Yet the slight awkwardness of the rhythm in line twenty indicates that his resignation is not total. If one more stanza were added one would expect it to be very regular, signifying a complete withdrawal from the courtly way of life into the life of the mind. For Wyatt such a stanza would be impossible. Retirement into the mind is just as evasive and perhaps just as boring as retirement to the provinces.

Donald M. Friedman has shown convincingly that Wyatt ultimately locates the source of instability, as well as, ironically, the desire for stability, in the fantasy within the mind.[27] However this contradiction was not the only one which plagued Wyatt for, as a humanist, his first concern was with action. That in turn required that the mind be coupled with language. He needed a rhetoric to go with his psychology. Michael Murrin has recently reminded us that there were two rhetorics available—a rhetoric of oratory and a rhetoric of allegory.[28] As Wyatt turns into the mind we should expect him to turn to allegory since this is the traditional rhetoric of wisdom and abstract thought. Indeed his speaker in "It may be good" begins to move in that direction. The confusion with which stanza two begins hints at the transition into a dream but by stanza three this move is leading him towards the hollow wordplay of the aureate tradition ("Assured, sure, suretie," and "prouff in vre"). Allegory may appear to explain the mind but really, from the

27. Donald M. Friedman, "Wyatt and the Ambiguities of Fancy," *JEGP* 67 (1968): 32–48. See also his "The Mind in the Poem: Wyatt's 'They Fle From Me,'" *SEL* 7 (1967): 1–13; "The Thing in Wyatt's Mind," *EIC* 16 (1966): 375–81; and "Wyatt's *Amoris Personae*," *MLQ* 27 (1966): 136–46.

28. Michael Murrin, *The Veil of Allegory: Some Notes Towards a Theory of Allegorical Rhetoric in the English Renaissance* (Chicago, 1969).

point of view of a humanist like Wyatt, it is, like scholasticism, just a tautological word game. The thinker must give way to the speaker, and with "Nay, sir" the speaker has jumped back from the pathway into the veiled world of allegory and has returned to the direct address of oratorical rhetoric. As in "They Fle From Me" (XXXVII), Wyatt chose here to present a speaker who might have said "it was no dreme: I lay brode waking" (line 15), but in both cases we are reminded of how close he still was to the allegorical tradition. He knew however that he could only solve his problem by getting outside his mind rather than by going deeper into it. He had to find a suitable way to link his wisdom with persuasive language. If allegory was not the answer neither was the crafty language of the court, for he had already noticed the weakness of that kind of language in such poems as "Ys it possyble"? In "It may be good" the dilemma even shows up in another way for his speaker is caught somewhere between the Rime Royal stanza of *Troilus and Criseyde* and the octosyllabic line of *The Romance of the Rose*. He had to find a new eloquence.

In his search for this new eloquence he turned of course to continental models. (I do not mean to imply anything about chronological order.) What he found there was a more sophisticated approach to the humanist dilemma but no resolution. In a loose translation of Petrarch's Italian, "The pillar perished is whereto I lent" (CCXXXVI), the speaker is deprived of a point of stability in the world of action and he can only respond:

> What can I more but have a wofull hart,
> My penne in playnt, my voyce in wofull crye,
> My mynde in woe, my bodye full of smart,
> And I my self my self alwayes to hate
> Till dreadfull death do ease my dolefull state?
>
> (lines 10–14)

Muir and Thomson note: "The only remark difficult to explain in personal terms is the self-hatred expressed in line 11."[29] Surely however this is the result of the same inability to act that in "It may be good" led him to lament: "My life thus I do wast / For dred to fall I stond not fast." He is reduced to writing and crying complaints that are no more effective in correcting the condition that has caused the problem than are allegorical analyses of the "unquyete mynde."

29. Muir-Thomson, p. 430.

If neither human thought nor speech can be trusted the only obvious course left for one who passionately desires stability would seem to be a leap to religious faith. "The Penitential Psalms" are an attempt to deal poetically with such a leap but we should not be too quick to conclude that Wyatt was entirely satisfied with the resolution he presents in that poem. We have seen what he did with such a leap in "Ys it possible," and at least one other poem that seems to counsel withdrawal and religious faith deserves some attention. "Who lyst his wealth and eas Retayne" (CLXXVI), partly translated from Seneca, ends: "Ber low, therforr, geve god the sterne / for sure, *circa regna tonat*" (lines 24–25). This poem has an inscription:

V. Innocentia

Veritas Viat Fides

Circumdederunt me inimici mei

Muir begins his commentary: "The last line [of the inscription] is adapted from Psalm xvii. 9. The references to enemies that compass the poet round about, the protestation of innocency, truth and faith, words which surround 'Viat' as though to protect him. . . ."[30] But this inscription is not just a charm. Wyatt is again being ironical; for the enemies who surround him are innocence, truth and faith as well as those people at court who have had him imprisoned. It is the desire of his mind for stability as much as his courtly companions which prevents him from living comfortably in the real world of eternal change. The inscription undercuts the statement of the poem and we are left once again with the indecisive stance that marks so much of Wyatt's poetry.

In the end neither the rhetoric of oratory nor the rhetoric of allegory offered a theory of language adequate to Wyatt's intentions. It was not, as Mason suggests, that the available theory was too advanced.[31] Wyatt demonstrates that he understood these theories perfectly well, so well that he recognised their limitations. What he was searching for was a theory of poetic structure that would reconcile the two rhetorical theories. He wanted to analyze the mind, not in itself, but in the world of action. When his poems succeed it is because of his great sensitivity to textual rhetoric (figures and tropes), which he could find in many of the rhetorical textbooks, and to rhythm and

---

30. Sir Thomas Wyatt and His Circle, *Unpublished Poems*, ed. from the Blage Manuscript by Kenneth Muir (Liverpool, 1961), p. xiv.
31. Mason, p. 66.

diction. These led him inductively, although he was sometimes assisted by the structure of the work he was translating, to find a new structure that worked for him. He could find discussions of arrangement or disposition in rhetoric books but they gave him no *a priori* idea of how to create the kind of structure he required to embody his indecisive stance. He attempted such a wide range of forms because every poem was a new search. I agree with Mason that "the Wyatt we should attend to is the author of poems that stand in a significant relation to the work of the Humanists,"[32] but there are more poems by this author than Mason allows. By restricting the term "Humanism" to translation Mason obscured an important continuity in Wyatt's work—his attempt, which he shared with all the important humanists, to find an eloquence that would reconcile thought and action so as to create a human society in which a man could participate without losing his self-respect.

32. Mason, p. 180; I have dropped Mason's italics.

3. Gascoigne's "Lullabie" and Structures in the Tudor Lyric

LEONARD NATHAN
UNIVERSITY OF CALIFORNIA, BERKELEY

O NE OF THE more diverting recent pastimes for those interested in Tudor lyrics is finding them a suitable taxonomy. Among the most notable—if not notorious—examples have been C. S. Lewis's Golden and Drab and Yvor Winters' Native and Petrarchan (or its less chauvinist version, Plain and Eloquent).[1] Helpful as these categories may be, they have, in their concern for stylistic discriminations, obscured other ways of making useful distinctions. One such way, structural, has been treated, if at all, in a most gingerly fashion.[2] The term *structure* itself has proved more slippery than most. I mean it here to signify the principle by which parts of a poem are related one to another, chiefly as regards larger units, for example, conclusion to body, subject or topic to the comparative material that may develop it.

It is my purpose in the following discussion to explore at least one characteristic Tudor poetic structure, and, further, to suggest that

1. See G. K. Hunter's "Drab and Golden Lyrics of the Renaissance," *Forms of Lyric: Selected Papers from the English Institute*, ed. Reuben Brower (New York, 1970), pp. 1–18. Professor Hunter, refining on both Winters and Lewis, makes his division along historical lines; he finds two modes: one is the plain-spoken social poem dominant at mid-century and dependent for its full meaning on its narrative context; the other, coming to prominence at century's end, is the aesthetically autonomous lyric, the emblem of some particular brilliant personality.

2. The exception is Douglas L. Peterson's *The English Lyric from Wyatt to Donne* (Princeton, 1967), in which structure is given a great deal of attention, but, alas, to the end of confusing the reader. For Professor Peterson seems sometimes to mean by structure a principle of arrangement, sometimes the arrangement itself; this shift of definition brings him to curious conclusions, not the least curious of which is the conflation of rhetorical with poetic intention when he reads certain poems from Tottel's *Miscellany* as though they were translations of the school rhetorics of the time (see, for instance, pp. 55–61). It is one thing to note that Tudor poets found rhetorical handbooks useful sources for arrangement, quite another to see some sort of equivalence between the rhetorical and the poetic usage of common material.

it represents an innovation that may distinguish a particular kind of sixteenth-century lyric from the dominant medieval type that preceded it far more radically than any quality of style. And I am using for my example George Gascoigne's "The Lullabie of a Lover," a poem that has been recently described as one "using medieval structure."[3] If style were the sole or even most significant determinant for understanding a poem, then such a judgment would seem right; but it is precisely in a poem whose surface might mislead on this score that the case can best be made for the conclusion that structural difference is perhaps all the difference.

An obvious characteristic of the medieval literary lyric is "enumerative" structure.[4] But how and to what end enumeration was used in these poems needs to be explained. The following "I Have Lived After My Lust," provides us, I believe, with a fair example of fifteenth-century poetic composition that can be called a typical handling of the topic:

Royal MS. App. 58

Now marcy, Ihe-su, I wyll amend
and neuermore displease the,
yff grace thow wylt me send.

My thoght ys full hevy
  and greuith me Ryght sore;
my synnys be pesy,
  whych repentyth me euer-more.
my flesh fast swetyng
  my paynys to Renew,
my body besely boylyng
  with hetys—lord Ihesu,

---

3. Professor Peterson again, who goes on to explain his judgment by asserting that "both the theme and the lullaby as a convention are common in collections of secular and religious medieval lyric" and that the "enumerative repetitive structure is also medieval" (p. 161). This reading engages in a gross reduction. The intention of the medieval poet in enumerating is, as I hope to show, far different from Gascoigne's intention in doing so; just as the view of poetry and of experience underlying medieval enumeration is different from that underlying Gascoigne's enumeration.

4. Professor Peterson's term (see note 3). It should be understood that I exclude from my consideration non-literary verse such as the popular song, occasional and practical verse since the Tudor lyrics under consideration were literary.

This haue I full surely
   for that I was vniust
to god, the sune off mary,
   and leuyd after my lust. Now mercy, Ihesu.

My fete, sume tyme more
   and lesse, they do swete;
my hert ys very pore,
   and besyly doth bete;
my hed ys all macy,
   and meruelowsly dothe werke;
my(n) yene dyme and dasy,
   my neke ys full sterke;
Thys haue I full surely
   (for that I was vniust
to god, the sune off mary,
   and leuyd after my lust. Now mercy, Ihesu.)

My hondys do me no good
   ne-dys must I ly so
and take no erthly fode

. . . .

now helpe me, goode lorde,
   my stomake ys full faynt;
I make to the acorde
   Vppon payne off a-taynt;
I wyll no more suerly
   to the be so vnjust
butt kepe thy lawes truly
   And put a-way false lust. Now mercy Ihe(s)u.[5]

Enumeration is clearly the dominant structural element here; the poem is a catalogue illustrating the consequence of the speaker having "leuyd after" his "lust." The illustrative material, set in the figure of repetition ("my synnys," etc.), works to amplify the theme for the sake of vividness and pathos. What is interesting about the structural character of the poem is that parts are interchangeable between its beginning and end. The poet shows no concern—and this is characteristic of his type—for composing what we like to call an organic form, or, for that matter, any form that lays claim to logical or se-

5. Carleton Brown, ed., *Religious Lyrics of the XVth Century* (Oxford, 1939), no. 139, pp. 213–14.

quential coherence. Thus what might seem to later poets an almost comic breach of decorum—the juxtaposition of feet and heart—seems not to trouble him. Indeed, structure to this poet is reduced to accumulation: one thing added to another. What seems to be the overriding determinant guiding the poet's choice (aside from prosodic considerations) is what things belonged to the topic. Those things belong in the poem somewhere between the opening and closing lines.

There is a further assumption here about the character of the topic itself: that is, the poet regards it as a thing unto itself, and as such, a settled affair with its own attributes. Perhaps because of the doctrinaire quality of medieval thinking, typical subjects for literary poems—love, age, morality, divine or significant persons, for instance—were not objects for exploration or discovery so much as fixed concepts that poets could amplify, ornament, or point to as exemplary. This static or categorical notion of topic leads to some predictable poetic behavior. Not only will topics be treated by the catalogue method, but the items that make up the catalogue will be arranged not because of their relations with each other, but because of their belonging to the topic; structural coherence, as we value it, is, then, beside the point. Further, topics themselves, seen as independent entities almost, will be presented with none but the most elementary relation to other topics, for example in the relation of comparison or contrast (as with youth to age). Often, whether his topic is secular or religious, the fifteenth-century poet's choice of stance is reduced to two: the encomiastic or the complaining.

It is perhaps too easy to see not just a way of perceiving literary composition, but also a way of social life, the aristocratic. Poetry, in this milieu, becomes a social pastime reflecting a rigid hierarchy in which status relationships ideally have precedence over and give value to personal relationships. It is no accident that the French *ballade* was so obsessively preoccupied with classes of things, of beautiful women, flowers, virtues, heroes, lovers; and that these individuals illustrate something typical about the class—its qualities or limits. Writing in this tradition, Lydgate provides us with an example of its English counterpart in the second stanza of an encomium to a lady:

> Wyfly trouthe with Penelope,
> And with Gresylde parfyt pacyence,
> Lyche Polixcene fayrely on to se,
> of bounte beaute having þ'excellence

> Of qweene Alceste, and al þe diligence
> Of fayre Dydo pryncesse of Cartage—
> Al þis haþe nature sett in your ymage![6]

Penelope, like all other elements of such lists, has no function beyond personifying a virtue and whether or not she precedes or follows Dido is not at issue. Her presence in the poem is simply to help exemplify and exhaust a certain category of women for the purpose of elementary comparison with the object of the poet's praise.

The limits of this method of composition are many and obvious, as any collection of fifteenth-century poetry will testify. The few truly gifted literary poets of the period manage, at best, charm and wit. The most important limit for our purposes, however, is that the enumerative structure, used in the way medieval poets tended to use it, implies a static and isolated treatment of topics. What makes "Lullabie" a Renaissance poem and not a medieval one is, as I hope to show, that Gascoigne's use of enumeration does not imply such a view of topics.

Before considering "Lullabie," however, I should like to discuss another poem, the well-known "The aged louer renounceth loue" by Lord Vaux. Its topic, like that of the medieval poem already quoted, is age and its attributes:

> I Lothe that I did loue,
>> In youth that I thought swete:
> As time requires for my behoue
> Me thinkes they are not mete,
>> My lustes they do me leaue,
> My fansies all be fledde:
> And tract of time begins to weaue,
> Gray heares vpon my hedde.
>> For age with stelyng steppes,
> Hath clawed me with his cowche:
> And lusty life away she leapes,
> As there had bene none such.
>> My muse dothe not delight
> Me as she did before:
> My hand and pen are not in plight,
> As they haue bene of yore.
>> For reason me denies,

6. Russell H. Robbins, *Secular Lyrics of the XIVth and XVth Centuries* (Oxford, 1952). From the poem titled "The All-Virtuous She," no. 131, pp. 129–30.

This youthly idle rime:
And day by day to me she cryes,
Leaue of these toyes in time.
　　The wrincles in my brow,
The furrowes in my face:
Say limpyng age will hedge him now,
Where youth must geue him place.
　　The harbinger of death,
To me I see him ride:
The cough, the colde, the gaspyng breath,
Dothe bid me to prouide.
　　A pikeax and a spade,
And eke a shrowdyng shete,
A house of claye for to be made,
For such a gest most mete.
　　Me thinkes I heare the clarke,
That knols the careful knell:
And bids me leaue my wofull warke,
Er nature me compell.
　　My kepers knit the knot,
That youth did laugh to scorne:
Of me that clene shalbe forgot,
As I had not ben borne.
　　Thus must I youth geue vp,
Whose badge I long did weare:
To them I yelde the wanton cup
That better may it beare.
　　Loe here the bared scull,
By whose balde signe I know:
That stoupyng age away shall pull,
Which youthfull yeres did sowe.
　　For beauty with her bande
These croked cares hath wrought:
And shipped me into the lande,
From whence I first was brought.
　　And ye that bide behinde,
Haue ye none other trust:
As ye of claye were cast by kinde,
So shall ye waste to dust.[7]

7. Hyder Edward Rollins, ed., *Tottel's Miscellany (1557–1587)* (Cambridge, Mass., 1965), I, 165–66.

The first stanza establishes a typical antithesis, youth against age. The antithesis is absolute: the attributes of the topic of youth are in no way seen as connected to or resulting in the topic of age. The former is perceived merely as contrastive material to heighten the interest of the latter. The antithesis, further, along with enumeration or accumulation, provides the structural principle of the poem which unfolds as a series of then/now contrasts, interspersed with descriptions of age.

There is in all this very little sense of logical or dramatic development. While it might be argued that there is something like a progress in the poem, the movement from stanza to stanza is considerably less than inevitable. Stanzas one through four serve as background representing the negative effects of the loss of youth; five is a transition between the first section and the next; six through nine present the character of age; ten, the proper stance toward age, though it overlaps five in this function; twelve intensifies the reason for the self-exhortation in eleven by offering a *memento mori* figure, though seeming to repeat the effects of six through ten; thirteen reverts to the opening stanza as a reminder that the vices of youth bring the troubles of age, perhaps as a preparation for the last stanza that generalizes the speaker's experience.

Though point by point, it is more lucid and its prosody is under better control than that of the usual among its fifteenth-century counterparts, "The aged louer renounceth loue," it is fair to say, hardly represents much of an advance on the late medieval literary lyric. Indeed, certain stanzas can be excised with no damage to the poem— one or two, three or four and five; twelve or thirteen. And if certain stanzas were shifted it would make no important difference: for instance, twelve back to eleven. The apparent looseness of the construction is to some degree concealed by the heavily patterned meter and clarity of each stanza, as well as by the familiarity of the topic. But measured against the structural integrity of, say, Marvell's "To His Coy Mistress," "The aged louer renounceth loue" is slack.

Its slackness, however, is less the result of incompetence than the poet's commitment to a principle of composition that gave him as structural means only the simplest kind of antithesis and enumerative accumulation, and, moreover, his commitment to a way of viewing experience that was static and categorical, so that topics like that of love and age could seem connected only by crude opposition.[8]

8. The opposition—a simplistic reading of Petrarch and a commonplace in the

The principle of composition arising from this view probably has little effect on epigrammatic verse; in longer poems enumeration and contrast are seldom enough to provide full structural control. Vaux, working from this principle, produces a series of sententious propositions about the dreadfulness of old age, vivified by a sort of low-profile personification, ending in the climactic apostrophe to the reader. That is, he has addressed a settled topic, located in it its characteristic attributes in a "poetic" fashion, and nothing more. This is the way of much poetry, of course, and particularly the literary lyric of fifteenth-century England.[9]

It is not the way of Gascoigne's "Lullabie." Yet a failure to see this is at least understandable, for Gascoigne composes in the same tradition as Vaux—at least with respect to topic, prosody, diction and figure—a tradition fixed primarily by Tottel's *Miscellany*, which includes "The aged louer renounceth loue." A cursory reading of "The Lullabie of a Lover" might suggest more likeness than difference between Gascoigne and Vaux:

---

anthologies—is handsomely represented in microcosm by two complementary epigrams of George Turberville:

> Maister George His Sonet of the Paines of Loue
>> Two lines shall tell the griefe,
>> that I by loue sustaine:
>> I burne, I flame, I faint, I freeze,
>> of Hell I feele the paine.

and

> Turberuile's Aunswere and Distich to the Same
>> Two lines shall teach you how
>> to purchase loue anewe:
>> Let reason rule where Loue did raigne
>> and ydle thoughts eschewe.

>> (Samuel Johnson, ed., *The Works of the English Poets* [London, 1801], II. 587.)

9. I do not mean to imply that poems informed by the principle of enumeration are necessarily slack or loose mixtures of these elements. Ralegh's "The Lie," written with a polemic intention, is but one example of enumeration working with powerful unitary effect. Any structural principle can be put to telling use. What separates "The Lie" from typical lyrics of the fifteenth century is that the latter, besides exhibiting less sophistication and skill, direct their language away from the experience they purport to encompass; to put it another way, they are all too often formularies. Because the poet sees poetic composition as gathering all that is appropriate to a topic, which is itself an abstraction, he can hardly help regarding his craft as something of a polite game. If religious poets were invested with more imaginative seriousness, they seldom show it except in the solemnity of their effort.

Sing lullaby, as women doe,
Wherewith they bring their babes to rest,
And lullaby can I sing to,
As womanly as can the best.
With lullaby they still the childe,
And if I be not much beguild,
Full many wanton babes have I,
Which must be stild with lullabie.

First lullaby my youthfull yeares,
It is nowe time to go to bed,
For croocked age and hoary heares,
Have wone the haven (within) my head:
With Lullaby then youth be still,
With Lullaby content thy will,
Since courage quayles, and commes behind,
Go sleepe, and so beguile thy minde.

Next Lullaby my gazing eyes,
Which wonted were to glaunce apace.
For every Glasse maye nowe suffise,
To shewe the furrowes in my face:
With Lullaby then winke awhile,
With Lullabye your lookes beguile:
Lette no fayre face, nor beautie brighte,
Entice you efte with vayne delighte.

And Lullaby my wanton will,
Lette reasons rule, nowe reigne thy thought,
Since all to late I finde by skyll,
Howe deare I have thy fansies bought:
With Lullaby nowe tak thyne ease,
With Lullaby thy doubtes appease:
For trust to this, if thou be styll,
        My body shall obey thy will.

Eke Lullaby my loving boye,
My little Robyn take thy rest,
Since age is colde, and nothing coye,
Keepe close thy coyne, for so is best:
With Lulla(b)y be thou content,
With Lullaby thy lustes relente,
Lette others pay which hath mo pence,
Thou art to pore for such expence.

Thus Lullabye my youth, myne eyes,
My will, my ware, and all that was,
I can no mo delayes devise,
But welcome payne, let pleasure passe:
With Lullaby now take your leave,
With Lullaby your dreames deceive,
And when you rise with waking eye,
Remember then this Lullabye.
Ever or Never.[10]

The typical metrical regularity, the addiction to alliteration, the reliance on repetition (enumeration) and personification—all these, as well as the deliberately idiomatic character of the language, show, if nothing else, that Gascoigne learned his lessons well and that one of his basic texts was *Songes and Sonettes*.

Yet the differences between "Lullabie" and its models are far more striking than the resemblances. First, there is the controlling metaphor of the poem, the invention of the lullaby, though this itself has been viewed as a proof of the poem's medievalness.[11] One might as well assert that the topic of *King Lear* marks it as somehow medieval because the fall of princes was a topic much used in medieval poetry. In fact, when the fifteenth-century literary poet used the lullaby it was not a metaphor in the strict sense but a literal attempt to represent what was regarded as an historical event in Christian lore; thus, in Harley MS. 2380, the poet exploits the topic to create a dramatic context for the doctrine he aims to communicate and the pathos he wishes to evince:

Sco sayd, 'sweit sone, wen sal þis be (don),
þat ȝe sal suffir al þis vo?'

10. George Gascoigne, *The Posies* in *The Complete Works of George Gascoigne*, ed. John W. Cunliffe (Cambridge, England, c. 1907), I, 44–45.

11. Professor Peterson regards this invention, as we have seen, as one mark of the poem's medieval character (see n. 3), but it is fair to say that he also finds it, as Gascoigne uses it here, part of what sets the poem off "as an example of the refined plain style," along with its "extraordinary control of the refrain technique" (Peterson, p. 162). Professor Peterson's preoccupation with the thesis of plain versus eloquent proposed by Winters makes him overlook important and, for his case, relevant points. By emphasizing questions of style in a way that seems to imply that Renaissance plain style is somehow more sophisticated than medieval, he further implies some sort of notion of progress as the underlying category for assessing poetry, when, in fact, as I am arguing, it is in some instances the far more radical matter of different modes of perception.

'Moder fre, al sal ӡe se
With xxx ӡer & thrio—
It is no nay.'
  He sayd ba-bay;
  sco sayd lullay,
  þe virgin fresch as ros In may.[12]

The lullaby here does no more than reaffirm a well-established and categorical relation between the virgin and her divine offspring. That relation was fixed and static with its appropriate attributes long before the poem was written. Nor did the poet tamper with it; his aim was to work within the limits imposed by such a tradition.

Gascoigne's use of the lullaby is far more complex and figures forth a relation between categories heretofore linked, if at all, only in the simple connection proposed by "The aged louer renounceth loue." If Vaux's speaker sees the acceptance of the miseries of age as the total and denunciatory rejection of the works of youth, Gascoigne, when he looks at the topic of age, sees something far less simple and, if one can use the phrase, less self-deceivingly facile. The metaphorical use of the lullaby is not quite paraphraseable, but it clearly establishes a relation between youth and age that is not simple contrast, but rather like that of the deepest kinship—mother to child—and the complex of feelings implied: fondness, indulgence, tenderness, irony, and a sense of duty. The topics are joined far more realistically or at least less abstractly than they are in Vaux. For men surely do not often give up their youth willingly; indeed, one suspects in Vaux's stance too much protest, an over-violent rejection of what, as Gasciogne plainly realizes, is part of one's self. Gasciogne's use of the lullaby, in fact, makes available to him a far more complex and accurate moral perception of the topic, an advantage reflected in his control and a complexity of tone as compared, say, to the flatness and simplicity of Vaux's voice.[13]

12. Brown, p. 6. It is interesting to compare John Phillip's "Lullaby," written before 1562, with both the fifteenth-century literary lullabies and Gascoigne's lyric (Norman Ault, ed., *Elizabethan Lyrics* [New York, 1949], p. 41). While Phillip uses the device for a secular poem and has achieved something like Tudor eloquence, his aim is perhaps even simpler than his fifteenth-century predecessors, though Gascoigne may have remembered Phillip's phrase, "I will not delay me," when writing "I can no mo delayes devise."

13. I think Professor Peterson insists on the wrong emphasis when he asserts (concerning the lines: "And lullaby can I sing to, / As womanly as can the best") that Gascoigne's "admission here that with the loss of those powers which have made him a vigorous lover he approaches effeminacy is nicely ironic" (Peterson, p. 162). Ironic yes, but not because of effeminacy. This is to overread the figure.

Gascoigne has, by his use of the lullaby metaphor, found a profound link between what before were perceived as mere opposites;
this link presupposes a specific way of seeing experience and how it
might be represented in poetry. And this way is far different from that
underlying the enumerative method. Topics here are not simply abstract conceptions by which to judge experience as if it could be isolated
into atomic units of significant substance. Thus, the possibility is
opened for a different kind of poem, a true alternative to the still preva-
lent literary modes of the fifteenth-century lyric: the cataloguing
encomium or complaint. Such poems might provide the wherewithal
to examine relationships not as if they were fixed and static, but rather
as the result of a process that paralleled the relational character of
actual experience. Many of Wyatt's poems are precisely the kind that
make relationship itself the center of interest, often the relation between the old way of composing and perceiving the experience of love
set against something new and painfully difficult to apprehend, which
he calls by many names, among them newfangledness or change.[14]
Newfangledness, as a topic, was long familiar to the medieval poets,
but never treated by them as fit for analysis in complex relation to
other topics. Like Wyatt, Gascoigne sees complex relationship itself
as a vital subject for poetry. More particularly, he sees that through
available poetic structure, he can connect apparently antithetical aspects of experience. The poet's task for him, then, is to invent a controlling figure of sufficient richness and appropriateness to give the poet
tonal scope to do justice to the complexity of the experienced relation.[15] And that "Lullabie" is not a mere accident is attested to by an-

---

The focus is on the relation between youth and age, not on Gascoigne's womanliness. Nor is he in any way making fun of the inability of age. Womanliness
is a counter to the youthful qualities personified as children. To make it anything
more is to misplace emphasis.

Another misreading of the lullaby metaphor is William Tydeman's "He sings
his declining faculties to rest, with the amused air of a content and mellowed
philanderer" (English Poetry, 1400–1580 [London, 1970], p. 62). This judgment
entirely ignores the moral understanding of the poem, enforced by the last
stanza; it also ignores the generous sympathy of the stance toward youth, rare
in a time when the commonplace position of the poet writing about age was a flat
condemnation of youth as a total waste, or worse.

14. See my "Tradition and Newfangleness in Wyatt's 'They Fle From Me,'"
ELH 32 (1965): 1–16.

15. This controlling figure may very well be what Gascoigne meant—but did not
have the terms for—when he speaks in "Certayne notes of Instruction" of invention that is posed against "oratione perpetua," which sounds suspiciously like
the sort of medieval poem I have described in which the poet's chief structural
principle is enumeration (see Gascoigne, I, 65–66).

other of Gascoigne's poems, "Woodsmanship," which links youth and age (or at least middle age) in a yet richer and more serious way.

A closer look at "Lullabie" indicates that, while the controlling metaphor does not provide Gascoigne with a particular means of organization, it does give him tonal control, stanza by stanza, throughout which he is able to maintain the stance of a mother singing her babes to sleep: a loving fondness made ironic by the underlying acceptance of the necessity to put youth to sleep. Moreover, it is wholly appropriate for the poet to make use of the principle of enumeration since a lullaby by nature is repetitive; so that if no other principle were at work in the poem the lullaby metaphor would have given Gascoigne considerable structural coherence.

There is another principle at work, however; the psychological, as understood by the Renaissance poet and his audience.[16] After the opening stanza that proposes the controlling metaphor, a second stanza extends the meaning of the metaphor to a literal situation; the next three stanzas are ordered so as to parallel the process involved in the experience of sexual passion. This artful organization is not in itself the inevitable sign of a Renaissance lyric, but the structural frame of the lullaby metaphor gives it a fine irony missing from the medieval lyrics. Thus what could have been—the middle stanza—medieval enumeration is indeed a witty little liturgy of renunciation, whose climax is the indulgently good-humored dismissal of "little Robyn," the most difficult and perhaps spoiled child of all. This, structured by the lullaby metaphor, achieves a complexity of perception simply unavailable through the conventions underlying fifteenth-century lyrics.

It remains to be said that the last stanza rounds off the poem in a summary statement qualified by the psychologically accurate admission that the speaker, because of his reluctance to give up his youth, has been inventing ways to forestall having to do so: "I can no mo delayes devise." This humane honesty is followed by an apostrophe accepting pain and a final farewell to his "babes," with the injunction

---

16. This fact has been noted before. See, for example, Tydeman who says: "Gascoigne . . . follows standard Renaissance sex psychology. The Elizabethans believed that love, contracted through the eyes, stimulated the passions, in alliance with the fancy, to gain control of the will, overthrow it, and achieve physical satisfaction" (p. 256). With some qualification and less summary simplicity, this was the general view of the literate Englishman of the sixteenth century. That "little Robyn," the sexual organ, should be treated in the favored climactic position is wittily proper, both to the allegory and to the then current view of the matter.

that they remember the lullaby when they awaken and, by implication, submit to the new dispensation.

Compared with this affectionately delicate and yet toughly candid poem, "The aged louer renounceth loue," seems flat and frigid. And this is not because Vaux is incompetent or Gascoigne the immeasurably superior writer. If "The aged louer renounceth loue" could do with some cutting and maybe even rearrangement, "Lullabie" is not flawless; for example, the last stanza, particularly in its sixth line, contains some unhelpful ambiguity. It is rather that the principles of composition—particularly with respect to structure—that inform "The aged louer renounceth loue" set very severe limits to what the practitioner can do with any topic. The principle of composition Gascoigne employs, however he came upon it, gave him an instrument of considerable range in dealing with common human experience. Moreover, each of these principles assumes a way of perceiving reality. The mannered and schematic tonality in Vaux's poem is the direct result of a categorical way of seeing reality, while Gascoigne's more open, subtle (though no less formal) voice is the direct consequence of a more fluid and relational way of seeing things. Indeed, it might be said that the topic of poems that come from this mode of seeing is always relationship itself. And it is this latter kind of poem that seems to me to appear in the Renaissance for the first time in numbers that suggest it is as characteristic of the time as it is uncharacteristic of fifteenth-century poetry. I have already mentioned its presence in Wyatt and have noted that Gascoigne's most impressive poem, "Woodsmanship," partakes of the mode, as does also Ralegh's "Even Such as Time," Sidney's "With How Sad Steps," and Jonson's "On My First Son." It might be argued that the structure of Shakespeare's great tragedies is akin to that of these poems, leading the auditor to a perception not of categories but of relationships. That may perhaps be too extensive a claim for one kind of structure; in any case, it is plainly visible at the end of the sixteenth century and carries over into some of the most important work of the seventeenth century in elaborate and subtle variations like Herbert's "The Collar" and Marvell's "The Garden."

At the beginning of this essay I asserted that enumeration was a characteristic structural principle of medieval poetry. At this point,

I think it is possible to go further: enumeration itself is based upon a more fundamental principle, what one might call the principle of simple juxtaposition in which the elements of a poem are related both in temporal order and conceptually on the basis of a nearly one-to-one comparison or contrast or both, and rarely anything between. This principle, which obviously leads to an accumulative structure of which enumeration is one kind, strongly persists into the sixteenth century; but along with it another principle comes into play which replaces the simple antithesis and catalogue of comparisons with a more complex relating of elements where the attention is not so much on any element as on the relation between them, as in the relation between youth and age in Gascoigne. This latter kind of mode differs also in that it is less concerned with stance (encomium, complaint, precation, exhortation) than with communicating a perception about experience, about how the parts of the world fit together.

It is understanding this mode that I think may give us at least as much help in understanding the sixteenth-century lyric as categories like Drab and Golden. Drab and Golden or Plain and Eloquent poets can also be looked at structurally with some benefit. For example, Sidney and Jonson turn out to share more than late Tudor sophistication by this criterion: a turn of mind that habitually seeks the meaning of relationship, that explores the discontinuities in experience for some connection that will hold, at least in poetry. It is perhaps for this reason that they, like Wyatt and Gascoigne, rely so heavily on irony, that figure which implies doubleness and ambivalence and which is so foreign to Lydgate, Orleans, Suffolk and the myriad minor writers of fifteenth-century lyrics. In any case, the poetry whose topic is relationship itself is one of the important kinds that appears in the sixteenth century. And, as I have tried to show, it can best be understood if we look to the principles that bind elements into coherency.

4. The Rhetoric of Fairyland

MICHAEL MURRIN
UNIVERSITY OF CHICAGO

O NE OF THE most suggestive remarks in Spenser criticism may
well be Coleridge's brief statement:

> You will take especial note of the marvellous independence and true
> imaginative absence of all particular space or time in the Faery
> Queene. It is in the domains neither of history or geography; it is
> truly in land of Faery, that is, of mental space.[1]

In this essay I will try to modify Coleridge's position, in some ways
fundamentally. While he describes properly our response to the allegorical levels of fairyland, he misconstrues Spenser's purposes and
explicit statements on the literal level of his epic. Particularly in Book
Two of *The Faerie Queene*, Spenser asks us to define the nature of his
fairyland and deliberately instigates a search which leads us into
strange realms. The search does not produce an interpretation of the
Legend of Temperance but rather reveals the radical nature of Spenser's art. On the literal or historical level of the poem we find a complex
euhemeristic amalgam, which in turn forces us to reconsider our own
relationship to the poem. Out of this reconsideration arise the allegorical levels, which finally concern not the poem but certain fundamental
human problems. Spenser manipulates us in such a way that he moves
us from wonder at his art to wonder at ourselves.

Spenser begins the search right away in his Prologue, itself a
rhetorical form and therefore apt for his purposes. Classical epic provides no precedent for Spenser's prologues, nor do Ariosto and Boiardo,
despite the direct address to the audience with which they begin their
cantos. In the Italian epic the speaker's address is not formally separated from the rest of the text but merges with the story. The narrator's comments usually have an informal, personal character to them.
Spenser, on the contrary, uses a public voice and a formal address.

1. Cited in John R. Elliott, Jr., *The Prince of Poets* (New York, 1968), p. 15.

Here in Book Two he defends himself against hostile critics, and his audience is the Queen herself. The only real parallels for this are the prologues of Roman comedy, where, as Trissino remarks, "the poet said what he wanted in his own voice."[2] Not through the intermediary of a narrator, whether naive or ironic, but directly, *in propria per sona*, Spenser discusses a number of different questions, and in this practice he follows Donatus' description of the prologue form.[3] The poet may explain something about the story, praise his own poem, or raise more complicated questions about his art. For Book Two Spenser does the third, a method particularly favored by Terence, who used prologues "only in order to defend himself from the criticism of his old rivals and mean poets. So in his prologues he didn't say anything relative to the development of the action . . . ."[4] It is typical of Spenser to turn comic forms, whether Terence's or Chaucer's, to serious purposes. The Prologue speaker, screaming to get attention from the noisy, milling crowds of the Roman festivals, would have been astonished to find himself elegantly introducing the high epic.

In this particular prologue Spenser claims objective status for his fairyland, an argument sufficiently outrageous to draw anyone's attention. To say that fairyland really exists, outside *The Faerie Queene*, should disconcert the most obliging audience, and yet Spenser asserts that we can find it ourselves:

> Of Faerie lond yet if he more inquire,
> By certaine signes here set in sundry place
> He may it find. . . .

(FQ 2. Pro. 4)

The negative corollary of this position should in turn upset the critics. With contemptuous language Spenser flatly denies *any* imaginative status for his poem. *The Faerie Queene* is not "the'aboundance of an idle braine" or a "painted forgery."[5] He would reverse Coleridge's

---

2. In *Theories of Comedy*, ed. Paul Lauter (Garden City, 1964), p. 45. Ariosto, of course, would talk to his patrons but always as narrator of the poem. See the discussion of the rhapsode convention in *Giraldi Cinthio on Romances*, trans. Henry L. Snuggs (Lexington, 1968), pp. 7–8, 36–37. See also Robert M. Durling's analysis of Ariosto and Spenser as narrators in *The Figure of the Poet in Renaissance Epic* (Cambridge, Mass., 1965), chaps. 5, 7.

3. In *Theories of Comedy*, p. 29.

4. Trissino, quoted in *Theories of Comedy*, p. 46.

5. *FQ* 2.Pro.1. All quotations from Spenser are taken from the three volume Oxford edition, edited by J. C. Smith and Ernest de Sélincourt (1909–10).

statement. What are we to make of a poet who vehemently denies that this most imaginative poem is imaginative?

We can at least understand why he is suspicious of the human imagination. In the House of Alma Spenser associates Phantastes with folly and madness (FQ 2.9.52). The flies which buzz about his chamber are idle thoughts and fantasies, and his walls are painted with a confused array of images:

> Infernall Hags, *Centaurs*, feendes, *Hippodames*,
> Apes, Lions, Ægles, Owles, fooles, louers, children, Dames.
>
> (2.9.50)

Reason and discrimination are absent here, and one can see the inherent dangers of solipsism and madness. Dependent on such an imagination, a mind, however healthy, could lose all contact with reality and believe in centaurs as well as apes. And it is this failing which in Book Two gives Acrasia her power. The Genius who presides over her bower deceives men by false phantoms, much as Archimago did the Red Cross Knight.[6] Of a threatening horde of sea beasts, the Palmer says:

> . . . these same Monsters are not these in deed,
> But are into these fearefull shapes disguiz'd
> By that same wicked witch, to worke vs dreed.
>
> (2.12.26)

In his fear and suspicion of the imagination Spenser expresses a standard Renaissance attitude. One need only read Gianfrancesco Pico's treatise on the subject or look at the manuals on witchcraft.[7] The devil controlled people through their imaginations, since he had no power over their intellects. Witches, who flew to sabbats, actually spent the nights at home in bed. One can understand why Spenser would wish to dissociate his poem from such a dubious power, but his stance creates serious problems. He cannot glory in his poem as an imaginative triumph, the way Giraldi Cinthio can in *The Orlando*

---

6. See *FQ* 2.12.48 and 1.1.45–2.6.

7. See, for example, Gianfrancesco Pico della Mirandola, *On the Imagination*, ed. and trans. Harry Caplan (New Haven, 1930), pp. 50–53 (solipsism), 56–57 (demonic action), 60–61 (madness). Chapter twelve details remedies to be taken against evil spirits. For another discussion of this same point, see my "The Varieties of Criticism," *MP* 70 (May 1973): 342–56.

Furioso; he has to defend it in some other fashion.[8] He must claim objective status for what we would consider fantasy.

Spenser models his argument on one used by Ariosto in similar circumstances. In Canto Seven of the *Furioso* Ariosto introduces Alcina's wondrous island with a contrast between what travelers see and what others believe.[9] His conclusion is Spenser's main point:

> Why then should witlesse man so much misweene
> That nothing is, but that which he hath seene?
>
> (FQ 2.Pro.3)

Englishmen should not doubt the existence of marvellous places like Peru merely because they have not been there. But an important difference separates Ariosto's argument from that of Spenser. Ariosto is urging his audience to read this particular tale of emotional experience allegorically. He is not arguing that Alcina's island really exists in the East Indies. Spenser, unfortunately, is. Fairyland is a definite place, one which we can find. Spenser found the true exemplar for his argument where he found Guyon, the hero of Book Two—in Jean of Arras' *Melusine*. Jean begins and ends his romance chronicle with a logical defence of faery, parallel to Spenser's.[10] He establishes possibility for faery by evidence of similar marvels, something he must do since his central character is a half-fay. And Jean carries the defence of faery to its furthest extremes. To deny faery is to ascribe limits to the divine omnipotence. Universal negatives are blasphemy.

As logic this argument falls apart, and Jean of Arras' exaggeration manifests its basic absurdity. If Spenser claims that a wondrous land exists, we can fairly demand some evidence. If he can adduce none, we certainly may reject his claims, however many undiscovered lands there may be. By this negative logic Spenser really begs the question. But if the argument collapses logically, it more than succeeds rhetorically. A scene in *Colin Clovts Come Home Againe* provides an exact paradigm for this kind of rhetoric. Colin Clout has been describing his trip to England, and Cuddie is surprised that another land exists be-

---

8. See *Giraldi Cinthio*, pp. 12, 49–51. He argues that feigned works are better than ones based on history and completely re-interprets Aristotle's remarks on Agathon's feigned tragedy, *The Flower*.

9. *OF* 7.1–2.

10. Like Ariosto he also appeals to the experience of travellers and to the wise. See A. K. Donald's edition for EETS, Extra Series 68 (London, 1895), pp. 2–6, 370–71.

sides the island where he lives (290–91). Colin answers him gently but amusedly with the same argument that Spenser uses in this prologue:

> Ah *Cuddy* (then quoth *Colin*) thous a fon,
> That hast not seene least part of natures worke:
> Much more there is vnkend, then thou doest kon,
> And much more that does from mens knowledge lurke.
>
> (*Colin Clout* 292–95)

We can laugh at Cuddie's naiveté and ignorance but may not realize that Spenser has put his critics in the same position. Whatever the quality of the logic, no one wishes to assume Cuddie's role.

Having developed this unusual argument and aroused the expectations of his audience, Spenser ends the Prologue in very mundane fashion and seems to close off discussion. Elizabeth can see her own realms *mirrored* in faery. So the wondrous lands reflect England, and any search seems unnecessary. But first of all, this identification would not apply to the narrative, where the characters are either natives of faery or British visitors from abroad. The poet does not identify the two. Moreover, such an identification would ignore Spenser's image and, therefore, collapse the distinction between the mirror and the object which it reflects. The substance of a mirror differs markedly from the diverse objects which it may image, and its shadow reflection *reverses* the position of the original object. We should not be surprised to find the mirror of England wonderful and splendid in a way that England could not be. And the relationship between the two is odd. In the Renaissance a person might argue that England mirrors an ideal order. He normally would not claim that the ideal mirrors the real, which is what Spenser asserts. This inversion of relations upsets a traditional, hierarchic structure, assumed for an aeon. So Spenser has not answered the questions of his critics, though he purports to do so. With his negative argument Spenser seems to say much about fairyland and at the same time gives us as little information about it as possible. The poet tantalizes his audience. He wants us to wonder about faery, to search for its traces. And he provides some remarkable clues.

The first of these occurs in the Prologue itself. Spenser hints at a possibility which dazzles. In his discussion of new worlds he includes, besides America, the moon and stars, twenty years *before* Galileo turned his telescope in that direction. Then the poet implies that Francisco de Orellana, when he sailed the wrong way down a

Brazilian river, proved the reality of the old Amazon myth. Do other classical myths mirror realities *not yet* discovered by man? The euhemerist critic saw these stories as reflections of a dim past. Spenser seems to be turning the mirror in the other direction:

> What if in euery other starre vnseene
> Of other worldes he [any man] happily should heare?
> He wonder would much more: yet such to *some* appeare.
>
> (*FQ* 2.Pro.3; italics are mine)

Augustine once had wondered whether some "process enables the future to be seen, some process by which events which have not yet occurred become present to us by means of *already* existing images of them."[11] Is Spenser making just such a claim? Or is he making the obvious statement that explorers discover new lands? The phrase is ambiguous. Spenser does not clarify the matter any further, nor need he. By his hints and negative argument, he has already accomplished his purpose. We are off on a hunt for faery.

The first stage of the search leads us out of the specifically rhetorical situation of the Prologue and back within the text. The poet ceases to address us and turns to his tale, while we look for clues, most of which are clustered at the beginning of Book Two and in the House of Alma. The preliminary explanation which this evidence warrants forms the literal and political levels of fairyland. We are concerned, in other words, with the relations of fairyland to history and to contemporary politics.

The first and most obvious question which we put to the Legend of Temperance has already been determined by the Prologue. We want to know where Spenser locates fairyland and what evidence he presents for its existence. We will take the question of location first, which Spenser answers quite succinctly. In the House of Alma Guyon reads of the faery beginnings:

> The first and eldest, which that scepter swayd,
> Was *Elfin*; him all *India* obayd,
> And all that now *America* men call.
>
> (*FQ* 2.10.72)

Fairyland is India and America. And here Spenser faithfully follows his sources, the Charlemagne romances. Since Spenser generally ig-

---

11. *Confessions*, R. S. Pine-Coffin (Baltimore: Penguin, 1961), 11.18, p. 267. Italics are mine.

nored Malory and imitated the Italian epics about Roland and Rinaldo, he found faery in the Near and Middle East. Boiardo strews the area with enchanted gardens, dragons, and fays, while with the episodes of Prester John and Alcina, Ariosto takes in the whole Indian Ocean. Boiardo even moves Morgan the Fay to the East.[12] There is one medieval Charlemagne romance which is of particular interest in this respect, since Spenser specifically refers to it in Book Two. *Huon of Bordeaux* clearly shows how faery drifts ever further east. In the original *chanson de geste* Huon meets Oberon on the way from Jerusalem to Babylon (Cairo), but in the continuations of the romance the marvels have receded beyond the Euphrates. When Huon finally arrives in Momure, the faery capital, he is in Hircania or the Elburz Mountains of North Persia. Arthur's new realms, which he receives from the dying Oberon, are further east, for they include Tartary or Central Asia.[13] So Spenser follows this eastward drift and locates faery in India and finally in America.

The inclusion of America resolves another potential dilemma. In contrast to the Charlemagne romances Arthurian tradition locates the wonders of faery in the west of Europe, in the Arthurian realm itself or still further west on the hidden isle of Avalon, where Morgan the Fay lives. Boiardo, however, put her realm in Asia. Since both Arthur and his sister Morgan rule lands which are both west and east, we can infer that fairyland itself can be found in opposite directions. Columbus sailed west to go east, and Orellana discovered the Amazon sailing east to go west. With a round world contradictory directions can be reconciled. Spenser includes both Indies in fairyland and so reflects the contemporary opinion that the American Indians migrated to the New World from Asia.[14] We can see that this equation of the newly discovered lands with fairyland is not farfetched if we look at Bernal Díaz del Castillo's reactions, when with Cortez' troops he first beheld Mexico City:

> During the morning, we arrived at a broad Causeway and continued our march towards Iztapalapa, and when we saw so many cities and villages built in the water and other great towns on dry land and

12. See *Orlando Innamorato* 2.8, for Orlando's first visit to Morgan's realm.

13. For Hircania, see *Duke Huon of Burdeux*, trans. Lord Berners and ed. S. L. Lee, EETS, Extra Series 40, 41, 43, 50 (London, 1882–87), pp. 595, 603. Material added to the original *chanson de geste* will be called the Huon Continuations.

14. See Isabel Rathborne, *The Meaning of Spenser's Fairyland* (New York, 1937), p. 111.

that straight and level Causeway going towards Mexico, we were amazed and said that it was like the enchantments they tell of in the legend of Amadis, on account of the great towers and cues and buildings rising from the water, and all built of masonry. And some of our soldiers even asked whether the things that we saw were not a dream. It is not to be wondered at that I here write it down in this manner, for there is so much to think over that I do not know how to describe it, seeing things as we did that had never been heard of or seen before, not even dreamed about.[15]

No quotation could better illustrate the discovery of fairyland.

The equation of faery with the Indies and America likewise establishes the political level of the allegory. Since 1580 both India and America were ruled by Philip of Habsburg and formed the first true world empire. To the Habsburgs with their immense power and Roman mystique of universal dominion, Spenser opposes a Crusader's myth. The Spaniards and Portuguese are interlopers in territories anciently visited by various English heroes. The mirror of Elizabeth's realm itself should belong to Elizabeth.[16]

On this level fairyland becomes wish-fulfillment. Harry Berger has shown how the chronicle of fairyland presents an ideal order, in striking contrast to the relative chaos of English history.[17] Similarly, in *Huon of Bordeaux*, where the earthly rulers are mostly weak and foolish, Oberon rules his faery realm justly and compassionately, and his commands are instantly obeyed.[18] In the Charlemagne romances this wish-fulfillment more frequently takes the form of military victory over the infidel. Orlando battles the forces of Agramant, and Guyon has for enemies the paynim brethren Pyrochles and Cymochles.[19] Huon of Bordeaux likewise spends most of his time fighting Saracens. With Oberon's aid and a few French knights he captures

15. *The Discovery and Conquest of Mexico*, trans. A. P. Maudslay, (New York: Noonday, 1956), pp. 190–91.

16. Spenser strongly supported the Virginia settlement and those like Ralegh who advocated imperial expansion. See Rathborne, p. 240.

17. *The Allegorical Temper* (New Haven, 1957), pp. 107–11, 113–14. I disagree, however, with Berger's sharp distinction between elves and human beings and between classical and Christian heroes.

18. Oberon three times forgives Huon: when the Frenchman first blows the ivory horn, when he lies to the guard at the First Gate of Admiral Gaudys' palace, and when he sleeps with Esclaramonde before the marriage service. See *Huon*, pp. 81, 152, 257.

19. The references are all in Canto Eight. The Argument calls them paynim, and so does the Narrator in 10 and 54, while the brothers swear by "Termagaunt" and "Mahoune" (30 and 33).

Cairo and makes it into a Christian fief. In the Huon Continuations the Egyptians get beaten again, this time by a newly Christianized Persian army. In this respect fairyland responds to the Christian sense of frustration after the Third Crusade and to their hopes in Prester John. For Spenser this function of faery would have a renewed application. Ariosto had already depicted an ideal victory over the Saracens by a gigantic Christian alliance, and Spenser looked forward to the battle of the Faerie Queene and Arthur with the paynim invaders of Britain. Englishmen were just recovering from the shock of the Armada and could well appreciate the general situation. Ariosto emphasized the fantasy involved in his details: an Ethiopian army crosses the Sahara; stones become horses; leaves, ships.[20] The myth contradicts the reality. In Ariosto's time the Turks moved from victory to victory, conquering Syria, Egypt, Rhodes, and Hungary. They seemed invincible. In Spenser's time reality had changed very little. Despite Turkish preoccupation with Persia and Christian victories at Malta and Lepanto, the Christians did not win back a single foot of territory, and Cyprus fell to the Turks.

In this manner the political level of the allegory differs from the literal. While both relate to historical reality, from one level to another the relation of myth to fact reverses itself. On the literal level fairyland reflects reality, the Asia of the Crusades. On the political level it contradicts reality. The grandiose vision of world empire compensates for political weakness. The Englishman fears for the survival of his nation, the Protestant worries for his faith, and the Christian perpetually loses to the Turk.[21] For the Christian, especially, the war had gone badly for hundreds of years, and an appeal to faery remained viable, whether made in the time of the Emperor Frederick II or in that of Queen Elizabeth.

Faery's continued existence over so long a period eventually gave it a status peculiarly its own, partially independent of any single literary text. This tendency appears first of all in the habit of cross-

---

20. *OF* 38.33–34; 39.26–28.

21. An appropriate passage in Tacitus shows the other side of this process (*Annalium* 15.31): "Concerned for Tiridates' interests, the Parthian king had sent envoys to Corbulo asking that his brother should not be exposed to any external signs of subjection—that he should keep his sword, be entitled to embrace governors, not be kept waiting at their doors, and at Rome receive a consul's honours. Vologeses was accustomed to foreign ostentatiousness. Clearly he did not understand how we Romans value real power but disdain its vanities." (Michael Grant, trans. [Baltimore: Penguin, 1956], pp. 347–48.)

reference. The Huon Continuations include references to two other romances. We learn that Reinold of Montalban captured Angora twenty years earlier and that Ogier the Dane destroyed Colanders en route to India. Spenser's remark about Huon and Guyon is the last in a series of such cross references:[22]

> Well could he [Guyon] tourney and in lists debate,
> And knighthood tooke of good Sir *Houns* hand,
> When with king *Oberon* he came to Faerie land.
>
> (*FQ* 2.1.6)

By such a method fairyland becomes an entity unto itself, a general place which draws together many different romances and chronicles and unites the matter of Britain with that of France. In *Huon*, when Arthur and his sister, Morgan the Fay, arrive at Momure, we learn that Morgan has newly married Ogier the Dane, who is now acting as Arthur's regent.[23] Spenser's choice of fairyland then has considerable artistic significance. In the other romances fairyland is a place visited amidst a number of adventures set in more mundane lands. In *Orlando Innamorato*, the most fantastic of the Italian romances, the heroes by the end are all drifting back to France. Spenser alone staged all his action there, in the land where all other romances cross over, one into another. Spenser has effectively made his epic into a *summa* of medieval and Renaissance romance, the last story which incorporates all the others. Here the dreams of faery isles and distant lands, of Avalon and Momure, achieve their final form.[24]

We have defined the where of faery, and in the course of this definition we have already worked through much of the evidence Spenser presents for its existence. The evidence itself, however, suggests that our answer to the where of faery needs revision. Fairyland is not simply India and America. However wonderful, Mexico and the

---

22. See *Huon*, pp. 72, 489. The imprecision of Spenser's reference is also typical of this method. Only on his first visit did Huon technically come to fairyland *with* Oberon, and then he did not knight anyone. The second time he found Oberon dying in Momure and had traveled there by himself.

23. See *Huon*, p. 601. For a number of similar examples, see Rathborne, pp. 186, 188, 212–14.

24. In this respect I would agree with Harry Berger's comment: "Spenser's poetry represents in its complex form all the phases which preceded it and which it, in effect, supersedes." But I would reject his evolutionary model and the general argument of this essay. See "Two Spenserian Retrospects: The Antique Temple of Venus and the Primitive Marriage of Rivers," *TSLL* 10 (1968): 7.

Moluccas do not contain marvels like Cleopolis and Acrasia's Bower. By his evidence Spenser suggests how we get from one to the other. We already know from Book One that the "antiquities, which no body can know" (FQ 2.Pro.1) are in Calliope's keeping, for she has the ancient rolls of fairyland put away in an "euerlasting scryne" or box (1.Pro.2). So we also know that Spenser is not talking of historical evidence in the normal sense of that term. The Muses do not preside over the Public Record Office. Guyon's experience at Alma's Castle further clarifies this assumption. In the Chamber of Memory he reads the "Antiquitie of Faerie lond" (FQ 2.9.60). Another answer then to the where of faery is anywhere that human beings exist. Fairyland is not a place *per se* but a memory in the mind of man, something preserved in books. Literary memory has this advantage over imagination, in that its images and data have already been filtered through reason. In Augustine's metaphor, memory is the stomach of the mind.[25] Books and chronicles express this difference clearly, for they result from a rational ordering of experiential phenomena. Now Spenser normally indicates what texts specially concern each book of The Faerie Queene: the Legend of St. George for Book One, or the *Canterbury Tales* for Book Four. For the Legend of Temperance the relevant books are three: *Melusine, Huon of Bordeaux,* and the traditional English chronicle history derived from Geoffrey of Monmouth.[26] Only the first two books treat of faery and need concern us here. Unfortunately, if we turn to these romances, we find another puzzle. Both *Melusine* and *Huon* (in its final form) are romance chronicles of particular families in Aquitaine. Neither has any demonstrable influence on the narrative of The Faerie Queene.[27] Spenser did not borrow any episodes, magical devices, or palaces from these sources. His appeal to them must have a different purpose.

A more likely explanation would be that Spenser wishes us to

25. *Confessions* 10.14.
26. See FQ 2.1.6 for the reference to Huon and Guyon. Arthur reads English chronicle history in the House of Alma (FQ 2.10).
27. One could make some case for *Huon.* Guyon's treatment of Tantalus resembles Huon's methods with Cain. They both elicit information from a damned person and then refuse to help him, out of respect for divine justice. Also, the first episode in Guyon's voyage recalls the beginning of Huon's second voyage East, where he passes over the Perilous Gulf and shipwrecks on the Castle of Adamant. What Huon experienced sequentially, Guyon does simultaneously, as he sails between the Gulf of Greediness and the Rock of Reproach (FQ 2.12.3–9). There the resemblance ends. Guyon escaped what Huon had to suffer.

see in these sources euhemerist analogues for his own poem. We can find out something about this if we look again at the episode in *Colin Clout*. Colin has been telling his friends about his little voyage to England:

> So to the sea we came; the sea? that is
> A world of waters heaped vp on hie,
> Rolling like mountaines in wide wildernesse,
> Horrible, hideous, roaring with hoarse crie.

(196–99)

What for an experienced person would be an uneventful trip Colin transforms into high heroics. We realize that the sea amazes and terrifies the shepherd because he has not seen it before. Therefore, while in our terms he exaggerates matters and wanders in hyperbole, he nevertheless conveys to us a genuine, authentic experience: his first view of the sea. One could argue that a similar process occurs in *Huon of Bordeaux* and explains its presentation of faery. At the battle of Rames Huon's valor stuns his Persian allies, and the narrator remarks:

> . . . he that had sene Houn howe he slewe and bet downe the Sarasyns and paynymes, wolde haue sayde that he was no mortall man / but rather a man of the fayrey, for the great prowes and maruayles that he dyd. . . .

(*Huon*, p. 598)

In fact, Huon wears powerful gems which make him invincible, so the judgment is appropriate. But the process of judgment is curious. Since Huon displays unusual abilities, he must be of "faery," despite the fact that he is of mortal birth and has not yet journeyed to Momure. Now invincibility need not warrant exaggeration but probably will. Following such logic, the author of the text could himself *invent* marvels to convey the quality of superior human achievement. If the history represents some such logic, then Oberon's faery wonders could be demythologized, and the chronicle would become another kind of euhemeristic narrative. And, whether the medieval authors of *Huon* and its continuations ever intend such distortions, Spenser, familiar as he was with Renaissance modes of exegesis, would probably have read *Huon* in this fashion. He could easily have seen that *Huon* conformed to a euhemeristic pattern. One of the most marvellous episodes occurs at the Castle of Adamant, where adherents to King Ptolemy besieged

Julius Caesar after he had set up Cleopatra in Egypt. Spenser could tell from Plutarch and from other classical sources that this event never happened. Caesar did not sleep with the Lady of the Privy Isle, command a troop of faery beings, and pass away his time in a castle whose "walles and toures were of fyne alabaster clere shynyng, and the towres rychely coueryd with fyne golde of Arabe."[28] If he wished to, Spenser could gauge with some precision the way *Huon* distorts reality into myth.

Spenser's own form of euhemerism is more complicated. He manufactures endless wonders but disengages them from his faery heroes. As Isabel Rathborne says:

> His good fairies are thoroughly humanized and rationalized. They possess, or at least exhibit, no supernatural powers that are not also possessed by the human characters. In fact the principal enchanted weapons in the poem belong to Britomart and Arthur, neither of whom is a fairy.[29]

Spenser manages to suggest simultaneously the original mundane hero (Guyon) and the effect of his career on others (the wonders with which the poet surrounds the hero). The process dramatizes the bases of euhemerism and explains the nature of Spenser's "evidence."

We have now come to a preliminary judgment on Spenser's faery. It is the literary expression of a complex mental experience. It begins with a person's response to an unfamiliar reality, the way Colin felt about the sea, the Persians about Huon's prowess, and the explorers about the two Indies. Therefore, in its very origins faery involves more than an external reality, it includes both perceiver and the thing perceived. This perceptual act is unique, for Colin's second or third experience of the sea will not have for him the same wonder and surprise as the first. The poet expresses the unity of this perceptual event by a restructuring of this whole process, which in turn stimulates a set of special reactions in us. We participate not in a firsthand experience, as in a romantic poem, but in its symbolic rearrangement, where the

---

28. *Huon*, p. 380.
29. Rathborne, pp. 172–73. Furthermore, Rathborne likewise points out on p. 142 that the genesis of fairyland is euhemeristic. It reflects Ovid's story of Prometheus in the *Metamorphoses*, which Golding sees as an analogue to the Genesis story of man's creation (see his Epistle to Leicester, 419–54). For additional information, consult Rathborne's remarks on E. K. and on Burton's *Anatomy* (p. 164) and on the way Melusine was euhemerized by Spenser's French contemporaries (p. 170).

whole landscape can look different, and impossible images rest next to everyday horses. To take one example, the great bridge of Cleopolis:

> . . . *Elfinor*, who was in magick skild;
> He built by art vpon the glassy See
> A bridge of bras, whose sound heauens thunder seem'd to bee.
>
> (FQ 2.10.73)

One first imagines a shining bridge stretched over a calm, or "glassy" sea, but then the syntax creates problems. Spenser identifies the bridge with thunder, which does not fit a calm day. Or, if we take the other syntactic possibility, how can a calm sea make thunderous noises? But if the bridge is really thunder and lightning, then the glassy sea suggests the apocalyptic sea of heaven. The description is already half-stellified. We cannot simply distinguish truth from hyperbole here or in many other scenes of *The Faerie Queene* because the formal vision does not represent an external reality; rather it mediates a perceptual process.

The blending of truth and hyperbole creates a peculiar rhetorical situation. Our response to Spenser's faery differs more than a little from Colin's wonder at the sea, and it is in this area that we come upon the allegorical levels of fairyland. We observe in Book Two certain phenomena which are ignored by the characters and by the narrator of the poem. We move, therefore, away from the literal level, where we dealt mostly with formal questions, matters of geography and sources. Now we must try to sift truth from hyperbole and enter the realm of psychology.[30] The questions which we will ask, the *whys* for which we will devise answers, provide the mechanism of transition. What we find at first is that Spenser systematically violates our notions of probability, in an ever increasing degree. What we make of these violations takes us out of the poem altogether.

To begin with, though Spenser has located fairyland in a definite place and, furthermore, given it a coherent time scheme, our predominant reaction to faery is quite different.[31] No one seriously wonders

---

30. For this distinction see my *Veil of Allegory* (Chicago, 1969), pp. 95–96, 127.

31. We know that Guyon was at Cleopolis, when Red Cross set off on his quest (FQ 2.1.19) and that he has been on his own quest for three months after he meets Red Cross again (FQ 2.2.44). Therefore, he left Cleopolis shortly after the Red Cross Knight. Arthur's chronology supports these inferences. When he rescues Red Cross, he has been searching for Gloriana nine months (FQ 1.9.15), but he has been out a year when he meets Guyon (FQ 2.9.7). Likewise we know that the

what road Arthur took from Orgoglio's Castle to the area by Mammon's vale or what happened at Medina's after Guyon left.[32] We feel that Medina with as much probability could cease to exist, once Guyon departs. Images and personifications appear and disappear in a largely deserted landscape. This dreamy sense contrasts markedly with the Italian romance epic. Tasso and Ariosto both present coherent societies with a real geography and history. We know exactly how to go from Paris to Arles, or from Palestine to Armida's Garden in the Canaries. Likewise we know that Jerusalem has its own history, both before and after the events narrated in Tasso's poem. Solyman's descendant will be Saladin.[33] Ariosto can leave Marsilio unpunished in Spain, confident that we will draw our own conclusions about Roncesvalles. The typical scene in *The Faerie Queene* generates no such probable illusions. It resembles more the vague, unending forest of adventures in which Malory's heroes wander. And Malory finally does not apply either, for two reasons. In a story like the Knight of the Cart, Malory can locate his events specifically and familiarly, near London. He can create a probable and real world, when he wants to. The other reason is more fundamental. Spenser, in places, makes his landscape deliberately incoherent.

The hag Occasion gives a fine example of what I have called elsewhere the Absurdity Principle.[34] When she instigates battle between Furor and Pyrochles, she uses a weird torch:

> His mother eke, more to augment his spight,
> Now brought to him a flaming fire brond,
> Which she in *Stygian* lake, ay burning bright,
> Had kindled. . . .

> (FQ 2.5.22)

Where could she get this prop all at once? It is ridiculous to assume that she kept it hidden and *burning*, while Guyon tied her up. But the other possibility is equally unacceptable. Who could imagine her

---

adventures of Red Cross occur in high summer, as Alastair Fowler points out. (See *Spenser and the Numbers of Time* [London, 1964], pp. 70–71.) But again our most pervasive feeling is the absence of seasons and specific times in *The Faerie Queene*.

32. I am indebted for this remark to one of my graduate students, Lynda Bundtzen. I have also discussed this matter in "The Varieties of Criticism" (see n. 7).

33. *Jerusalem Delivered* 10.22–23.

34. See *The Veil of Allegory*, pp. 146–48, 149–50.

suddenly running off to Hades and back again, all in an instant, un-
noticed either by the other characters or by the narrator? The scene
violates probability. Then there is the episode where Guyon literally
padlocks her tongue (*FQ* 2.4.12). Or take another, less obvious example.
Who can seriously imagine Guyon sailing for two days over the open
sea—in a rowboat? (*FQ* 2.12.2) But these are minor "lapses" compared
to the systematic violation of all probability which Spenser achieves
with his major characters. If he is so concerned over the objective truth
of faery, why does he have characters interact who could never have
met? Arthur is a fifth- or sixth-century personage, Huon lived in the
eighth and Guyon in the twelfth century. Arthur's "contemporaries"
are backward projections from the distant future. And all these dates
are assumed in the chronicles, not invented by modern historical research. What would we make of a play or film with a fourteenth-
century setting whose major characters were Edward II, Henry VIII,
and Sir Winston Churchill?

There was precedent for such anachronism in classical and Renaissance epic. Dido and Aeneas made love despite the four hundred
years separating their lives, and Ariosto could take a twelfth-century
ruler of Damascus and move him back to the time of Charlemagne
(or at least use the name).[35] But both of these were isolated incidents,
while Spenser has made his central and continued action anachronis-
tic. Perhaps no epic or romance poet ever grounded his plot on such a
radical principle. Spenser made poetic license the focus of his epic.

Isabel Rathborne tried to explain this phenomenon in *The Meaning of Spenser's Fairyland*. She associated fairyland with the classical
Elysium, the place of the famous dead.[36] She thus could explain with
precision how renowned heroes from different periods could meet one
another. The Christian version would be heaven and hell and would
have an additional value, for it would rationalize our psychological
apprehension of faery. Aquinas had argued that man in the Beatific
Vision apprehends many things at once, while now we think succes-
sively and by means of many ideas.[37] This was a conventional notion,
not one peculiar to Aquinas, and could help to explain why in *The
Faerie Queene* we perceive several different times at once.

Unfortunately, Rathborne's theory, though attractive, does not

35. I refer to Norandino (Nur ed-Din, the father of Saladin).
36. Rathborne, pp. 143–44.
37. *Summa theologica* 1.12.10.

really apply to Spenser, or at least not in the manner in which she formulates it. Such a hypothesis cannot explain the everyday activities of faery. Guyon lives a life of chivalric action, by which he acquires fame. Heaven and Elysium, on the other hand, are rewards for such virtuous action. They are not places where one makes oneself a hero or a devil. Therefore, moral choice does not exist in these afterworlds, and good and evil are separated from each other. In fairyland the condition is just the opposite. Guyon and Arthur are constantly making moral choices and the bad mingle with the good.[38]

We can still keep much of Rathborne's theory, however, if we give to it a different basis. We must look not to the *meaning* of fairyland but to a rhetorical set of relationships, namely those between ourselves and the poem. While reading *The Faerie Queene* we experience the interaction of Guyon and Arthur with perfect ease, while on reflection all the difficulties appear. When we try to rationalize what we have experienced in Spenser's poem, we stumble and talk inaccurately.[39] Somehow we can understand the coexistence of times in a literary form but not in philosophical discourse. Or theological discourse, for that matter. If we can sense how Guyon and Arthur interact, we approach dimly to the divine comprehension of history, to the interaction of Abraham and Christ. Unlike a romantic poet who might image in his poetry *how* his mind grapples with the primary data of experience, Spenser transforms this perceptual process. He makes us think of the conditions for perception, the whatever which underlies our mental processes. It is one thing for the mind to understand a mathematical theorem or a perceived object like a cat. It is quite another thing for the mind to understand why it understands, to comprehend its own form, particularly when the problem turns on the contrast between mental and external time.

Here we must make a short digression to clarify the next point. By the Renaissance philosophic discourse on time had become extremely subtle and complicated. A few examples will suggest some of the dimensions of the problem. Plotinus, with his Alexandrian love for hierarchy, has insisted that eternity must be defined first, since it is the precondition for the temporal order.[40] The caveat is logical but makes an already difficult question almost impossible. Who can talk

38. Rathborne has her own suppositions on this problem. See p. 145.
39. See n. 24.
40. *Enneads* 3.7.1.

about not-time? Augustine, perhaps, did it better than anyone, when he tried to explain how the mind can comprehend past, present, and future simultaneously.[41] By the Middle Ages Aquinas, drawing on such late classical speculation, could weave a set of truly fine distinctions. One could argue that the term *eternity* applied to God alone and then find a new term for various intermediary beings. So *aeviternity* was applied to changeless beings which nevertheless approach change in limited ways. Thus, one could distinguish immortal beings from an eternal being, those which had a beginning but will never end from the One who was, is, and ever shall be.[42] For a complex set of abstruse problems Aquinas used a clear and precise terminology, of the sort possible only when there has been sustained disputation over a long period. But for us this discourse remains unsatisfactory for a number of reasons. Aquinas inherits the Alexandrian love for endless intermediaries, none of which are part of normal experience, and today we have different assumptions and philosophies. Perhaps any rational explanation will be inadequate. Augustine says: "What, then, is time? I know well enough what it is, provided that nobody asks me; but if I am asked what it is and try to explain, I am baffled."[43] And yet the problem is very much our problem. Somehow we exist in two worlds at once, an eternal and a temporal world.[44] The second world we understand, not the first, which we define negatively (not-time), as unlike the second and yet somehow its *precondition*. Through a specialized

---

41. See *Confessions* 11.14–31.

42. This we may take as a representative example of this kind of discourse: "We say then that since eternity is the measure of a permanent being, in so far as anything recedes from permanence of being, it recedes from eternity. Now some things recede from permanence of being, so that their being is subject to change, or consists in change; and these things are measured by time, as are all movements, and also the being of all things corruptible. But others recede less from permanence of being, forasmuch as their being neither consists in change, nor is the subject of change; nevertheless they have change annexed to them either actually, or potentially. This appears in the heavenly bodies, the substantial being of which is unchangeable; and yet with unchangeable being they have changeableness of place. The same applies to the angels, who have an unchangeable being as regards their nature with changeableness as regards choice; moreover they have changeableness of intelligence, of affections, and of places, in their own degree. Therefore these are measured by aeviternity, which is a mean between eternity and time." (*Summa theologica* 1.10.5.) The translation is the older one by the Fathers of the English Dominican Province (New York, 1947), I, 43–44.

43. *Confessions* 11.14, p. 264.

44. I use the term *eternal* loosely here, as not-time, and will avoid technical, scholastic vocabulary like *aeviternity*.

literary form Spenser has demonstrated the reality of this second world. To perceive the coexistence of times in his poem is to have the viewpoint of eternity on time. Spenser has thrown us outside the temporal flux and into that area of our mind which we cannot define but can experience: a non-temporal perspective on the temporal.

We are now in a position to recall Coleridge's famous remark and develop further his notion of mental space. Spenser reorganizes primary mental experience symbolically for rhetorical purposes. In response to faery we move outside the poem and try to know ourselves. Later we attempt to formulate this understanding philosophically. And for Spenser or for anyone in the Renaissance our reaction should also involve cosmic speculation. We apprehend the eternal of which this temporal order, this universe of earth, stars, and planets, is but a moving image.

There may also be a theological level to fairyland, for Spenser's characters create more than temporal problems. So far we have examined fairyland literally as a place and its characters rhetorically. On the philosophical level we devised theories to explain our response to the characters in the poem. On the theological level we will assume the same rhetorical situation as we did on the philosophical, but our attention will be directed to another set of discrepancies, quite as notorious as Spenser's anachronisms.

Horace's rules about characterization delineate the problem most clearly. In the *Ars Poetica* he demands a complete consistency of characterization:

> You should either stick to tradition
> Or invent a consistent plot. If you bring back Achilles,
> Have him say how laws don't apply to him, have prowess
> Prevail over status, make him ruthless, impatient and fierce,
> And ANGRY! Let Medea be wild, inconquerably so,
> Ino tearful, Io "lost"; let Ixion
> Go back on his word; let Orestes be sadly depressed.
> If it's something as yet untried you put on the stage
> And you dare construct a new character, you must keep
> To the end the same sort of person you started out with,
> And make your portrayal consistent.[45]

45. The first sentence is an interpretation by the translator, Smith Palmer Bovie, in the *Satires and Epistles of Horace* (Chicago: Phoenix Books, 1959).

Now one could argue plausibly that Spenser follows the latter part of this advice. Within his poem he keeps his characters reasonably consistent.[46] The problem comes with the first part of Horace's advice. The Roman poet wants the dramatist to keep famous characters consistent to the preconceptions of the audience. A timid and quiet Achilles would empty the theater very quickly.[47] This is sound rhetorical advice and recognizes the fact that for many works of art there exists what the French call a *prétexte*. If an author wishes to depict a famous hero, he must conform to the traditional type of that hero. Now Spenser put some famous heroes into his poem, heroes like Arthur and St. George, but they might as well be new characters like Britomart—despite their names. The change is deliberate, for it is more difficult to establish inconsistency in romances and yet Spenser does so. Unlike the characters of tragedy the heroes of romance have far less developed personalities. They lack the necessary monologues and dramatic speeches. Physical oddities and repeated actions normally define them. In *Melusine*, for example, Guyon has one eye higher than another, and Huon in his tale always disobeys Oberon.[48] Even so, Spenser has managed completely to disengage his heroes from their literary tradition.

Consider the case of Arthur. Who would recognize in the romantic lover of Gloriana, whom he saw only once, the experienced knight, perpetually out on quest, with his horse Spumador and his sword Morddure,[49] or who would recognize the adolescent who pulled the sword from the stone and married Guinevere? Or who could find the Arthur of Geoffrey's *Historia Regum Britanniae*, who spent money so fast that he had to attack the Saxons for plunder?[50] Spenser's Arthur supposedly *precedes* these figures, yet he resembles rather accomplished knights like Orlando or Lancelot. Guyon presents the same problem. Where is the boy who followed his brother to Cyprus and became King of Armenia? The two Guyons relate to each other so little that scholars have wondered whether Spenser used *Melusine* or not, and yet the two figures relate to each other as well as the two

46. A number of critics have done studies of characters in *The Faerie Queene*, something which would be impossible, if Spenser had constructed inconsistent personalities. The most notable example is T. K. Dunseath, *Spenser's Allegory of Justice in Book Five of The Faerie Queene* (Princeton, 1968).

47. See Aristotle's criticisms in *Poetics* 1454a27–33 concerning the needless degradation of a famous character. His remarks involve two plays of Euripides.

48. *Melusine*, p. 103.

49. For a reference to Spumador, see *FQ* 2.11.19; for Morddure, see *FQ* 2.8.21.

50. See the beginning of Book Nine.

92

Arthurs. Why should Spenser insist on historical figures and then give them almost complete changes of personality?[51]

I do not think that we in the twentieth century would have any obvious response to this problem other than general dismay. Although modern writers have much concerned themselves with fluid personalities, they have not by and large worried about the theological dimensions of this problem. In the Renaissance, however, a theological conception of discontinuity did exist and was accepted by all, whether Protestant or Catholic. A Christian then would define a person not only as an identifiable individual who lives a certain span of time here but as one who after death lives a transformed existence in heaven and hell. This idea involves as radical a discontinuity as we find in Spenser's historical characters. I am not suggesting, of course, that Guyon or Arthur somehow signify the saints in heaven. Quite different. The discontinuity which we observe in Spenser's characters parallels logically the discontinuity a Christian would perceive in his own existence. Paul's analogy for the risen body clearly demonstrates this. The glorified body of a human being relates to his earthly body as the plant does to its seed.[52] Now in form a seed does not remotely resemble a tree or flower, though we understand their hidden continuity and ordinarily give to them the same name. We buy *aster* seeds and *tulip* bulbs. Similarly, a Christian would ascribe the same name to what appears drastically different. It is still Paul, whether on earth or in heaven.

Personal names would be the normal way to indicate such a continuity in discontinuity. We know that such words signify unique personalities, which we get to know gradually but never completely. Our initial judgment usually depends upon givens, the accidents of birth. Belphoebe is beautiful and Arthur is strong. It takes years to guess at the use of these gifts and so to approach the more unique aspect of a person. Nevertheless, some kind of reasonable judgment can finally be made here on an individual, a judgment which is succinctly expressed by the old Greek proverb: "Call no man happy until death."[53]

---

51. To argue that Spenser needed creative freedom in his handling of Arthur and St. George is nonsense. He could always have used invented characters like Britomart.

52. 1.Corinth. 15:35–44.

53. The proverb concludes many Greek tragedies including *Oedipus Rex* and is paraphrased by Solon in his discourse with Croesus. See Herodotus, *The Persian Wars* 1.32.

We cannot assess the value of a man's life or come to know it properly until we perceive it teleologically. We have to know the man's complete record, how his story ends. Only then can we say we know, as much as we are able to know any particular, what the name of that person really denotes. But in the Christian tradition we can never achieve such a perspective. If someone believes in resurrection, then the life of the individual literally has *no end*, and teleology becomes impossible.[54] It is as if we were limited to the prologue of a story. Time will fade before eternity, and each individual person will be transformed, will become like angel or demon. Augustine relates a conversation which he had with his mother, shorly before her death, and his narrative shows affectively the mystery of that future life which by its brilliance annihilates this present existence:

> Our conversation led us to the conclusion that no bodily pleasure, however great it might be and whatever earthly light might shed lustre upon it, was worthy of comparison, or even of mention, beside the happiness of the life of the saints. As the flame of love burned stronger in us and raised us higher towards the eternal God, our thoughts ranged over the whole compass of material things in their various degrees, up to the heavens themselves, from which the sun and the moon and the stars shine down upon the earth. Higher still we climbed, thinking and speaking all the while in wonder at all that you have made. At length we came to our own souls and passed beyond them to that place of everlasting plenty, where you feed Israel for ever with the food of truth. There life is that Wisdom by which all these things that we know are made, all things that ever have been and all that are yet to be. But that Wisdom is not made: it is as it has always been and as it will be for ever—or, rather, I should not say that it *has been* or *will be*, for it simply *is*, because eternity is not in the past or in the future. And while we spoke of the eternal Wisdom, longing for it and straining for it with all the strength of our hearts, for one fleeting instance we reached out and touched it.[55]

In response to Spenser's poem we have gone through a similar process to that described by Augustine. We went from things mundane to an eternal viewpoint on the temporal order in which we live and theologically we got some intuition of what our personalities look like

54. Augustine makes a similar observation about time as the measure of a sound: "In fact, what we measure is the interval between a beginning and an end. For this reason a sound which has not yet come to an end cannot be measured." See *Confessions* 11.27, p. 275 in the Penguin translation.

55. *Confessions* 9.10, pp. 197–98.

from the other world. But the vision does not last, it wavers and soon vanishes. As Augustine goes on to say:

> Then with a sigh, leaving *our spiritual harvest* bound to it, we returned to the sound of our own speech, in which each word has a beginning and an ending—far, far different from your Word, our Lord, who abides in himself for ever, yet never grows old and gives new life to all things.

Back in this mundane world, where we live and die and where works of art have finite limits, we, nevertheless, have left with us a new vision of ourselves and of our daily life. The simplest and most insignificant acts throw long shadows into eternity. By his denigration of this world the Christian simultaneously transvalues it. On the one hand, it is a brief prologue to eternity. On the other, human existence here assumes an importance so great that it is difficult to express in words. In allegory this vision reveals itself in two seemingly contradictory character types. There are the shadowy personifications and half-developed characters of *The Faerie Queene*, perfect emblems for the unfinished personalities which we have in this temporal life. There are likewise the realistic characters which Auerbach found in the *Divine Comedy*, realistic because they are the essence of an individual's total life, its consummation in eternity.

If the heavens are so far away from earth, the gap which must be bridged by a name is too great, and the mind cannot comprehend it. Not so in some of the classical stories. When Odysseus crossed the Ocean Stream to Hades, he found there the same personalities which he had known at Troy. Though they were insubstantial shadows of themselves, Achilles could not refrain from making outrageous remarks and Ajax still could not forgive Odysseus.[56] But for the Christian the whole set of connections between here and there had become labyrinthine and yet fundamental to his whole vision. We do not see in the girl next door a glorified saint or a damned thing, but the Christian had to call them by the same name. A familiar example from literature might help here.[57] When we read the *Divine Comedy*, it is difficult to see any relation besides the name between Beatrice Portinari of Florence and the glorious creature Dante meets in the Earthly Paradise, clothed in living flame and riding a griffon-drawn chariot. But, when they looked at each other, the pilgrim recognized his old love.

56. *Odyssey* 11.465–567.
57. *Purgatorio* 30.22–48.

5. Shakespeare's Sonnet 15 and the Art of Memory

RAYMOND B. WADDINGTON

UNIVERSITY OF WISCONSIN, MADISON

Sonnet 15

When I consider everything that grows
Holds in perfection but a little moment,
That this huge stage presenteth nought but shows   3
Whereon the stars in secret influence comment;
When I perceive that men as plants increase,
Cheerèd and checked even by the selfsame sky,   6
Vaunt in their youthful sap, at height decrease,
And wear their brave state out of memory:
Then the conceit of this inconstant stay   9
Sets you most rich in youth before my sight,
Where wasteful Time debateth with Decay
To change your day of youth to sullied night;   12
    And, all in war with Time for love of you,
    As he takes from you, I ingraft you new.[1]

T HE EXTENT OF the treasure still adrift in the Sargasso Sea of the *Sonnets,* despite the constant depredations of freebooting cranks and critics, remains a cause for astonishment. While the more spectacular pieces of flotsam have been seized—94 by the piratical Empson, 116 by Burckhardt, 129 by Peterson—or encircled by rival claimants, the sheer number of the *Sonnets* and their consistent poetic complexity have conspired to delay the exploration of more quietly-impressive achievements. To my knowledge, until the publication of

1. In quoting the *Sonnets* I use the text edited by Douglas Bush and Alfred Harbage in The Pelican Shakespeare series (Baltimore, 1961).

Stephen Booth's much praised *An Essay on Shakespeare's Sonnets,*[2] no extensive analysis of Sonnet 15 has been available. Concerned to demonstrate the multiple organizational patterns ("formal, logical, ideological, syntactic, rhythmic, and phonetic") of the *Sonnets,* Booth offers the discussion of 15 as "a summary demonstration" of his argument about Shakespeare's use of sonnet form and tradition (pp. 174–86, 209–14). And, indeed, the analysis of 15 does epitomize the strengths and weaknesses of the book. Booth's largely linguistic method slights more historical considerations germane to understanding this sonnet and the *Sonnets* generally. Playing Tuve to Booth's Empson, I wish to discuss those aspects of Sonnet 15, principally the rhetorical situation it projects and the related intellectual and metaphoric traditions, necessary to a fuller comprehension of its technique and meaning. Moreover, by reconstruction of the relevant historical contexts, I, too, hope to use this sonnet as a demonstration piece, illustrating the way in which certain kinds of reflective lyrics should be read.

The speaker of Sonnet 15 strikes a posture of contemplative analysis, syntactically structuring his rumination upon the logical pattern "when/then." In the first quatrain he reflects upon the transience and mutability of all life; the second particularizes the reflection to human life and activity; the third applies the lesson in an expression of fear for the change which the Youth must undergo; the couplet offers the consolation of immortality through the speaker's love: "And, all in war with Time for love of you, / As he takes from you, I ingraft you new." The process, then, is this: the speaker reflects upon the knowledge his previous experience of life has provided, uses that knowledge to illuminate his present situation (recognition that the object of his love cannot retain static perfection), and moves to a resolution of future action (as Time destroys the Youth, he will renew him). Sonnet 15 deliberately provokes comparison with 12 ("When I do count the clock that tells the time") by its construction upon the same radical pattern of syntax. Further, Shakespeare in both sonnets completes the octave with an appositive,[3] beginning the second quatrain with a parallel "when" construction; makes the "turn" in the third quatrain with "Then"; starts the couplet with "And." The formal and

2. New Haven, 1969. For one of the most influential and laudatory responses to this book, see Frank Kermode, "A New Era in Shakespeare Criticism?" *New York Review of Books* 15, no. 8 (5 November 1970): 33–38.

3. As Booth notes, pp. 42, 208.

verbal similarity is designed to intensify the reader's awareness of flat difference in statement. Whereas 12 also begins with the speaker's knowledge of the inescapable mutability of nature and moves to the Youth's condition ("Then of thy beauty do I question make / That thou among the wastes of time must go"), the solution is "breed." Sonnet 15 makes, and very deliberately, the first break with the pro-creation group, initiating the new theme of immortality through the poet's love and art.

The thought process underlying 15 and the logical formula which orders it may seem an inevitable resource of the Petrarchan tradition, but the heritage of "When I consider everything that grows" lies elsewhere. Petrarch's *Rime* yield two sonnets which superficially might appear to serve as models for the Shakespearean type. "Quando mi vene inanzi il tempo e 'l loco" (175) describes the way in which the poet can summon up the circumstances of his surrender to love, and so recreate the identical emotions he then felt. The sun of his beloved even now burns so strongly "Che la memoria ad ogni or fresca e salda / Pur quel nodo mi mostra e 'l loco e 'l tempo."[4] In short, this records a two-stage process, the past acting upon the present through the agency of memory, without the application to future which completes the process of Shakespeare's sonnet. A similar activity may be observed in "Quand'io mi volgo in dietro a mirar gli anni" (298), which is set in time after the death of Laura. Here, in a manner more directly analogous to Shakespeare's 12 and 15, the poet reflects upon the experience of time to focus upon the central fact of the loss. The moral he extracts might be glossed poetically with Shakespeare's 64: "Ruin hath taught me thus to ruminate / That Time will come and take my love away." But, whereas the Shakespeare 15 moves from application to present situation to resolution for future action, Petrarch's 298 goes no further than understanding of present condition, ending with a simple lament:

> O mia stella, o fortuna, o fato, o morte,
> O per me sempre dolce giorno e crudo,
> Come m'avete in basso stato messo!

While the rudiments of the "when/then" sonnet construction may come to Shakespeare from Petrarch, one must seek elsewhere for its union with the tripartite temporal analysis.

4. Petrarch, *Sonnets and Songs*, trans. Anna Maria Armi and intro. T. E. Mommsen (New York: Universal Library, 1968), p. 266; and, for 298, p. 420.

An obvious and fruitful possibility is the arsenal of rhetorical and psychological conventions available to Shakespeare through the English plain-style tradition. For instance, Lord Vaux's "On the Instability of Youth" does supply, in an extended form, just such a three-part temporal process as we have isolated in Shakespeare 15:

> When I look back and in myself behold
> The wandering ways that youth could not descry,
> And mark the fearful course that youth did hold,
> And mete in mind each step youth strayed awry,
>   My knees I bow, and from my heart I call,
>   O Lord, forget these faults and follies all.[5]

Vaux assesses the errors of past behavior from the vantage point of his present maturity; recognizing his character is so spotted that future salvation can be attained only through God's mercy, he prays for forgiveness. The remainder of the poem amplifies the pattern encapsulated in this first stanza: stanzas two and three give variant descriptions of his offenses and appropriate petitions; these accounts of youth's errors are balanced in stanzas four and five by the enumeration of instances of God's infinite mercy; and stanza six draws the whole to a fitting conclusion by an expansion of the prayer. The careful symmetries of construction exemplify the median position of the speaker, caught midway between youth and age, the Janus-like figure of the present weighing past follies against his store of grace in that future accounting.

The formula which Vaux employs for a religious end was adapted to amorous verse by Surrey:

> When youth had led me half the race
> That Cupid's scourge did make me run,
> I looked back to meet the place
> From whence my weary course begun.
>
> And then I saw how my desire
> By ill guiding had let my way. . . .[6]

This seemingly serious beginning is soon undercut by the triviality of the "lesson" which the speaker draws from his experience. By too conspicuously revealing his ardor (with four more stanzas of evidence in the "when" construction), he "Had lost me many a noble prey."

5. *English Renaissance Poetry*, ed. John Williams (Garden City: Anchor Books, 1963), p. 42.
6. *English Renaissance Poetry*, p. 50.

Finally Love teaches him "To blind their eyes that else should see / My sparkled cheeks with Cupid's hue" and he now "worships Cupid secretly."

A more impressive use of the pattern, because of the more acute psychological perception, can be found in the poem which begins "When raging love with extreme pain / Most cruelly distains my heart. . . ." Surrey neatly inverts the pattern which we have traced, using the reflection upon past experience to justify continuation in the same course of action. In the depths of despair for love, the speaker reminds himself of the magnitude and consequences of the Trojan War; since all of this occurred for love of a woman, he must learn to think his life well spent in suffering for love. The firm logical structure ("When . . . I call to mind. . . . Then think I thus. . . .") without the tedious amplification which vitiates the potential wit of "When youth had led me half the race," and the amusing portrait of the humorless, obsessed lover who imagines he serves a "worthier wight" than Helen gives point to the reversal of our expectations of the time formula.

In these poems Vaux and Surrey are exploiting the tradition of Prudence, which coordinates the three forms or aspects of time—past, present, future—with the faculties of memory, intelligence, and foresight to choose a reasoned course of action. For the Renaissance the seminal account of Prudence was that which occurs in Cicero's *De inventione* wherein he divides the concept of virtue into four parts, *prudentiam, iustitiam, fortitudinem, temperantiam*, later to become known as the cardinal virtues. Of the first Cicero writes:

> Wisdom [*Prudentia*] is the knowledge of what is good, what is bad and what is neither good nor bad. Its parts are memory, intelligence, and foresight [*memoria, intelligentia, providentia*]. Memory is the faculty by which the mind recalls what has happened. Intelligence is the faculty by which it ascertains what is. Foresight is the faculty by which it is seen that something is going to occur before it occurs.[7]

Prudentia or the prudent man, therefore, uses the three modes of time to inform the faculties of the mind, preparing it with a knowledge of what is likely to happen or enabling it to work toward a desired outcome. The three forms of time can easily be equated with the conventional three ages of man, as they are in Titian's *The Allegory of Prudence*, depicting three human heads—an old man presented in profile

7. Trans. H. M. Hubbell, Loeb Classical Library (Cambridge, Mass., 1960), II.lii.160, p. 327.

and turned to the left, a mature man of middle years in full front, and a very young man in profile turned to the right. Above the heads is the inscription, arranged with its phrases grouped spatially to accord with the appropriate portrait: *EX PRAETERITO / PRAESENS PRVDENTER AGIT / NI FVTVRV ACTIONEM DETVRPET.*[8] Such an anthropomorphic visualization of the forms of time readily explains the attractiveness of the prudence *schemata* as a structural principle in the poem, like those by Surrey and Vaux, which takes stock of a man's life in mid-course. The implied age relationships in the Shakespeare *Sonnets*, taken as a group, are rather more complex. The poet constantly projects an image of himself as a middle-aged, or even outright old, man, while exaggerating the youthfulness of his beloved. Thus, 37, "As a decrepit father takes delight / To see his active child do deeds of youth," or, to cite the inescapable example, 73, "That time of year thou mayst in me behold." The extended situation sustains the dramatic relationship of the older man constantly assessing the fruits of his own experience for his friend's benefit. While he foresees the remaining course of his own life (in the sense of being philosophically resigned to it), he does not try to alter that course. Instead he actively directs the knowledge acquired through Prudence toward the future life of the young man with whom he identifies (62). This modification of the Prudence formula from univocal application to dramatic interplay is one means by which the poet succeeds in imparting an experiential density to even such a routine performance as "When forty winters shall besiege thy brow" (2) and of course to the sequence as a whole.

When these psychological and syntactic patterns are borrowed from the discursive Tudor lyrics and fitted to the sonnet form, the most obvious gain is compression. From "when" to "then" clearly designates a movement that is sequential in both logical and temporal terms (thereby reinforcing the temporal progression of the Prudence analysis). Without the control of such an exacting form the amplification

8. I am conspicuously indebted to Erwin Panofsky, *Problems in Titian, Mostly Iconographic* (New York: Phaidon, 1969), pp. 102–08, and plates 117–27. See also his *Meaning in the Visual Arts* (New York, 1955), pp. 146–68. Panofsky translates the inscription as follows: "Instructed by the past, the present acts prudently lest the future spoil its action" (*Problems*, p. 103). Beneath Titian's human heads, of course, are an animal trinity, deriving from Macrobius' identification of the three-headed animal companion of Serapis with the forms of time. It should be noted that some personifications depict a two-headed figure, like Janus, looking to the past and future while taking for granted existence in the present. See, e.g., Cesare Ripa's figure of "Prudenzia" (*Iconologia*, Rome, 1603, p. 416).

of Surrey's "When youth had led me" or even the fourth and fifth stanzas of Vaux's much more skillfully constructed "When I look back" results in shifting to a paratactic structure,[9] a confusion which weakens the effectiveness of these poems. Shakespeare's 15 avoids the danger of merely additive structure in the apposition of the second quatrain, employing it, instead, as the middle integer in a sequence of general to particular, which acts in counterpoint to the temporal sequence of past to future. The speaker first considers "everything that grows" (line 1), focuses his reflection on "men," who "increase" as do plants (line 5), and turns the lesson to a personal application: "the conceit of this inconstant stay / Sets you most rich in youth before my sight" (lines 9–10).

If, as Paul Fussell has maintained, imbalance (between octave and sestet, quatrain and couplet) must be considered the essential formal characteristic of the sonnet,[10] the function of the multiple organizational patterns in the sonnet, and particularly the Shakespearean sonnet, will be to *almost* correct that radical imbalance. The first two stages of the general-to-particular sequence ("everything" and "men") are here confined to the octave and the third ("you") to the sestet; conversely, in temporal sequence, one form of time (past) occupies the octave and two the sestet (or, more precisely, present in the third quatrain and future in the couplet), the two patterns thus counterbalancing. The last line of the octave, "And wear their brave state out of memory" summarizes the first stage of the Prudence analysis. The phrase "out of memory" means not only "until forgotten" (Bush's note), but signals the process that has been taking place; the reflections of these two quatrains have been created out of memory. The consciousness of the speaker now moves to the Youth. Typical of the multiplying complexities in this poem, the action of this quatrain is one of continued recollection; the speaker "sees" the Youth only in his mind's eye, but the memory is of the Youth as he exists in the present. The alliance of Time and Decay to "change his day of youth" exists at the present moment (they "debateth" now); his rich perfection, however, as yet remains unaffected. That they inevitably will waste and sully his beauty is the inference the speaker has drawn from

9. For a good, brief discussion of paratactic and sequential structures, see Barbara Herrnstein Smith, *Poetic Closure: A Study of How Poems End* (Chicago: Phoenix Books, 1970), pp. 96–139.

10. Paul Fussell, *Poetic Meter and Poetic Form*, Random House Studies in Language and Literature (New York, 1966), pp. 113–33.

his remembered experience of life. Continuing the dual time-scheme which prevails throughout (the entire sonnet is cast in a narrative-present tense), the speaker responds to this conspiracy of nature by a course of action which—since we know the assault has not yet become tangible—we must understand to occur in the future: "As he takes from you, I ingraft you new." The resolution to future action corresponds to foresight, *providentia*, thereby completing the Prudence sequence.[11]

Number 15 is not Shakespeare's only reflective sonnet which employs the "when/then" logical pattern and shows the influence of the Prudence tradition in the organization of its psychological progression: witness 2, 12, 30, and 64. Looked at purely from the standpoint of effective use of the tradition, however, none of these equals the achievement of 15, largely because of difficulties in moving from *intellegentia* to *providentia*, that is, from illumination of the present situation by the past to resolution of the future. "When I have seen by Time's fell hand defaced" (64) might be excepted from the generalization because the deviation is deliberate. He uses memory to comprehend the present, but, as with Petrarch's "Quand io mi volgo in dietro a mirar gli anni," that understanding evokes only a lament: "This thought is as a death, which cannot choose / But weep to have that which it fears to lose." The point is that there is no consolation, which surely exploits the reversal of his reader's expectation that he will look to the future with either a plan of action or philosophic resignation. This reversal of expectation results in a more powerful conclusion than that of the better-known 30, "When to the sessions of sweet silent thought," which does use the complete past-present-future sequence to reach an altered state: "But if the while I think of thee, dear friend, / All losses are restored and sorrows end." For some readers, at least, this couplet's optimistic resolution is a too-facile attempt to counterbalance the pervasive melancholy of the preceding twelve lines.[12] Sonnets 2 and 12 also evidence full use of the three modes of

---

11. Shakespeare's dramatic use of the Prudence tradition has been demonstrated convincingly by Barry B. Adams, "The Prudence of Prince Escalus," *ELH* 35 (1968): 32–50. For the currency of the tradition in the late sixteenth century, see especially pp. 38–43.

12. See, for instance, Douglas L. Peterson, *The English Lyric from Wyatt to Donne* (Princeton, 1967), p. 235, who charges that ". . . it is flat, formulary, and unpersuasive because it stands in context as an undeveloped assertion." See also Yvor Winters, "Poetic Styles, Old and New," *Four Poets on Poetry*, ed. D. C. Allen (Baltimore, 1959), pp. 48–49. Barbara Smith, *Poetic Closure*, pp. 214–20,

time within the framework of the "when/then" construction; but the conclusion in both (beget a son), whether meretricious or simply an exercise,[13] fails to satisfy modern readers.

To support my assertion that the *providentia* stage of Sonnet 15 escapes the triviality of 2 and 12, the inadequately prepared-for reversal of 30, or, indeed, any of the other weaknesses in the couplet which readers have found in the *Sonnets*, will require an examination of the sonnet's figurative language. Let me begin by rehearsing Stephen Booth's analysis of the metaphors in the sonnet: "The terms in which the speaker presents his meaning, the 'things' of the poem, are from a variety of ideological frames of reference, and the reader's mind is in constant motion from one context to another." Three dominant metaphors are introduced in the first quatrain—*grows* (line 1), *stage* (line 3), and *stars* (line 4). These are, according to Booth, unrelated, "new" metaphors. "That the matter-of-fact tone withstands coexistence with three distinct metaphors would be remarkable if each new metaphor were not introduced into the reader's mind as if it were already there." As he reads the poem, elements of the formal structure, specifically syntactic and logical parallelisms, serve to insinuate a relationship between the metaphors, which ideologically does not exist. Our awareness of the disparity of intellectual contexts creates a tension only partially relieved by the formal assertions of similarity. "The three metaphors pull both apart and together."[14] But, in fact, he is mistaken. Properly understood, the three metaphors are constituent members of one figurative construct and derive from one coherent ideological frame of reference.

First, let us consider the relation of logical structure to figurative language or structure of images. I have bracketed Sonnet 15 with the sonnets built upon the same syntactic pattern to illustrate the varying

---

qualifies Winters' general judgement somewhat but does not discuss this particular sonnet. One ought to consider the possibility that 30 was not designed to be convincing—i.e., as psychological portraiture its point lies precisely in the speaker's waning faith in the power of redemptive love.

13. By "meretricious" I refer to the old biographical chestnut that Shakespeare was hired to persuade a recalcitrant young nobleman to marry, and composed the "marriage group" of sonnets before becoming personally involved, etc. Peterson, *The English Lyric*, p. 72, has noted that the thesis of whether it is good to marry was a popular one for rhetorical exercises. Ricardo J. Quinones, *The Renaissance Discovery of Time* (Cambridge, Mass., 1972), pp. 300–11, sensibly relates the marriage sonnet themes of "increase" and "husbandry" to the larger issue of Time.

14. The quotations have been taken, in proper order, from pp. 181–82.

degrees to which they employ a common process of psychological analysis. All of these sonnets are intimate in tone. They present an overheard speaker attempting to understand a present situation by juxtaposing recollections of the past. He speaks directly to no more than one person, the young man, or only to himself. 64 is a soliloquy; while 15 does address the Youth, the direct address occurs after the speaker has projected his presence through memory, suggesting that it, too, may be considered a soliloquy. In these poems *time* sounds the thematic keynote and, because of the adaptation of the Prudence tradition, *memory* plays an extraordinary part. Although the Scott-Moncrieff translation of Proust's novel may cause us, adventitiously, to think of memory in these sonnets as associative, it is not. Rather, it is used in accordance with the precepts of classical rhetoric as they were transmitted to Shakespeare by his own age.

Memoria had a *prima facie* importance as one of the five major divisions of classical rhetoric; beyond this, however, Cicero's disposition of memory as one of the three parts of *Prudentia* gave it a special status in rhetoric. As Harry Caplan has observed, ". . . the course which wisdom should take is an important consideration in both deliberative and epideictic speaking."[15] In the Middle Ages, with the Christianization of Cicero's cardinal virtues, memory was transferred to the field of ethics, thus strengthening the position accorded to it in rhetoric. Albertus Magnus and Thomas Aquinas, for instance, both quote Cicero's definition of Prudence in their important treatises.[16] Even before this, however, Augustine, the most influential of the Church Fathers during the Renaissance, had transformed the Ciceronian rhetoric on which he was trained to a Christian rhetoric, and—apparently influenced directly by Cicero's treatment of memory—had written that extraordinary account of memory in Book X of the *Confessions*, which begins,

> I will soar therefore beyond this faculty of my nature, still rising by degrees unto him who hath made both me and that nature. And I come into these fields and spacious palaces of my memory, where the treasures of innumerable forms [*imaginum*] brought into it from these

15. "Memoria: Treasure-House of Eloquence," *Of Eloquence: Studies in Ancient and Medieval Rhetoric* (Ithaca, New York, 1970), pp. 196–246; quotation, p. 211.

16. See Frances A. Yates, *The Art of Memory* (Chicago, 1966), pp. 50–81, for this transferal and the significance of memory in *De bono* and the *Summa theologica*.

things that have been perceived by the senses be hoarded up. There is laid up whatsoever besides we think, either by way of enlarging or diminishing, or any other ways varying of those things which the sense hath come at: yea, and if there be anything recommended to it and there laid up, which forgetfulness hath not swallowed up and buried. To this treasury whenever I have recourse, I will demand to have anything brought forth whatsoever I will.[17]

The reform of Ciceronian oratory into Christian eloquence which Augustine describes in Book IV of *De doctrina christiana* has no extensive account of memory but the *Confessions* supplied this lack for Christian rhetors. In an impressive analysis of the theory of eloquence underlying John Donne's sermons Dennis Quinn has concluded:

> It is the memory which Donne most often addresses in his sermons. Donne's conception of memory as a faculty of great spiritual significance derives directly from the Augustinian tradition, which makes memory the instrument of self-knowledge, which is in turn the key to the knowledge of God.[18]

The importance assigned to memory by these three eloquent men, Cicero, Augustine, Donne, springs in large part from their common Platonic philosophical orientation. Cicero proclaims his belief in the Platonic doctrine of reminiscence in the *Tusculan Disputations*, in which, as Miss Yates remarks, he uses an orator's technical vocabulary to prove the immortality of the soul. "It is as a Christian that Augustine seeks God in the memory, and as a Christian Platonist, believing that knowledge of the divine is innate in memory."[19] And, hundreds of years later but in an unbroken line of intellectual descent, Donne preached sermons on the belief that "The art of salvation, is but the art of memory."[20]

17. *St. Augustine's Confessions*, tr. William Watts, Loeb Classical Library (Cambridge, Mass., 1961), X.viii; II, 93–95. Augustine's knowledge of Ciceronian Prudence seems implicit in his account of how times past and future are now present. See *Confessions* XI.18.

18. Quinn, "Donne's Christian Eloquence," *ELH* 27 (1960): 276–97; quotation, p. 283. See also Robert L. Hickey, "Donne's Art of Memory," *Tennessee Studies in Literature* 3 (1958): 29–36. For Augustine's struggle to reconcile Ciceronian eloquence with Christian truth, see Erich Auerbach, *Literary Language and its Public in Late Latin Antiquity and in the Middle Ages*, trans. Ralph Manheim (New York, 1965).

19. *The Art of Memory*, p. 48; see pp. 44–49 on the Platonism of Cicero and Augustine.

20. *The Sermons of John Donne*, ed. E. Simpson and G. Potter (Berkeley, 1955), II, 74. See Quinn's discussion of this sermon, "Donne's Christian Eloquence," pp. 289–93.

Rhetorica

Bronze figure from Antonio Pollaiuolo's *Tomb of Pope Sixtus IV* (1493). She holds an oak branch in her left hand and with her right points to a Ciceronian inscription: "Aperta et ampla oratione ex quaelibet disciplina pro tempore assumo apte dico suadeo vel dissuadeo."

As Cicero provided the starting-point for this sketch of the memory tradition, so—in one of those splendid historical confusions which dot the chart of Renaissance thought—he also concludes it. The main source for the classical art of memory, the *Rhetorica ad Herennium*, enjoyed an enormous prestige throughout the Middle Ages and the early Renaissance because it was thought to be a work by Cicero. As Miss Yates explains,

> . . . the Middle Ages grouped the *De inventione* with the *Ad Herennium* as both by Tullius; the two works were known respectively as the First and Second Rhetorics of Tullius. Tullius in his First Rhetoric states that memory is a part of Prudence; Tullius in his Second Rhetoric says that there is an artificial memory by which natural memory can be improved. Therefore the practice of the artificial memory is a part of the virtue of Prudence.[21]

The artificial memory or mnemonic system detailed in the *Ad Herennium* operates on a pronounced visual basis. It requires the use of images set against backgrounds or places (*loci*). The ideas which one wishes to remember are associated with images—figures, marks, portraits which are strikingly memorable and bear some appropriate relation to the ideas. These images are set in backgrounds, like the wax tablets upon which letters are inscribed; the backgrounds should form a series so that ideas can be remembered in proper order from any starting point.[22] Quintilian's *Institutio oratoria* (XI.ii.17–22) gives additional detail on the most popular type of background, the architectural, which is admirably suited for the spatial separation of images, as well as the sequential arrangement. Quintilian explains how the symbols may be distributed among the various rooms of a spacious house, through which the subject is to imagine himself walking; but the exercise can be done equally well, he tells us, with public buildings, the ramparts of a city, with pictures or with a journey, with places either real or imagined (XI.ii.21).[23] Sidney observes in his *Defence of Poesie* that ". . . euen they that haue taught the Art of memory haue

21. *The Art of Memory*, p. 21. Caplan explains that "Raphael Regius in 1491 positively divorced the work from Cicero's name" ("Introduction to the *Rhetorica ad Herennium*," *Of Eloquence*, p. 3). But such legends are not dispelled overnight.

22. *Ad Herennium* III.xvi.28–xxiv.40. See also the discussions by Caplan, pp. 228–31, and Yates, pp. 4–17.

23. On buildings as *loci*, see Yates, pp. 3–4; also, pp. 21–26 on Quintilian. Caplan (p. 235) considers it especially significant that for Quintilian, Cicero, and the author of *Ad Herennium*, ". . . the memory of words was subordinate to *memoria rerum*."

shewed nothing so apt for it as a certaine roome diuided into many places well and thoroughly knowne."[24]

Or with a theatre. In a sequence of brilliant scholarly performances Miss Yates has shown us how, in the context of Renaissance Neoplatonism and occultism, the classical art of memory underwent a radical transformation. While the images and *loci* continued to be used according to the rules from the rhetorics, the function of the art was elevated from that of a relatively simple mnemonic technique to the idea of a symbolic representation of the cosmos. No longer mere aid to the forgetful, but a glimpse of the underlying order of the universe permitting the visionary to understand its nature from the perspective of its Maker, perhaps through that understanding to even partake of his powers. In this fashion the theatre, the "memory place" in which the orator literally stood as he delivered his speech, was metamorphosed into a symbolic "Memory Theatre," such as the famous one actually constructed by Giulio Camillo:

> Camillo brings the art of memory into line with the new currents now running through the Renaissance. His Memory Theatre houses Ficino and Pico, Magia and Cabala, the Hermetism and Cabalism implicit in Renaissance so-called Neoplatonism. He turns the classical art of memory into an occult art.[25]

There can be no doubt that the artificial memory systems came to the Elizabethan poets as a part of their rhetorical heritage.[26] Hamlet's courtly sarcasm about Laertes' virtues rests on common knowledge: ". . . to divide him inventorially would dozy th' arithmetic of memory" (V.II.112–13). Well into the seventeenth century references to the art remain casual and offhand: Burton recommends its study as an antedote to melancholy (*Anatomy* II.ii.4); and Herrick skewers a pedantic fraud in his epigram, "Upon Parrat":

> Parrat protests 'tis he, and only he
> Can teach a man the *Art of memory.*
> Believe him not; for he forgot it quite
> Being drunke, who 'twas that Can'd his Ribs last night.[27]

24. *Elizabethan Critical Essays*, ed. G. Gregory Smith (Oxford, 1904), I, 183.

25. Yates, *The Art of Memory*, p. 151. See also her *Giordano Bruno and the Hermetic Tradition* (Chicago, 1964) and *Theatre of the World* (Chicago, 1969).

26. See Carroll Camden, "Memory, the Warder of the Brain," *PQ* 18 (1939): 52–72; especially, pp. 61–72.

27. *The Poetical Works of Robert Herrick*, ed. L. C. Martin (Oxford, 1963), p. 186.

While the evidence of literary response to the occult art of the Memory Theatre is rather more sketchy, what we have is most suggestive. Ariosto and Tasso both lauded Camillo's achievment for its importance to poetry.[28] Giordano Bruno by his person and writings directly introduced Hermetic memory art into the circle of Sir Philip Sidney, an interesting association, considering the attention Sidney gives to memory in the *Defence*.[29]

Miss Yates' most controversial argument, that the engraving of a memory theatre illustrating Robert Fludd's *Ars Memoriae* bears a direct relation to Shakespeare's Globe Theatre, has made relatively few converts.[30] More convincing is the demonstration that the revival of Vitruvian architectural theory, with its underlying principle that public buildings, temples and theatres, should reflect cosmic and human proportions in geometrical terms, parallels and conflates with the symbolic theatres of "astral memory systems" which "attempt to organize memory by harnessing it to the forces of the cosmos."[31] These two revivals and transformations of classical theory serve to explain, by supplying philosophic justification for, the enormous popularity of the venerable *theatrum mundi* metaphor in the Renaissance. From Pico della Mirandola's declaration of independence in the *Oration on the Dignity of Man* to the dramas of Calderon and Shakespeare the cry that "all the world's a stage" resounds.[32] These ideas are so pervasive

28. See Yates, *The Art of Memory*, p. 169.

29. On this see Yates, *Giordano Bruno*, and *The Art of Memory*, pp. 260–319. Sidney makes an analogy between the spatial allocation of images in the memory place and the distribution of words in a controlled form which constitutes poetry (Smith, I, 183). It must be noted, contra Yates (p. 264), that most scholars date the *Defence* prior to Sidney's contact with Bruno. J. A. van Dorsten, taking off from Yates and Sidney, suggests a connection between poetic and mnemonic uses of imagery. See "The Arts of Memory and Poetry," *ES* 48 (1967): 419–25. Van Dorsten further sees the fixed sonnet form as an analogue to the room in which such images are placed (p. 422).

30. See, e.g., Leah Scragg, *Shakespeare Survey*, 24 (1971): 166; and D. S. Bland, *Ren. Q.* 23 (1970): 482–85. While rejecting the Fludd argument, Bland also emphasizes the importance of *theatrum mundi* to Renaissance thought and accepts Yates' view of the symbolic design of Renaissance theatres.

31. *Theatre of the World*, p. 142.

32. On *theatrum mundi*, see *inter alia* E. R. Curtius, *European Literature in the Latin Middle Ages*, trans. W. R. Trask (New York, 1953), pp. 138–44; Richard Brenheimer, "*Theatrum Mundi*," *Art Bulletin* 38 (1956): 225–47; Jean Jacquot, "Le Théâtré du Monde," *Revue de litterature comparée* 21 (1957): 341–72; Anne Righter, *Shakespeare and the Idea of the Play* (London, 1962); Herbert Weisinger, "*Threatrum Mundi*: Illusion as Reality," *The Agony and the Triumph: Papers on the Use and Abuse of Myth* (East Lansing, Mich., 1964), pp. 58–71; D. C. Allen, "*Rex Tragicus*," *Image and Meaning*, rev. ed. (Baltimore, 1968), p. 138–51;

that the symbolism need not literally have been built into the physical structure of the theatre. Even without that, "His theatre would have been for Shakespeare the pattern of the universe, the idea of the Macrocosm, the world stage on which the Microcosm acted his parts."[33]

We have seen already the way in which the logical structure of Sonnet 15 operates in terms of time and memory; Shakespeare, in fact, organizes the poem, using the topics of Prudence in a manner similar to that recommended by the *Ad Herennium*.[34] It should not be surprising that he would select a basic metaphor and develop his pattern of imagery from a closely related sphere of thought: the metaphor is the theatre of the world, and the time/memory link comes from its association with the art of memory. The lyric strategy of this poem has a close narrative analogue in "The Castle of Alma" episode of *The Faerie Queene* (II.ix). There Guyon and Arthur are taken to the turret of the castle to meet in three different rooms Alma's counsellors:

> The first of them could things to come foresee,
> The next could of things present best advise,
> The third things past could keep in memory,
> So that no time nor reason could arise
> But that the same could one of these comprise.
>
> (II.ix.49.1–5)[35]

The three sages are personified as Phantastes, "a man of years, yet fresh" with a Saturnine, prophetic temperament; "a man of ripe and perfect age" surrounded by pictures of judges, governors, scientists, "And all that in the world was aye thought wittily"; and Eumnestes, "an old, old man" in a library: "His chamber all was hanged about with rolls / And old records from ancient times derived." Though the order

---

and Yates' chapter, "The Theatre as Moral Emblem," *Theatre of the World*, pp. 162–68. For the argument that theatre of the world is essential to the dramatic constructions of Shakespeare and Calderon, see Lionel Abel, *Metatheatre: A New View of Dramatic Form* (New York, 1963), pp. 59–72, 76–83, 107–13; and Jackson I. Cope, *The Theatre and the Dream: From Metaphor to Form in Renaissance Drama* (Baltimore, 1973).

33. *Theatre of the World*, p. 189.

34. "We shall be using the topics of Wisdom [*prudentiae partibus*] in our discourse if we compare advantages and disadvantages, counselling the pursuit of the one and the avoidance of the other; . . . or if we recommend some policy in a matter whose history we can recall either from direct experience or hearsay— in this instance we can easily persuade our hearers to the course we wish by adducing the precedent" (III.iii.4). Trans. Harry Caplan, Loeb Classical Library (Cambridge, Mass., 1964), pp. 163–65.

35. From *Books I and II of The Faerie Queene*, ed. Robert Kellogg and Oliver Steele (New York, 1965); see their note, p. 343, on Spenser's use of Prudence.

is reversed for narrative requirements, one easily recognizes Cicero's triad of *memoria, intellegentia,* and *providentia.* Spenser wittily places the "images" of these words against suitable memory places, the rooms of a building, culminating the process with a visual pun by displaying "the chamber of memory" as Memory is a chamber.[36]

Whereas in Spenser's narrative the images and place of *ars memoriae* illustrate the concept of Prudence and the faculties of the mind, Shakespeare particularizes the psychological process of remembering with a nexus of images drawn from the memory art. Lines 1–2 state a general proposition, "When I consider everything that grows, / Holds in perfection but a little moment," devoid of imagery,[37] which is then cast in figurative terms and amplified. The grammatical construction poses lines 3–4, "That this huge stage presenteth nought but shows / Whereon the stars in secret influence comment," as an alternative statement of what the speaker considers. Reinforcing the appositive construction, rime asserts an identity between the two thoughts here (*grows/shows*), just as consonant alliteration and parallel placement in lines 4–5 emphasize the link between *stage* and *stars.* The shows presented upon "this huge stage" of the world, therefore, are a dramatic mimesis of the proposition that everything living is mutable and transient. How are we to interpret the role of the secretly influential stars, as audience or as director? Booth chooses the former possibility— "[they] are to the world-stage roughly as the powerless speaker was to the mortal world in line 1" (p. 182). Yet to observe that the speaker is "powerless" fixes the point of difference in his role from that of the "influential" stars. Presumably Booth regards the influence as deriving from the actors' desire to please the audience and gain their applause ("Cheerèd and checked even by the selfsame sky"); even so, this makes untenable the mirror relationship he describes. The alternative possibility, that the stars direct the action on the stage, suggests the milieu of the astral memory systems such as the cosmic memory theatres of Camillo and Fludd.[38]

36. Caplan, *Of Eloquence,* pp. 214–16, summarizes the line of imagery, stemming from Quintilian, which figures memory as a repository of some sort— treasure-house, storehouse, chest, mine, magazine, vessel, cask, purse, cell, closet, chamber, etc.

37. Although Booth regards *grows* as an active metaphor which "carries a vaguely botanical reference over into line 2" (pp. 181–82), strictly speaking botany does not enter until line 6.

38. I do not imply that Shakespeare was an occultist; only that the ideas were

In the Hermetic version of the creation, made accessible to the Renaissance in Ficino's translation of the *Pimander*, the Christian myth of the Fall undergoes a sea-change: "This is what happens to man in the *Pimander*; the interior man, his *mens*, created divine and having the powers of the star-rulers, on falling into the body comes under the domination of the stars, whence he escapes in the Hermetic religious experience of ascent through the spheres to regain his divinity."[39] Continuing the theme of astrological knowledge from 14, the speaker thus reflects on man's material bondage to the stars. This bondage, with the loss of that original divinity, puts him on the same deterministic plane as plants which take their form and identity (as revealed by "signatures") from the sympathetic correspondence with the stars which "influence" them.[40] So these actors, "men as plants," will increase and decrease, "Cheered and checked even by that selfsame sky"; as they increase, they will "Vaunt in their youthful sap," then decrease "And wear their brave state out of memory." The last phrase, as I remarked earlier, signals the conclusion of the memory stage of the analysis; it also renders overt the presentation of the "theatre of the world" as a memory theatre. Booth observes, "The syntax of the line presents *memory* as if it were a place, but its sense makes it capable of comprehension only in terms of time" (p. 185). It is a place. The memory theatre, and of course the whole conception underlying the memory systems, permits the subject to visualize the processes of time as occurring spatially. Marvell's phrase, "deserts of vast eternity," nicely epitomizes the concept. The conflict between the expected use of "out of memory" as referring to the past and the actual future reference (in terms of the lives of the imagined actors) here, as Booth comments, "allows the reader an approximation of actual comprehension of all time and space

sufficiently current to provide viable poetic material and that they were philosophically consonant with the generally Platonic tenor of the sonnets addressed to the young man. Formerly Hermeticism was considered to be only an aberrant strain of Renaissance Neoplatonism; but, since the work of Miss Yates, the tail now wags the dog.

39. *The Art of Memory*, pp. 146–47; see also the fuller exposition in *Giordano Bruno*, pp. 20–43.

40. On "signatures," see Walter Pagel, *Paracelsus: An Introduction to Philosophical Medicine in the Era of the Renaissance* (New York, 1958), pp. 148–49; also, 218–26. For Paracelsian theory and imagery in Shakespeare's plays, see W. A. Murray, "Why was Duncan's Blood Golden?" *Shakespeare Survey* 19 (1966): 34–44, and Richard K. Stensgaard, "*All's Well that Ends Well* and the Galenico-Paracelsian Controversy," *Ren. Q.* 25 (1972): 173–88.

in one" (p. 185). This is the intention, exactly, behind the cosmic memory theatre. Booth's formal analysis here confirms the inferences I have drawn from the figurative language of the sonnet.

The "conceit" of line 9 punningly alludes to the entire figurative construct, the theatre of the world with its stage full of motley players (*conceit* as *concetto*); the lesson "of this inconstant stay" which the speaker extracts from it (*conceit* as *idea*); and comments on the blind self-absorption of the actors in their vaunting bravery (*conceit* as vanity). This "conceit" with its multivocal suggestions of implicit comment on character, "Sets you most rich in youth before my sight," which is to say, the juvenile lead enters from the wings and takes his place on the stage. The phrase "rich in youth" associates him with both the plant-like men of "youthful sap" and the richness of costume ("brave state") worn for their pathetic strutting and bellowing. The boards of Roscius lead but to oblivion.

The engagement of the speaker's understanding with memory has led to a perception of the fate awaiting the young man. With the problem thus defined, the solution can only be to reform it altogether. Having suited his words to the action of life, the speaker now suits his action to the words. Discarding his previous role as a contemplative Jacques, he imagines himself, like Hamlet rescripting the voyage to England,[41] altering the nature of the stage play: it becomes battle, rather than progress. One of the new elements that Sonnet 15 introduces to the procreation group is the shift from a resolution whereby the speaker advises action to one in which he acts. Line 13, "all in war with Time for love of you," projects himself as dramatic protagonist; he and Time are figured as rival lovers. Petrarchists both, no doubt, warring for the favors of the young man esteemed as a love-object but, significantly, now cast in a secondary part. An obvious function of the symbolic cosmos represented in the Hermetic memory theatres was to aid the mind of the viewer to recognize the divine knowledge it once had and to draw power from the cosmic images into the memory. By so doing, the viewer could escape his mundane domination by the stars and resume his rightful divinity. In this way does man become, to pursue the theatrical metaphor, a director, or, in the vocabulary of the occultists, a Magus. Shakespeare later would unite

41. For Hamlet as a director-actor, see the interesting remarks of Abel, *Metatheatre*, pp. 40–58.

the two under the proper name of Prospero.[42] In Sonnet 15 the transformation of the speaker from passive observer to resolute planner and do-er suggests that the art of memory has been the catalyst for a similar regeneration in him.

Booth concludes,

> The last six lines of the sonnet are more abstract than the first eight, and the three metaphors become more separable from each other, from a new metaphor of warfare, and from the abstract statements that they figure forth. . . . The couplet describes a facile and fanciful triumph over time. (Pp. 185–86)

The increased abstractness of the sestet reflects the stage of psychological process; rather than *memoria*, with its images and places, the speaker's mind has reached the stage of rational analysis. This understanding, however, as well as the resolution which results from it, remains very intimately involved with the *theatrum mundi* metaphor that triggered the entire process. The dilemma is to rescue the young man from the influence of the sinister stars and their minion Time before he is entrapped in their realm of "sullied night." The couplet announces the speaker's counterplot: he will "solve" the dilemma by recourse to a device oddly reminiscent of a rhetorical training procedure in the Elizabethan grammar schools, the "paraphrase" exercises of turning poetry to prose or one poetic meter to another.[43] One might call Shakespeare's invention the translation through genres.

"As he takes from you, I ingraft you new." *Ingraft*, the final change capping a sequence of words (*influence, increase, inconstant*) threatening change, means "to graft" in the horticultural sense, of

---

42. In Harry Levin's summation, "*The Tempest* is concerned with illusion, as fabricated by magicians and playwrights and 'all which it inherit,' the illusory stuff that dreams and dramas and life itself are made of (IV.i.154)." "Two Magian Comedies: *The Tempest* and *The Alchemist*," *Shakespeare Survey* 22 (1969): 51.

43. "The precedent for teaching the exercise of paraphrase at St. Paul's School was established by Erasmus in his *De ratione studii* (1511) where he recommends the turning of poetry to prose and prose to poetry, and the turning of poetry from one meter to another, as Milton gave the theme on early rising in elegiacs and in choriambics. Even Ascham grudgingly admits that paraphrase from prose to verse or from verse to prose has classical sanction and is better than paraphrase from one prose version to another." D. L. Clark, *John Milton at St. Paul's School* (New York, 1948), p. 180. Clark also notes that the approval which Ramus and Talaeus afforded to paraphrase led to its use in most English grammar schools (see pp. 178–79). See also T. W. Baldwin, *William Shakespeare's Small Latine & Lesse Greeke* (Urbana, Ill., 1944), II, 385–88 for the prose-to-verse practice.

course; and so ironically echoes the previous theme of procreation. But only ironically because grafting is not a natural means of procreation, and Shakespeare has in mind no bastard "gillyvors" here. In this sense the speaker's promise to "ingraft you new" can only be understood figuratively, as Bush's note, "graft, infuse new life into (with poetry)," takes for granted. How else could a poet perpetuate the identity of a male friend?[44] This figurative sense, however, becomes the primary and literal meaning of the statement when we recognize the probable pun of *ingraft*: it means "to write." The now primary meaning of *graft* originally was a figure of speech, deriving from the resemblance of the scion or shoot used in the grafting process to a stylus, pencil or similar writing instrument (*graphium*).[45] The pun, like that on *conceit* earlier, technically is an example of *syllepsis*, which Sister Miriam Joseph defines as ". . . the use of a word having simultaneously two different meanings, although it is not repeated."[46] Indeed, considering the simultaneous connotations of gardening and writing, there is the more remote possibility of a compound pun: like those astral gardeners, what he now has the power to write is the "signature" of identity in this mortal plant.

The poet, like Hamlet with "the table of my memory" (I.v.98), heeds the dictum of the *Ad Herennium* (III.xvii.30–31) that the memory images are as inscriptions on a wax tablet. "Writing the young man new" means composing the sonnet itself, a graffito on the face of history saying "Kilroy (or W. H. or Someone) was here." Time is rightly cast as the antagonist in the poet's new plot. Implicit in the *theatrum mundi* metaphor is the awareness so evident in Aristotle's *Poetics* that drama is a temporal, processive medium. Later, in such plays as *Antony and Cleopatra* and *The Tempest* Shakespeare will try his hand at a kind of drama which breaks out of temporal limitations;

44. See Curtius, pp. 476–77, for some notes on perpetuation through poetry.

45. See OED, s.v. *graff; graft; engraff, ingraff; engraft, ingraft*. Booth, pp. 182–83, argues for another Latinate pun in *consider* ("*sidus, sider-, star*"). Rosalie Colie, "My Ecchoing Song": *Andrew Marvell's Poetry of Criticism* (Princeton, 1970), p. 152, suggests that puns function "as anamorphic pictures do," i.e., they alter point of view. Thus the speaker contemplates "with the viewpoint of the stars" and ingrafts, "acts as a writer." Shakespeare uses *ingraft* conventionally in Sonnet 37: "I make my love ingrafted to this store."

46. *Shakespeare's Use of the Arts of Language* (New York, 1947), p. 166. She describes *syllepsis* as the "most subtle of the figures of ambiguity" (p. 168). For Puttenham the figure is "the Double Supply," ". . . conceuing, and, as it were, comprehending vnder one, a supplie of two natures, and may be likened to the man that serues many masters at once. . . ." *The Arte of English Poesie*, ed. G. D. Willcock and A. Walker (Cambridge, 1936), p. 165.

but the plays of the 1590s, the period with which the early sonnets are associated, are immensely time conscious.[47] To defeat Time, to protect the young man from his ravages, the poet translates him from the public, temporal genre of theatre to the private, non-temporal dimension of the immortalizing sonnets. As line 13 intimates, Time's love for the young man is natural; and, as the grafting connotations suggest, in a sense the poet's love is unnatural. He wants to take the young man out of nature or, to follow the implications of the memory theatre more precisely, *above* nature. It is an escape into art, and at this point in the sequence our wonder is evoked by the suddenness of both assertions—the power of art and the poet's confidence in his mastery of it. The emphatic double closure (the GG rime, "you"/"new," repeated in the last two syllables of line 14, "you new") counters the potential inconclusiveness of the couplet's logical statement, which looks forward to an action not yet begun (it is, remember, only foreseen). More than this, however, the strong identification of *you* and *new* emphasizes the change, even beyond the transcendence of temporal dimension, that will be effected through the poet's ingrafting. Though the theme of the young man's human imperfections has not yet entered the sequence, the solution to that problem is already clear. In Sidney's words, "Nature neuer set forth the earth in so rich tapistry as diuers Poets haue done. . . . Her world is brasen, the Poets only deliue a golden."[48]

In the argument of this essay I have tried to follow the course of prudent scholarship, which is to say, I have used the past, in the form of certain traditions, to illuminate the present, our current comprehension of one Renaissance poem. It seems only appropriate to complete the paradigm by giving the future its due. Accordingly, I want to exercise *providentia* to the end of suggesting certain ramifications this reading might have for better understanding similar kinds of poems.

For twenty-five years Rosemond Tuve's magistral study of *Elizabethan and Metaphysical Imagery* has remained the starting point for any serious discussion of poetics in Renaissance English poetry. Miss Tuve sought to prove that poetic theory underwent no radical changes in this period; that the theory was comprehensive enough to accommodate, via the principle of decorum, the shift in style identified with

47. See, e.g., Quinones, pp. 297–300. The time consciousness, of course, is not always negative. C. L. Barber, *Shakespeare's Festive Comedy* (Princeton, 1959), deals with the comedic alliance of society's and nature's time.
48. *Elizabethan Critical Essays*, I, 156.

Metaphysical poetry; and to suggest that the shift in style could be accounted for by the influence of Peter Ramus's reform of logic and rhetoric. Her first contention, the continuity of poetic tradition from Wyatt to Marvell, has been widely accepted; the correlative thesis, that Ramistic logic and rhetoric are responsible for the "dialectical toughness" of Metaphysical poetry, widely disputed. Miss Tuve labored under the handicap of writing before Father Walter J. Ong's definitive study of Ramus; and, a few years after the publication of her work, Louis Martz offered, in *The Poetry of Meditation*, a more plausible explanation for the emergence of the so-called "Metaphysical" school. As one reviewer observes, Martz' study ". . . suggests a non-Ramistic and convincing source in the older meditational tradition for exactly the elements of Metaphysical style which Tuve traces to the impact of Ramism."[49] Elsewhere in this volume Thomas Sloan argues that the Ramists do provide a causational link between Elizabethan and Meditational poetry, although in a way other than that advanced by Miss Tuve. According to Sloan, the Ramist reorganization of rhetoric forced to the surface a problem always latent in traditional rhetoric, the question of the proper use of the passions in rhetorical discourse. The poets of the late sixteenth century, left by the Ramists without their very stock-in-trade, turned from rhetoric to meditational theory, in which they found sanctions for their use of passionate discourse through self-directed rhetoric, projecting a voice which the poetic audience only overheard.

In a discussion of Shakespeare's Sonnet 121 as an example of "closure without resolution," Barbara Smith comments on those sonnets which are not addressed to any particular audience and seem to represent the poet in the process of thought:

> . . . certain of the sonnets begin to sound more like soliloquies than set speeches and are generated by principles not easily accommodated by the formal structure of the English sonnet. The speaker in these poems moves from point to point as does Hamlet or Richard II in those troubled monologues in which at critical moments the character ponders his condition, or his relation to the world about him, or the possibilities of action and attitude open to him.[50]

49. Jackson I. Cope, *The Metaphoric Structure of Paradise Lost* (Baltimore, 1962), p. 29. I am indebted to Cope's resume of the scholarly controversy over Ramism (see pp. 27–35).
50. Smith, *Poetic Closure*, p. 143.

The "dialogue of one" (to appropriate Donne's phrase), the quality of self-examination, the indefinite or overheard speaker-audience relationship, all of these things in Ms. Smith's description are the characteristics which, since Martz, we have come to identify with meditational poetry. I would observe (waiving the particular point about closure, which is a variable) that the description applies equally well to those serious sonnets, 15, 30, 64, that I have associated with the Prudence tradition.

The definitive characteristics of meditational poetry, as laid down by Martz, require the presence of a three-stage sequence—composition of place, analysis, and colloquy. This sequence derives from the "three powers of the soul," memory, understanding, will, as described by St. Ignatius Loyola in his *Spiritual Exercises*, a trinity of powers explicitly regarded by religious writers as analogous to the Holy Trinity. Martz writes:

> All these parts of a given exercise will, when properly performed, flow into one inseparable, inevitable sequence: the imaginative "composition" will in the meditation proper be recalled by the memory, whose responsibility is to "lay open to the view of our understanding the persons, wordes, and workes contained in the first point," thus "setting before our eyes the point or Mysterie on which we are to Meditate." Similarly, the acts of the colloquy are inseparable from the affections of the will. Without expecting any hard and fast divisions, then, we should expect to find a formal meditation falling into three distinguishable portions, corresponding to the acts of memory, understanding, and will—portions which we might call composition, analysis, and colloquy.[51]

Now, although *prudence* is not a word which occurs in Martz' study, it is impossible not to observe a close correspondence between Martz' Ignatian trinity of memory, understanding, will and the Ciceronian trinity of memory, intelligence, foresight. The first two components in the sets of faculties are, in fact, identical; the half-step transforming *foresight* to *will* may reflect the contamination of rhetorical with psychological terminology; or it may simply make overt the tendency, always present through the Platonic context of the Prudence tradition, to equate knowledge with the will to act. To know the good is to do it.

51. *The Poetry of Meditation*, rev. ed. (New Haven, 1962), pp. 37–38; see pp. 25–39.

Sir Thomas Elyot, for instance, takes pains to identify just such a will to act with the concept of *providentia* in his discussion of Prudence:

> Providence is, whereby a man not only foreseeth commodity and incommodity, prosperity and adversity, but also consulteth and therewith endeavoureth as well to repel annoyance, as to attain and get profit and advantage. And the difference between it and consideration is that consideration only consisteth in pondering and examining things conceived in the mind, providence in helping them with counsel and act.[52]

The likelihood that the procedures of Ignatian meditation and the three parts of Prudence share common origins in classical rhetoric is strengthened by Martz' admission that

> the meditative process would, of course, be working in cooperation with many other elements to form the character of this poetry. In particular, the principles of Renaissance logic and rhetoric would be in evidence, for these methods of meditation are in themselves adaptations of ancient principles of logic and rhetoric.[53]

I am willing to conjecture that the point at which religious meditation by the three powers of the soul emerged from the mainstream of rhetorical tradition occurred sometime after Augustine's efforts to convert Ciceronian rhetoric to the service of Christianity. It was, after all, Augustine who in the *De trinitate* first defined the powers of the soul as memory, understanding, and will, describing these three faculties as the image of the Trinity in man, and, in so doing, according for the first time such importance to the faculty of memory.[54]

52. *The Book named The Governor*, ed. S. E. Lehmberg, Everyman's Library (London, 1962), p. 81.

53. Martz, p. 38. He cites the example of the *Scala Meditationis* by Wessel Gansford, which ". . . is filled with references to the logical and rhetorical methods of Aristotle, Cicero, Raymond Lull, Rudolf Agricola, and others" (p. 39). Note that Lull figures prominently in the artificial memory tradition. See Yates, *The Art of Memory*, pp. 173–98.

54. *De Trinitate* X, 11–12; *Select Library of the Nicene and post-Nicene Fathers of the Christian Church*, ed. Philip Schaff (Buffalo, 1887), "On the Holy Trinity," trans. Rev. A. W. Haddan, III, 142–43. Augustine's originality here is remarked by Caplan, *Of Eloquence*, pp. 199–200, and Yates, *The Art of Memory*, p. 49. St. Bonaventura, *Itinerarium Mentis ad Deum* III.1–5, follows Augustine's version of the three powers. In *The Paradise Within* (New Haven, 1964), Martz gave full attention to the possibility of an Augustinian strain of religious meditation, which operates through the agency of memory, as a dominant influence upon certain religious poets, Traherne, Vaughan, and Milton, whose structures could not be satisfactorily described by the Ignatian pattern. However, Martz' amorphous description of Augustinian meditation as an intuitive process with no

If we can see poems which derive their logical structure from the meditative tradition and those which rely upon the Prudence tradition as closely related variants of the same process, we can understand why, for instance, Vaux's "On the Instability of Youth," which I have analyzed as organized upon the Prudence process, might be susceptible, as well, to a meditative analysis (as might also Vaux's "Bethinking Himself of his End, Writeth Thus"). Or why Bishop Joseph Hall's writings should include *The Arte of Divine Meditation* on the one hand and, on the other, a description of the parts of Prudence in his *Characters of Virtues and Vices*.[55] Or why Martz can claim Milton's "When I consider how my light is spent" (Sonnet 19), as a specimen of the "Meditative Poem,"[56] when Milton unmistakably employs a past-present-future time sequence in correspondence with the memory-understanding-foresight analysis. Indeed, "patience to prevent / That murmur" (lines 8–9), which voices the answer to the poet's questioning, comes very close to functioning as a personification, a Patience who is a palpably Christianized avatar of that once-pagan notion of Prudence. Martz' appropriation of Sonnet 19 particularly underscores the close relationship of Meditation and Prudence, since both the phrasing and cadence of Milton's opening suggest that he is echoing Shakespeare's 15.

Perhaps we may eventually conclude that with these and with related kinds of poems (those employing the *ars memoriae*, for example), it is less important to attach precise labels to the stages of mental process than to observe the large role of memory establishing an immediacy of felt experience upon which the poet's understanding then freely ranges. Given this process of retrospection and interior analysis, the rhetorical situation will be invariably private; the speaker talks to himself or, what is the same thing, to an imagined presence, human or divine; the reader, perforce, becomes eavesdropper. It is this simulation of overheard thought which lends such poems this extraordinary quality of "sincerity," a rhetoric of unpremeditated presentation.

---

set procedures; the lack of necessary historical grounding (as, for instance, in the unexplained differences between his account of Augustinian memory and Quinn's); and the intractability of some of the poetry he examines conspire to make this study a less valuable one than his first. See the review by John M. Wallace in *JEGP* 64 (1965): 732–38.

55. On Hall's meditational treatise, see *The Poetry of Meditation*, pp. 331–48. His use of the Prudence tradition is commented upon by Adams, "The Prudence of Prince Escalus," p. 40.

56. In his anthology, *The Meditative Poem* (Garden City: Anchor, 1963).

None of this is new. What would seem new and would perhaps explain the heightened emphasis on the role of memory in poetic process is the altered consciousness of time itself in the Renaissance. For a number of reasons, of which secularization, urbanization, and technological advancement are only the most obvious, the human consciousness of time underwent a marked change in this period of history. Ricardo Quinones has commented,

> For the men of the Renaissance, time is a great discovery—the antagonist against which they plan and plot and war, and over which they hope to triumph. . . . It is a force of their consciousness by which they themselves indicate the differences that set apart their new awareness of the world and their place in it from an older one.[57]

And, given this new force of consciousness, one means of understanding, and thereby vanquishing it, for the poet, for everyman, is through memory.[58]

57. Quinones, pp. 3–4. He also observes that ". . . time figures prominently in the formation of middle-class values" (p. 349), which may explain the attraction of Prudence.
58. This study was completed during my tenure as a visiting member of the Institute for Research in the Humanities at the University of Wisconsin.

6. Samuel Daniel:
A Voice of Thoughtfulness

ANTHONY LaBRANCHE

LOYOLA UNIVERSITY, CHICAGO

Our first reaction, like Jonson's, to Samuel Daniel's poetry is that, regrettably, true poetic talent and a certain kind of honesty cannot coexist: "Samuel Daniel a good honest man, but no poet." Instead of persuasive techniques Daniel appears to have moments of sincere self-revelation, issuing through a voice of thoughtfulness, and we allow that these moments are eloquent, but not really poetic or poetically engaging. This is, of course, an oversight on our part, and on Jonson's. There is a poetry of sincere self-expression which manages to discover its own particular rhetorical techniques and can become as well the object of our study as the more exaggerated postures which poets habitually assume. But even this last assertion raises further questions, which Daniel in his prefatory poems to *Musophilus* recognized implicitly.

> But here present thee, onelie modelled
> In this poore frame, the forme of mine owne heart.[1]

Does thoughtfulness, or honesty, or the "forme of mine owne heart" search out a rhetoric proper to it, or *is* it its own rhetoric in the sense that it provides a mutual association between speaker and reader which forms the basis for further specific rhetorical conduct?

As poet and defender of learning Daniel respects the public image of honesty, the image that must be strengthened and guarded with weapons from the armory of persuasiveness. Like Sidney's Astrophil who lives in fear of words uttered mechanically, divorced from an "inward touch," Daniel's speaker is sensitive to the conflicting demands of well-speaking and truth-saying. Daniel's choice and handling of

---

1. *Poems and A Defence of Ryme*, ed. A. C. Sprague (London, 1950), 67.

123

the speaking voice, consequently, are important aspects of his rhetorical technique which Jonson passed over and which, generally, we neglect in favor of a rather disjunctive examination of rhetorical figures according to criteria of persuading and delighting. The rhetorical procedures which we attach to these criteria I will call "accepted" or "recognized," for our discovery of them at work amplifying and advancing favorite poems has encouraged us to speak about Renaissance poetry too exclusively, I believe, in terms of epideictic and forensic argument. We neglect the difference between argumentation in verse and the poetic representation of an argument in a poem—the voice of the thinking, deliberating speaker. This last event is a dramatic rehearsal, and it has more to do with the speaker's tone of voice, his presentation of a recollected self to us, and our feeling of closeness to or distance from that voice, than it has to do with our mastery of "accepted" rhetorical procedures. I hope to show that Daniel's notion of a speaker confronts most sensitively the problem of just where persuasion lies, whence it issues, how it makes itself heard and take on significance— problems which cannot be reduced to the choice and control of verbal technique, while excluding all consideration of the posture out of which the rhetorical figures emerge.

Given more time and patience, we might redress the imbalance of scholarly investigation by studying Kierkegaard's anguishings over direct and indirect communication, over the inward consistency of irony, and over the basically ironic vein of man's thinking.[2] Moving closer to Daniel himself, as I hope to show presently, we can fight this oversimplification by remembering Montaigne's struggle to express *his* particular kind of "honesty." With what is the sincere or honest speaker keeping faith when he confronts his audience with a particular speaking voice which hardly says the whole truth about his own thoughtful abstraction from us? The whole autobiographical enterprise is evasive and misleading, even ironic, in its effort to represent through a particular speaking presence the thoughtful abstraction or absence of the speaker. For, "To be conscious is, among other things, to be somewhere else."[3]

Daniel offers a significant example in this perplexing matter of

2. *The Journals*, ed. Alexander Dru (New York, 1959), pp. 129–216; *The Point of View for My Work as an Author*, ed. Benjamin Nelson (New York, 1962), pp. 25–27, 142–51.

3. Maurice Merleau-Ponty, "Reading Montaigne," in *Signs*, trans. Richard C. McCleary (Evanston, 1964), p. 200.

the dramatic speaker, for often we describe our relations to Daniel's speaker as "honest" rather than "poetic" or "dramatic," without recognizing that this "honesty" is first of all a careful poetic creation of the autobiographical speaker. The mode or manner of this voice is established by Montaigne and his imitators, freely-ranging and confessional, and we have seen that the basic irony of that voice arises from the problem of how to be both thoughtful to oneself and present to one's audience. This is the first and most basic problem of the poet who expresses himself through any speaker. But the problem requires, first that we recognize details of the poet's style and technique.[4] I would like to examine, in this opening section, some of Daniel's favorite rhetorical strategies, just to make sure that we see how he is selecting and modifying the traditional figures to create a particular tone of speech. In a later part of my study I will try to describe the effort of creative imitation which lies behind Daniel's inventive use of "accepted" rhetorical procedure in his verse epistles. Although we cannot hope to answer all the general questions we have raised concerning the dramatic speaker, perhaps we may profit from a deeper experience of one poet's creation of the speaking voice.

1

The rhetorical figures which Daniel uses to proclaim those urgent moments when man must face some moral question, seem to operate in balanced periods of flow and interruption. Into the smooth river of his *thus . . . and, who, which* and *that* clauses, Daniel introduces exclamations, interrogations and word-repetition which, aided by rhyme, impose a new and heightened rhythm on the narrative. It is evident that the "moments" which we have mentioned are outbursts or emphatic underlinings which show through the otherwise regular and sober narrative.

> Percy, how soone, by thy example led,
> The household traine forsooke their wretched Lord!
> When, with thy staffe of charge dishonoured,
> Thou brak'st thy fayth, not steward of thy word,
> And tookst his part that after tooke thy head;

---

4. Two welcome beginnings have been made by C. C. Seronsy, "Well-languaged Daniel: A Reconsideration," *MLR* 52 (1957): 481–97, substantially reprinted in *Samuel Daniel* (New York, 1967), and *The Civil Wars*, ed. L. Michel (New Haven, 1958), pp. 24–48.

When thine owne hand had strengthned first his sword
"For, such great merits do upbraid, and call
"For great reward, or thinke the great too smal.

(Civil Wars, 1609, II, 2)

The figures of exclamation and interrogation usually appear at those instants when the argument has reached a local climax or temporary dead-end; by adopting an excited attitude the speaker asks us to reconsider the irony, injustice or paradoxical nature of events. This technique applies often, as above, to the structure within a stanza as well as to the relatively large patterns of interruptive stanzas within whole sections of narrative. In the *Panegyrike Congratulatorie* (1602), for example, stanzas 17–21 operate markedly by this process of interruption. These are traditional figures of rhetoric exhorting to action or persuading to an opinion.[5] But in Daniel they become a means of articulating second thoughts and calling to our attention a speaker who is definitely involved with moral issues. The dramatic situations of the first, second and fifth books of the *Civil Wars* (here given in the text of 1609) lend themselves to the amplifications and word-play which accompany such contemplative moments. The word-play indicates a deliberative effort as well as an emotional heightening of the incident. The poetic justice of Percy's reward, given above, is worked out in a series of ironic qualifications suggested by the words *brak'st, word, took'st, part, after tooke, head, hand, strengthned first,* and *sword.*

Thou brak's thy fayth, not steward of thy word,
And took'st his part that after tooke thy head;
When thine owne hand had strengthned first his sword.

It is this tone marking the presence of this particular speaker that critics have been at pains to define, but they have neglected to specify the origins of the tone. Terms such as "sober," "well-languaged Daniel" indicate a kind of dramatic presence, most carefully defined by particular moments of emphasis—or at times lack of emphasis. Ideally, as we move down the interminable list of rhetorical devices we might gradually grow to see them in a more organic, organizational light— something resembling the imaginative adaptation of an orator's em-

---

5. H. D. Rix, *Rhetoric in Spenser's Poetry* (College Station, Pa., 1940), p. 70. For definition and description of the figures I have relied on Henry Peacham, *The Garden of Eloquence* (1593), ed. W. G. Crane (Gainesville, 1954).

phatic stance rather than merely as tools of public address itself. One such trait, which operates very near to the ironies of word-play, is what Henry Wells discussed long ago as "sunken imagery."[6] Such imagery, in Daniel's hands, avoids witty similarities and resemblances while plunging down to a level of natural and unavoidable (rather than striking) association, and it creates often the tone of sober, tenacious contemplation. The breaking of the staff of steward, and the breaking of Percy's loyalty to Richard, the taking of parts and the taking of heads ("And took'st his part that after tooke thy head"), the acts of forsaking and of strengthening, all point to a seriously ironic level of association among events and imply a speaker who is reflecting upon his discourse before us, not merely declaiming a dissertation.

Especially in those poems where the poet appears to speak his mind, or where we are given a speaker deeply concerned with a continuing line of thought—the dedicatory pieces "To the Reader" (1607), the dedication of *Philotas* to Prince Henry, and in "To the Right Reverend . . . James Montague"—we hear the freely discursive, self-commemorating monotone which strikes many of Daniel's less patient readers as prosaic. Actually no prose or stance could be more ingratiating than this one, and too little attention has been given to the artful representation of second thoughts and qualifications through unusual syntax and word repetition.

> Though I the remnant of another time
> Am neuer like to see that happinesse,
> Yet for the zeale that I haue borne to rime
> And to the Muses, wish that good successe
> To others trauell, that in better place,
> And better comfort, they may be incheerd
> Who shall deserue, and who shall haue the grace
> To haue a Muse held worthy to be heard.
>
> (Preface to *Philotas*, 66–73)

The word-repetition, to which our eyes have become accustomed, provides emotional shading as well as structure to the central portion of the passage. The uncertainty of the long opening appositive, "I the remnant of another time," is contradicted by the emphatic phrases of the dangling, ruminative construction that follows ("to rime/ And to the Muses"; "that in better place,/ And better comfort"; "Who shall

---

6. *Poetic Imagery* (New York, 1924), ch. 3; cf. Seronsy, pp. 490 ff.

deserue, and who shall haue the grace/ To haue a Muse"). Among the further peculiarities of style which readers have noted in Daniel's use of the word *that*—possibly both as a demonstrative and a correlative conjunction intermixed in this case—"wish that good successe/ To other trauell, that in better place . . . they may be incheerd."[7] The same appearance of correlated or even "fused" thinking is achieved in the emphatic restrictive clauses at the end of our passage with their curious play on *deserue, haue, held* and *heard.*

This correlative, loose-jointed manner, curiously reminiscent of Latin and Romance relative clauses, by its very nature makes use of what linguists call the syntagmatic figures of speech—horizontal patterns (subject-verb-complement) which stress regular structural similarities—rather than the shocking selection of a single word or metaphor (paradigmatic).[8] We shall see that in Daniel the syntagmatic extends to his overall musing upon a subject; it stresses the activity of finding similarities and relationships and reflects the rhetoric of a mind in associative action rather than a voice delivering polished arguments or striking exaggerated postures. And like the tantalizingly unrealized imagery of the passage above, it operates on us through the example of a speaker intent upon pursuing a course within himself rather than upon swaying our opinion.

We might sum up by saying that Daniel's rhetoric is not really oratorical in purpose and tone, but it is a rhetoric of thoughtfulness, creating a poetry that presents habits of mind through certain rhetorical signals, a mind given in this case to tracing cause and effect, analogy, recapitulation and the like. This overall presence, when captured by the poem, is a truly rhetorical discovery. It is truly a tone of voice, not just the intrusion of a haphazard honesty into the argument of the poem—even when the speaker appears to be uttering the poet's own feelings. I mean that this speaking presence is a deliberate device no matter how closely the poet stands behind it—as in the memorable passages of *Musophilus* and of the various epistles and dedications.

---

7. See Seronsy, pp. 485–86, and C. C. Seronsy and R. Kreuger, "A MS of Daniel's *Civil Wars* Book III," *SP* 63 (1966): 157–62. Another start, though unclear, in the observation of Daniel's syntax is made by Donald Davie, *Articulate Energy* (London, 1955), pp. 45–50. The suggestion has been made to me that in the passage I have cited Daniel may be following Latin and Romance precedent in repeating the conjunctive *that* after a verb of volition.

8. G. N. Leech, "Linguistics and the Figures of Rhetoric," *Essays on Style and Language*, ed. Roger Fowler (London, 1966), pp. 135–56.

In fact the semblance of closeness to the poet's own mind and feelings, as well as the rhetorical mannerisms which reflect that mind, are embodiments of that "inward consistency" toward which Daniel (like his predecessor Sidney) is striving. This portrait of a mind discoursing, reconsidering, reacting, is Daniel's sober representation of the eternal struggle between truth of subject matter and the arts of persuasion by which the poet must present that matter.[9] The arts of persuasion have come under scrutiny and have been submerged in favor of the speaker's recollection of himself. Out of Daniel's "imitation of a discourse" emerges not clear precepts or propaganda, but man's tenacious effort to persist in confronting truth, whatever that may be, in its many guises. This becomes what the rhetorician would call Daniel's *ethos*. Having glimpsed this, we may go on to our more specific task of describing Daniel's epistolary imitations.

2

If we were to compare Jonson's "Epistle to Katherine, Lady Aubigny" (*Forest*, 13) which Wesley Trimpi calls "plain, intimate and urbane"[10] and Daniel's "To the Ladie Lucie, Countesse of Bedford" (1603), we would be struck by differences in the order and procedure which each poet deems appropriate to his poem. Jonson's strategy is to win the reader's belief in his sincerity at the outset by describing the setbacks he has suffered in praising virtue and condemning vice (1–20) and his fiercer determination now to proceed in his encouragement of virtue, "Nor feare to draw true lines, cause others paint" (20). Jonson, or his speaker, can assure Lady Aubigny directly that his praise will be truth, not flattery, and there follows a list of qualities he will *not* praise (while mentioning how favorably they are disposed in her)—beauty, wealth and position (21–42). But what really concerns the poet is her mind, that is her virtues, and these virtues all reside in her resolution to shun the dissoluteness of court life (which 59–88 describe in variety and detail) and to embrace a chaste domestic life. This life is subject for celebration by the poet and will shower a reward of fruitfulness, domestic love and unity upon the happy pair (99–120). The Lady will see that her resolution promises a lasting and virtuous

---

9. Joan Rees, *Samuel Daniel. A Critical and Biographical Study* (Liverpool, 1964), chs. 6–8.

10. *Ben Jonson's Poems: A Study of the Plain Style* (Stanford, 1962), p. 139. See Arnold Stein's interesting review, *ELH* 30 (1963): 306–16.

course by consulting the poet's "truest glasse" (122). We must agree
with Trimpi that the poem is urbanely calculated and that the castiga-
tion of courtly vice and glorification of plain virtue are amalgamated
into a single discourse. Jonson proceeds by vivid, even exaggerated
illustration and assertion, not analytically; he seeks to move the emotions by praise and ridicule. The importance of cogent descriptive
exempla in this operation cannot be overestimated; and other poems,
for example the epistle to Sir Robert Wroth (*Forest*, 3), proceed in
much the same manner.

Daniel's "Epistle to the Ladie Lucie, Countesse of Bedford," on the
other hand, adopts an entirely different approach to its advisory or hor-
tatory task, and the result is an entirely different kind of epistolary discourse. For the opening twenty-five lines the speaker remains on a level
of generality as he describes the effectiveness of a virtue according to
the position of its practitioner. The entire movement of the poem is toward the problem of virtue's "abilitie" to affect other people. Only then
does the speaker bring his discourse to its particular application.

> And therefore well did your high fortunes meete
>   With her, that gracing you, comes grac't thereby
>   And well was let into a house so sweete
> So good, so faire; so faire, so good a guest,
>   Who now remaines as blessed in her seate,
>   As you are with her residencie blesst.
>
> (26–31)

The basis of this "vertue" is knowledge which is achieved through
study, "the'onely certaine way that you can goe / Unto true glory, to
true happiness" (34–35). The poet offers by way of development an
excursus of false appearances (36–39), then a commendation of knowledge as the key to enfranchising the fair sex from the prison of false
appearances (40–49), and an extraordinarily extended account (*aetio-
logia*) of how the mind is the seat of all good (50–82)—interrupted
only in time for the conclusion which returns us to the subject of books
as a directive to knowledge and the addressee's "cleerenesse" in choos-
ing this "Rightest way" (83–97). As we consider this strange and un-
prepossessing structure we are struck by the truth that though Daniel
appears digressive, even evasive, he is more tenaciously analytical than
Jonson. Daniel's speaker continues to examine the worth of studies,
their relation to the mind and to knowledge; Jonson's speaker leaps

from example to example of praise or blame with an orator's persuasiveness of "application."[11] In other words, the sum of Jonson's individual sections is a rather self-consciously cogent act of persuasion,
whereas Daniel's more evasive and parallel lines of exposition (e.g.
the emphatic "digressions"[12] of 36–39 and 50–82) provide a more
subtle embodiment or reenactment of his cardinal feelings. He ends
by capturing a "voice" somewhere nearby, not just a formal witty
posture. One poem sets out wilfully to persuade by example, the other
by repetition and parallel movement provides a contemplative structure which addresses the reader's attention and sympathy. This may
be the moment, if ever, to venture that Jonson's epistle in the plain
style is cogent and decorous, perhaps even moving, but not very
thoughtful. This is one defect of his version of classical plain style
and sufficient warning not to judge his attempts in the epistolary
genre by the square of the poems alone.

Most of Daniel's rhetorical traits, his word-play, sunken imagery,
and tenacious if syntactically loose-jointed pursuit of a theme, point
to the welcoming of a thought process as the basic activity of his
poetry—the poetic imitation of an argument rather than the argument
itself.[13] And to the purposefully-minded reader his poems may seem
muted and removed, pre-occupied with an autobiographical working-
out of favored ideas, rather than a full-blooded attempt to convince a
worldly audience. They seem to do something slightly different from
what they should be doing, and they owe greater allegiance to a single,
continuing philosophical discourse within themselves than they do to
the call of social need or of external occasion. In a sense they perform
for themselves, or to themselves, and we are permitted to witness the
show. Daniel's best passages are most profoundly passages of presence, illuminations of a highly imitative and allusive kind. And the
highly "imitative" uses to which he puts the normal devices of apos-

11. A full account of the orator's use of example is given in *Ad Herennium*,
trans. Harry Caplan (London, 1954), bk. 4.

12. Some critics have questioned whether digression can properly be said to
occur in poetry, where there is a less stringent notion of argument than in
certain kinds of prose. See D. L. Clark, *Rhetoric and Poetry in the Renaissance*
(New York, 1922), p. 30.

13. One Italian critic, Speroni, argues "The enthymeme of oratory is a more or
less imperfect effigy of the probable syllogism, and the probable syllogism is an
image of a perfect demonstration. . . . Should it not be inferred that rhetorical
persuasion is a picture and imitation of opinion, and opinion an imitation of
science?" See Baxter Hathaway, *The Age of Criticism: The Late Renaissance in
Italy* (Ithaca, N.Y., 1962), pp. 68–69, 160.

trophe, exclamation and self-examination in shadowing forth a sincere and earnest speaker have discouraged our critical attention. It is this lack of rhetorical aggressiveness which has deceived us into describing Daniel's performances largely in negative terms. But we are far from describing that performance which we *are* called upon to witness and to complete.

Some light in this case may be thrown upon Daniel's poetic performance by sizing up the genre in which he is working. Where did Daniel find the impetus to an intimate, epistolary yet un-Horatian kind of poetry which presents alternately the personality of an immediate speaker and that lofty moral attitude "written from above" which Auerbach remarks of Tacitus?[14] This style or mode may be one more example of Renaissance imitation—that eclectic and contemporary recreation of classical and continental models which inspires so much of Renaissance poetry and which reveals indirectly much of the disposition of Renaissance poetic minds. Jonson himself observes that among Daniel's "pilferings" stands the ever-fashionable Montaigne, and modern scholars have detected some of those borrowings from Montaigne and, behind him, from Seneca.[15] The interesting point which has remained unmentioned, however, is that Daniel's sense of organization also may owe something to Montaigne's loose, discursive intimate essay style—a version of the Senecan mode which affected matter over manner. Daniel appears to have caught the mainstream of the Senecan revolt with its insistence on "inward consistency" yet with its often contradictory passions to express a balanced overview of man's moral history. The progression from *Rosamund* (1952) to *Cleopatra* (1594) to the *Civil Wars* (1595) and on to the later *Epistles* and *Defense of Ryme* (1603) could bear some scrutiny for this trend.[16]

14. *Mimesis*, trans. Willard Trask (Princeton, 1953), ch. 2.
15. Jonson's comments are gathered by Trimpi, p. 268 n. 34. See R. Himelick, "Montaigne and Daniel's 'To Sir Thomas Egerton,'" *PQ* 36 (1957): 500–04; "Samuel Daniel, Montaigne and Seneca," *N & Q* 3 (1956): 61–64; J. I. M. Stewart, "Montaigne's *Essays* and a *Defence of Ryme*," *RES* 9 (1933): 311–12; and Camilla Hill Hay, *Montaigne: Lecteur et Imitateur de Sénèque* (Poitiers, 1938), especially pp. 167–74. Hay's findings have recently been questioned by Jean-Pierre Boon, "Emendations des emprunts dans le texte des essais dit 'stoiciens' de Montaigne," *SP* 65 (1968): 147–62. The opening of Daniel's "To the Lady Lucie . . ." recalls the opening of Montaigne's "Of the Institution and Education of Children."
16. The flexibility of Daniel's rhetorical adaptation during this period is illustrated by the 1594 additions to *Rosamund* (see A. C. Sprague ed., *Poems and A Defence of Ryme* [London, 1950], pp. 197–201) and Richard Carew's awkward, if rhetorically exact, rendition of Tasso in the same year, both of which stand as background to the amplification and word-play of the *Civil Wars*.

Our immediate approach to this tone of voice is through Daniel's possible borrowing in 1603 from Montaigne, who "Yeeldes most rich pieces and extracts of man; / Though in a troubled frame confus'dly set" ("To my deere friend M. Iohn Florio," 80–81).[17] Both Croll and Williamson describe Montaigne's mature style as "loose" or a combination of loose and curt elements whose "progression adapts itself to the movements of a mind discovering truth as it goes, thinking while it writes."[18] Analogously, the structure of the essays avoids the oratorical and strives toward the organic: "le dialogue externe de Platon se transforme chez Montaigne en un monlogue intérieure."[19] This may be the reason behind the "troubled frame" which Daniel mentions in his poem to Florio, and it may be also the impulse by which he transforms his own more orotund "public" discourses, filled as they are with conditional and causal periods, into a more appealing, personal ruminative genre, "the forme of mine owne heart."

Montaigne's art of interior monologue (and in less rambling fashion Bacon's more curt *Essays*) offer an interesting analogy, then, to Daniel's adaptation of the *genus humile*—a concentrated effort to capture the new (in 1600) serious orientation to moral concerns and to a responsible speaker, concerns traditionally assigned to the province of Jonson's plain style. In Book I. 38, "Of Solitarinesse," an essay which Himelick notes supplies background to some of Daniel's pronouncements on integrity, virtue and fit audience,[20] there occurs the following passage. This passage does not move in the loose style of the later essays, and yet it shows (in Florio's version)[21] something of the system of association and emphasis within an extended periodic structure which Daniel's ethical verse also creates.

> We should reserve a store-house for our selves, what need soever change; altogether ours, and wholly free, wherein we may hoard up and establish our true libertie, and principall retreit and solitarinesse,

17. See Roger E. Bennett, "Sir William Cornwallis's Use of Montaigne," *PMLA* 48 (1933): 1080–89; George Williamson, *The Senecan Amble*, (Chicago: Phoenix Books, 1966), pp. 105–09.

18. See Williamson, pp. 145–9; Morris Croll, *Style, Rhetoric, and Rhythm*, ed. J. Max Patrick and Robert O. Evans, with John M. Wallace and R. J. Schoeck (Princeton, 1966), pp. 221, 22–30.

19. Floyd F. Gray ,*Le Style de Montaigne* (Paris, 1958), p. 187.

20. "Samuel Daniel, Montaigne and Seneca," see n. 15, above. "Of Solitarinesse" is numbered I. 29 in most editions of Montaigne.

21. Florio was well into his translation of Book I of the *Essays* by 1598 and dedicated that book to the Countess of Bedford. See Frances A. Yates, *John Florio* (Cambridge, 1934), pp. 214–20.

wherein we must go alone to our selves, take out ordinarie enter-
tainement, and so privately that no acquaintance or communication of
any strange thing may therein find place: there to discourse, to medi-
tate and laugh, as, without wife, without children, and goods, without
traine or servants; that if by any occasion they be lost, it seeme not
strange to us to passe it over; we have a minde moving and turning in
it selfe; it may keep it selfe companie; it hath wherewith to offend and
defend, wherewith to receive, and wherewith to give.[22]

The excesses of ornament and expansion which Matthiessen and Yates
remark of Florio's translation are held to a minimum in our passage,
but Florio's natural redundancy relieves some of the curtness of the
original.[23] The passage proceeds by appositions, associations, loosely
conjunctive members: *what need soever, wherein, and, wherein, and so,*
and the like.[24] It is freely extended, yet sober and regular. The same
rhythms and the appearance of extending his thoughts while he writes
occur in Daniel's epistle "To the Countess of Bedford." Each unit of
three or four lines is loosely conjoined to an earlier theme or concern
through the topics of definition, division (subject and adjuncts) and
causality.[25]

> *Since all* the good we haue rests in the mind,
>   *By whose* proportions onely we redeeme
>   Our thoughts from out confusion, and do finde
> The measure of our selues, and of our powres.
>   *And that* all happiness remaines confind
>   *Within* the Kingdome of this breast of ours,
> *Without whose* bounds, all that we looke on, lies
>   *In* others Iurisdictions, others powres,
>   *Out* of the circuit of our liberties.
> All glory, honor, fame, applause, renowne,
>   Are not belonging to our royalties.
>   But t'others wills, *wherein* th'are onely growne.
> *And that* vnless we finde vs all *within,*
>   We neuer can *without* vs be our owne:
>   Nor call it right our life, *that* we liue *in.* . . .

          (50–64)

22. World's Classics ed. (London, 1919), I, 287–88.
23. Yates, ch. 10; F. O. Matthiessen, *Translation: An Elizabethan Art* (Harvard, 1931), ch. 4.
24. In the loose style, on the other hand, Williamson remarks "no phrase
provides an obvious cue to the syntax" (p. 225).
25. See Sister Miriam Joseph, *Rhetoric in Shakespeare's Time* (New York,
1962) ch. 7; Croll, p. 220.

The phrases I have put into italics are all means of furthering the discourse in a curiously additive manner; despite their gestures toward causality and definition, they give the appearance of a freely expanding rumination extending outwards and onwards. This loosely appositive expansion within a periodic framework *is* the essential progression of the passage.[26] And the aim of this manner of progression is not just to offer precepts and example, but to show the self extending itself into a question, into a position facing the predicaments of life. The members of the passage are fairly regular, if isolated from each other; they create a feeling both of deliberateness and of associative freedom, of serious commitment to the "life we live *in*" and of speculative expansiveness regarding its challenges. And they create the presence of a speaker engaged in an expansion-discovery, such as is indicated by the series of *and that* clauses all relating to the *finde* of the third line. The use of word-play and of word-repetition (*within, without,* and the final relative *that* following upon the insistent *and that*) reveals a speaker who is anxious to describe himself, in his well-timed dilations, by the qualifications of balance, contrast and irony.

It is only too evident that Daniel's application of the ruminative manner, based on the premise "gentle Reader, myselfe am the groundworke of my booke," results in a curious compromise which for many readers robs Daniel's poetry of clarity and decisiveness. Daniel sees the poet's task as morally directive, through ancient authority, and this task demands an elevated, even orotund style, a voice issuing an overview, rather than an intimate, informal, ironic confession to the reader, like Montaigne's above. One might accuse Daniel's speaker of a certain doubleness or bad faith—he engages us at the level of argument, but ends by giving us autobiographical revelation. This doubleness creates a breach of contract in the rhetorical relationship which Daniel's speaker seems eager to acknowledge as the basis of clear and honest social intercourse.

In the passage we have selected for analysis, and throughout the *Epistles,* Daniel's style is essentially formal even though his speaker's presence is intimate, or as Coleridge remarks "grave and easy." This style is reminiscent in tone and rhythm of Hoby's *Courtier,* and, for

---

26. An interesting discussion of distorted grammaticalness as a kind of syntactical strength is Allan Rodway's "By Algebra to Augustanism," in Fowler, *Essays on Style and Language,* pp. 53–67.

1603, it appears more Isocratean than Senecan.[27] But I have stressed Daniel's new modification, his tendency to revise, extend and qualify the basic syntactic regularity out of a need to approximate in his own terms the "dramatic sentence of a mind thinking."[28] As a result Daniel's epistolary style is both humble and formal, immediate and distant, intimate and authoritative, and I believe, in reply to Daniel's critics, that this was a poise or balance toward which he was striving, albeit with varying success. The *Epistles* and prefatory pieces, for that matter the longer poems too, present a test of true balance, perspective and insight which we must pass in order to qualify as morally sensitive beings. The curiously ambiguous intimacy of the speaker is the largest challenge of these addresses. We sense a less intimate personality in Daniel's speaker than we do in Montaigne's, perhaps to the extent that he doesn't quite carry off the autobiographical dimension of his discourses, but the speaker's voice is not really distant. The speaker appears so persistently concerned throughout the poem with thinking as a valid mode of action that we have the illusion of a close intellectual companionship with him, a familiarity with his "thinking" presence—precisely one concern of the loose mode. Here Daniel's style, as formal as we know it to be, is also truly plain in that it assumes the stance of having no artistic concern for itself.

3

Our few insights into Daniel's style, alone or placed in the relief of Jonson's or Montaigne's, should guard us from too simple a notion of rhetorical procedure, and particularly from the notion that such a procedure when singled out by us could describe the style and principal direction of a poem. It is important that we allow ourselves to see Renaissance poetry as poetic representation rather than simply oratorical persuasion. Many of Daniel's rhetorical figures become meaningful only in context of the larger gestures of the poem. For example, his reiterative word-play stresses ironic contrasts of attitude, but also a certain continuity of concern in the poem, the concern embodied in a tone of voice and a presence which apply themselves gravely to the "topics" of life as they arise. That is, word-play may support certain

27. Croll, ch. 6 *passim*; Williamson, ch. 1; G. K. Hunter, *John Lyly: The Humanist as Courtier* (London, 1962), p. 272; Herbert G. Wright, *The First English Translation of the "Decameron"* (1620) (Cambridge, Eng. 1953), pp. 216–17.

28. Williamson, p. 149; Croll, pp. 224–26. For a version in Daniel's prose see *A Defence of Ryme*, ed. Sprague, lines 60–81.

ironic contrasts in local passages, but it also represents the continuing process of thought and commentary which is the major subject of the poem and which sets its "pitch" and tone. Such word-play is not merely ironic, interruptive and fragmenting, but indicates the continuing concern of the speaker for his subject, his continuing struggle to be present to life. It gathers together and harmonizes the individual addresses of thought, the transitions, extensions and reservations of attitude which extend the length of Daniel's poems.

The original, and larger question, however, is that of the dramatic speaker's presence to us and our presence to him—that bond of relationship which gives rise to our understanding the rhetoric of the situation. If the problem of communicating one's *thinking* to an audience is a problem of the absent-present, the nearby-distant, then the normal criteria of rhetorical description, expansion and argument are not exactly to the point, and we will not achieve through their terms an adequate description of Daniel's style and poetic accomplishment. Vividness and concreteness, for example, are only momentary accomplishments and smack of necessary falsification to the gravely speculative mind. Is "honesty" either vivid or concrete? There are other kinds of patience than the patience of careful illustration and clarity which Jonson epitomizes. The "plainer," more basic kind of patience may be a humility in pursuing the process of thinking itself, a feeling for the deep irony of its activities, and an autobiographical consciousness which bows to the limits placed on truth by man's preoccupation with living. This may be the organizing mentality of the honest or thoughtful style. The question posed by Daniel's version of the poetic speaker contrasted with Jonson's, for example, is not a superficial one of appeal to or intimacy with an audience. It is Montaigne's nagging question of why he should expose himself at all, why he should come forward, when the inevitable result will be the falsification of his most inward thinking and at the same time a failure to acquiesce in an audience's thirst for vivid entertainment and flashy argument. Daniel's answer strikes us as less maturely resolved or thought out than Montaigne's, but it is still too honest to answer the demand of many readers for vivid performance in poetry. The voice in Daniel's poetry is aware of this, but too often that voice gets no further than letting us share the biting irony of the thimker's predicament, fighting back despair with whatever arguments seem to offer some ray of hope.

The latter part of this study has tried to suggest the kind of imaginative effort required to seek out a style for the speaker whom Daniel was set on representing, a style which involves in its distant-engaged tone an ingenious imitation of the essay-style and of which we can note traces as early as *Cleopatra* (1594). In this deeper sense of imitation all of Daniel's maneuvers to present a sympathetic and per-suasive speaker can be viewed as a fictionalization, and so an extension of the struggles of the autobiographical "I" to retain balance, self-awareness, and perspective. The term "dramatic" does justice only to the external features of this process, for the curious "presence" of Daniel's best poetry reveals that the speaking voice is an extension of psyche as well as a verbalization of it. This double activity—first, the extension of this active center within us, and second, the excitement inherent in its portrayal and verbalization—are the continuing actions in most of Daniel's poetry. I believe he shaped his style to reflect this activity. And so, as much as they are concerned with precept and dis-course, his better "moral" passages also create the presence of a voice speaking near to us.

To speak, for Daniel, is to capture this predicament—or rather to reflect upon one's speech-act is to capture it. The sound of one's voice lends assurance that one is individual, yet savingly entangled in a net-work of human appositions, extensions, qualifications, antitheses. To speak is the first and, for Daniel, the most serious step toward our embodiment in the world. To this step or commitment the conventions of vividness and concreteness add little: "I know I shal be read, among the rest / So long as men speake english." This is why his poetry ap-pears both engaging and forgettable, to many readers, and possesses at times the poignancy of a telephoned farewell which we soon feel to be "unreal" though it was terribly near to us while it was happening.

At the level of technique Daniel seems bent upon selecting and adapting rhetorical strategies so as to turn them from their normally emphatic clarifying role toward the non-public, personal and "directly expressive." Once again the sensitive reader may feel in Daniel a deep conflict—a respect for the presence of inward thoughtfulness crossed by the desire to imitate that thoughtfulness, and so publicize it, as carefully as his knowledge of literary devices permitted. His speakers are more deeply concerned with literary composition than with poetic effectiveness, the former being the more personal, the latter the more satisfying. We are hesitant to determine where the speaking voice is issuing *from*, and so we say it is the man himself. We must be getting the "poet himself." Or are we getting only his concern with the question of being present to himself and to the "questions" of living in the world? This latter concern would militate against a vivid sense of location, for all thinking is undeniably "here"—and elsewhere.

Rhetorically considered, the formation of this style depends on an eclectic mingling of figures, being as they are common tools, but always, hopefully, with that Sidneian "inward touch." that inspection of the relation of honest feeling to its artistic expression which so absorbed the attention of Astrophil. Such a style cannot be considered in Daniel's case a mingling of poetic figures with prosaic matter. Much of the rhetoric is directed to specific representations of the speaker's stance, balance, and manner of discourse, rather than to isolated vivid turns and "effective" argumentation.

My main interest has been to arouse our more imaginative instincts when approaching these signals, and to ask once again what is a speaker's "voice," out of what sense of our worldly entanglement does it issue, how does it draw us to it? One way to start on this problem is through a more sensitive observation of Renaissance imitation, such as that which is suggested by the various genres which Daniel methodically undertook from *Delia* to *Musophilus*. Although Daniel turned entirely to prose history after 1612, for the last ten years of his life, we should not let this pronounce the final word on his earlier accomplishments in verse-essay, beginning around 1594, which ask us to revise our notions of poetic rhetoric and behind that, of imitation —that deepest kind of imitation in which the novelty, energy, perhaps meaning of the Renaissance poem often reside.

7. Donne and "The Extasie"

ARTHUR F. MAROTTI

WAYNE STATE UNIVERSITY

The Extasie

1. Where, like a pillow on a bed,
   A Pregnant banke swel'd up, to rest
   The violets reclining head,
   Sat we two, one anothers best;

2. Our hands were firmely cimented   5
   With a fast balme, which thence did spring,
   Our eye-beames twisted, and did thred
   Our eyes, upon one double string,

3. So to'entergraft our hands, as yet
   Was all our meanes to make us one,   10
   And pictures on our eyes to get
   Was all our propagation.

4. As 'twixt two equall Armies, Fate
   Suspends uncertaine victorie,
   Our soules, (which to advance their state,   15
   Were gone out,) hung 'twixt her, and mee.

5. And whil'st our soules negotiate there,
   Wee like sepulchrall statues lay;
   All day, the same our postures were,
   And wee said nothing, all the day.   20

6. If any, so by love refin'd,
   That he soules language understood,
   And by good love were growen all minde,
   Within convenient distance stood,

7. He (though he knew not which soule spake,   25
   Because both meant, both spake the same)

140

Might thence a new concoction take,
And part farre purer then he came.

8. This Extasie doth unperplex
(We said) and tell us what we love,   30
Wee see by this, it was not sexe,
Wee see, we saw not what did move:

9. But as all severall soules containe
Mixture of things, they know not what,
Love, these mixt soules, doth mixe again,   35
And makes both one, each this and that.

10. A single violet transplant,
The strength, the colour, and the size,
(All which before was poore, and scant,)
Redoubles still, and multiplies.   40

11. When love, with one another so
Interinanimates two soules,
That abler soule, which thence doth flow,
Defects of lonelinesse controules.

12. Wee then, who are this new soule, know,   45
Of what we are compos'd, and made,
For, th'Atomies of which we grow,
Are soules, whom no change can invade.

13. But O alas, so long, so farre
Our bodies why doe wee forbeare?   50
They'are ours, though they'are not wee, Wee are
The'intelligences, they the spheare.

14. We owe them thankes, because they thus,
Did us, to us, at first convay,
Yeelded their forces, sense, to us,   55
Nor are drosse to us, but allay.

15. On man heavens influence workes not so,
But that it first imprints the ayre,
Soe soule into the soule may flow,
Though it to body first repaire.   60

16. As our blood labours to beget
Spirits, as like soules as it can,
Because such fingers need to knit
That subtile knot, which makes us man:

17. So must pure lovers soules descend   65
    T'affections, and to faculties,
Which sense may reach and apprehend,
    Else a great Prince in prison lies.

18. To'our bodies turne wee then, that so
    Weake men on love reveal'd may looke;   70
Loves mysteries in soules doe grow,
    But yet the body is his booke.

19. And if some lover, such as wee,
    Have heard this dialogue of one,
Let him still marke us, he shall see   75
    Small change, when we'are to bodies gone.[1]

L IKE "THE CANNONIZATION" or "A Valediction: Forbidding Mourning." "The Extasie" has long been a touchstone for discussions of Donne's poetry. Drawing together motifs scattered throughout his verse—the mystery of love, the body-soul relationship, the reflection of the macrocosm in the microcosm—this lyric, in its Byzantine complexity of argument, intellectual allusiveness, and rhetorical subtlety, is quintessential Donne. Coleridge thought it the quintessential metaphysical poem—a literary work that gathers into itself the energy of a large sensibility, reshaping and transforming its intellectual and poetic materials to create a rare artistic synthesis. Creatively derivative, it is a unique and original poem.

Between Pierre Legouis' view of it as the performance of a scholastic Don Juan and Helen Gardner's antiseptically philosophical reading lies a crazy-quilt of interpretive exercises.[2] What is usually at stake

1. John Donne, *The Elegies and The Songs and Sonnets,* ed. Helen Gardner (Oxford, 1965); all quotations from the love poetry are taken from this edition. I accept Miss Gardner's text of "The Extasie" with the exception of the word "That" (line 67), which has absolutely no manuscript authority. I have restored the commonly accepted reading, "Which," in its place. In quoting from Donne's other works, I use the following: John Donne, *The Satires, Epigrams, and Verse Letters,* ed. W. Milgate (Oxford, 1967); John Donne, *The Divine Poems,* ed. Helen Gardner (Oxford, 1952); *The Complete Poetry and Selected Prose of John Donne,* ed. Charles M. Coffin (New York, 1952)—for the other poetry, some letters and the miscellaneous prose works; *The Sermons of John Donne,* ed. George R. Potter and Evelyn Simpson, 10 vols. (Berkeley and Los Angeles, 1953–1962).
2. Pierre Legouis, *Donne the Craftsman* (Paris, 1928), pp. 61–71; Helen Gardner, "The argument about 'The Ecstasy,'" in *Elizabethan and Jacobean Studies*

in such readings is the individual critic's conception of Donne and his art; so the debate has, consequently, been a heated one. The stress has fallen upon the argument of the "dialogue of one" (line 74) and the conclusion it reaches about the nature of the love relationship. Critics have combed the works of Plato, Aristotle, Aquinas, Ficino, and the writers of the sixteenth-century *trattati d'amore* for material to illustrate Donne's love-metaphysic; but they have discovered, finally, that "The Extasie" presents an unremarkable truth: soul and body involve each other and both have a necessary part in the love experience. If this is what the poem offers, the wrapping is more precious than the gift. Although the place of physicality in the most sublime type of love was a live issue for Renaissance love-philosophers and poets, Donne, I suspect, has much more in mind than the articulation of a truism.

Attention has been focussed too exclusively upon the content of the poem's argument to the neglect of the way that argument is presented. At this point, we would do well to examine closely the whole reader-poem relationship, particularly those devices that condition our responses to the supposedly "objective" meaning of the work. Within this larger context, I would like to offer a new reading of "The Extasie" —not new in the sense of discovering fresh literary or philosophical antecedents, but new in the way I shall extrapolate from details of the poem's content and method to point to a specificity of meaning no one has yet dared (or been foolhardy enough) to claim; for I shall assume the existence of a kind of poetic control even the most microscopic readings have been reluctant to posit. Briefly, I see this poem as a rhetorically sophisticated defense of conjugal love, written originally, perhaps, as an exercise in literary imitation, but, nevertheless, rooted in Donne's deepest personal experiences and designed for a coterie audience familiar with *both* his life and his art. My interpretation is

---

Presented to Frank Percy Wilson (Oxford, 1959), pp. 279–285, summarizes the critical debate up to the late 1950s. Since then the major discussions of the poem have been the following: A. J. Smith, "Donne in His Time: A Reading of *The Extasie*," *Rivista di Letteratura Moderne e Comparate* 10 (1957): 260–75; Michael McCanles, "Distinguish in Order to Unite: Donne's 'The Extasie,'" *SEL* 6 (1966): 59–75; N. J. Andreasen, *John Donne: Conservative Revolutionary* (Princeton, 1967), pp. 168–78; Charles Mitchell, "Donne's 'The Extasie': Love's Sublime Knot," *SEL* 8 (1968): 91–101; René Graziani, "John Donne's 'The Extasie' and Ecstasy," *RES* NS 19 (1968): 121–36; Earl Miner, *The Metaphysical Mode from Donne to Cowley* (Princeton, 1969), pp. 76–83.

unashamedly biographical; but for a poet like Donne, who wrote primarily for his friends, such a perspective is, I believe, both inevitable and necessary.

1

Donne's best poems are linear, rather than iconic. Bearing what Lowry Nelson Jr. calls the typical mark of the Baroque lyric, an *evolving* rhetorical situation,[3] they carefully manipulate reader response as they twist their meaning one way and another, to end either with a surprisingly logical conclusion or simply with a surprise. They challenge our intellectual stamina and agility. Some, as Donne characterized his prose paradoxes, sound "alarums to truth," presenting deliberately outrageous arguments for which readers must produce the antidotes. Others pretend merely to entertain us and flatter our assumptions while they tease us unsuspectingly, into a new awareness, mocking our ignorance and insensitivity. Others treat us as enemies and close us out of their worlds, forcing us to beg admission. And still others address themselves to our capacity for sympathetic involvement, to reward us with insight and an experience of civilized emotion —they sharpen our sensitivities. Although Donne says in the preface to his scornfully satiric *Metempsychosis*, "I would have no such Readers as I can teach," his poems do transmit a forcefully didactic impulse. Poetry with such a recurrent and strong argumentative element could not do otherwise.

"The Extasie" is Donne's most complexly argued lyric; and, if for no other reason, it has exerted a lodestone pull on critical minds. We follow its train of thought, which, like Donne's sermons, proceeds largely by seemingly casual association, until we assent to its natural conclusion before we actually realize what the poem is saying or appreciate its implications. Before the argument proper, however, the first seven stanzas locate us in a complex narrative, dramatic, and rhetorical framework, conditioning our responses in important ways.

The initial stanzas, with their telescoped description of the traditional *locus amoenus* or pleasaunce and their erotically suggestive

3. *Baroque Lyric Poetry* (New Haven, 1961), p. 91; see his remarks on Donne, pp. 121–37. David Novarr, " 'The Extasie': Donne's Address on the States of Union," in *Just So Much Honor: Essays Commemorating The Four-Hundredth Anniversary of the Birth of John Donne*, ed. Peter A. Fiore (University Park, 1972), pp. 219–43, appeared too late to be used in this study.

word-choice ("pillow on a bed" [line 1], "Pregnant" [line 2], "reclining [line 3], "propagation" [line 12]) lead us to expect a scene of love-making.[4] We notice, furthermore, that the lovers change from a sitting to a lying position: the verb "sat" of line four becomes "lay" in line eighteen. The hand-holding and eye-gazing are depicted in an exaggeratedly physical way: the hands are "cimented" (line 8) and "enter-graft[ed]" (line 9); the eyes are threaded "upon one double string" (line 8). These are the first courses in a banquet of sense that should culminate, as the lovers' moist palms suggest,[5] in sexual union. Most of this has been noted before. But the fourth and fifth stanzas employ a conceit whose erotic implications have not been noticed:

> As 'twixt two equall Armies, Fate
>   Suspends uncertaine victorie,
> Our soules, (which to advance their state,
>   Were gone out,) hung 'twixt her, and mee.
>
> And whil'st our soules negotiate there . . . .

> (lines 13–17)

With his characteristically hard-nosed critical attitude, Yvor Winters complains about this military metaphor: "a false comparison," he writes, "for the two souls are not in conflict, but are about to unite."[6] Despite his misreading (the bodies are the combatting armies, the souls the individual negotiators), he is onto something important. Donne utilizes the amatory topos of love's war (the title of one of his elegies), and, therefore, reinforces the erotic suggestions of this section of the poem, though we lack here the "close thrusts and stabs" of sexual battle.

At this point in the action, however, the subject has shifted to that of a spiritual, rather than a sensuous, ecstasy, and, as Winters begins to perceive, tenor and vehicle clash in this metaphor. Considering the work Donne seems to assign his conceit—the spatial placing of the souls outside the bodies in a separate transaction of their own—it

---

4. Shakespeare assumes similar expectations in the scene in *A Midsummer Night's Dream* in which the eloping Hermia and Lysander select their first resting place in the forest (2.2.35–65). For the *locus amoenus* topos, see Ernst Robert Curtius, *European Literature and the Latin Middle Ages*, trans. Willard Trask (New York, 1953), pp. 195–200.

5. Legouis, pp. 62–63; cf. K. G. Cross, " 'Balm' in Donne and Shakespeare: Ironic Intention in *The Extasie*," *MLN* 71 (1956): 480–82.

6. *Forms of Discovery* (Denver, 1967), p. 76. Mitchell, p. 96, notices the metaphor, but misses its implications.

overreaches itself to create a kind of incongruity that characterizes this poem. In the first five stanzas alone, there are several examples of this phenomenon. The bold image of twisted eye-beams and pierced eyeballs alerts us to one such case; its violent physicality jars against the refinement of the Petrarchan convention it exploits.[7] The poetic elaboration of the hand-holding seems out of all proportion to the apparently minor significance of the gesture. The Homeric image of Fate's scales and the simile of the "sepulchrall statues" (line 18) creates comic hyperboles that undercut the seriousness of the ecstatic experience. The whole section, in fact, is one large mismatch of image and meaning; for the fifth stanza contradicts the clear suggestions of the previous four as it brings physical (erotic) activity to a standstill (or a lie-still): "All day the same our postures were, / And wee said nothing all the day" (lines 10–20). We are told, in no uncertain terms, that this is no amorous dalliance. We have been deceived by appearances.

We realize, then, that the poem has an elaborate false start; so we must orient ourselves to a new situation. The sixth and seventh stanzas facilitate this process, as they transfer our attention to a world as emphatically spiritual as the previous one was physical. They also introduce, as a hypothetical witness of the spatially and temporally over-literalized ecstasy, a third party, whose exaggerated purity matches the hyperbolic character of the event:

> If any, so by love refin'd,
>   That he soules language understood,
> And by good love were growen all minde,
>   Within convenient distance stood,
>
> He (though he knew not which soule spake,
> Because both meant, both spake the same)
> Might thence a new concoction take,
>   And part farre purer then he came.

(lines 21–28)

This third party must be considered carefully in any interpretation of the whole poem; but, for the present, I would like simply to examine his effect on the rhetorical situation.

Through all but the last three words of stanza four we are in the comfortable position of most readers of Renaissance love poetry:

---

7. Donald Guss, *John Donne: Petrarchist* (Detroit, 1966), discuss Donne's habitual literalization of Petrarchan conceits.

by the rules of the game, we are allowed to enter the fictional world of love unseen to observe what passes there between a lover and his mistress. All the "we"s and "our"s of the first fifteen lines create the impression that a man is speaking to the woman he loves of some past experience they shared. In such a situation of intimacy, the reader is imaginatively an eavesdropper. The pronoun "her" of line sixteen changes all this, making it impossible for the poem to be addressed to the speaker's beloved.[8] We must assume, then, the existence of a fictional listener to whom the words are addressed, one whose aesthetic distance on the world of the lovers mirrors the reader's own.[9] In fact, for all intents and purposes, the reader and his fictive auditor merge and *both* are reflected in the hypothetical witness of the ecstasy the poem twice mentions—in stanzas six and seven and in the final four lines. The reader is moved back and forth between the poles of sympathy and judgment, first drawn into the scene of intimacy the narrative presents, then reminded of his outside position as the poem tells him, in effect, that it knows he is both looking and listening.

In one sense, the first seven stanzas are one large attention-getting device, the effect of which is to draw us imaginatively into the poem's world while, at the same time, making us self-conscious about our aesthetic act. But these introductory lines prepare us for vicarious participation in a past event by another means, the manipulation of verb tenses. The poem begins in the dramatic present, a vantage point from which we can view the experience that occurred in the past. Thus, the speaker employs narrative past tenses. The actual verbs, however, denote states of being rather than dynamic action: "sat," "were cimented," "was," "were gone out," "hung," "lay," "were." They slow physical activity and temporal progression to a halt and support the notion of a near-timeless ecstasy. Our sense of pastness is weakened, so we barely notice the shift to the historical present in line

8. John Carey, "Notes on Two of Donne's *Songs and Sonets*," *RES* 16 (1965): 52, pointed out this obvious fact. The surprising thing is that most critics have discussed the poem as though it were spoken to a woman.

9. Earl Miner remarks: ". . . a Metaphysical poem . . . does not have a single audience but, potentially at least, three different kinds: the speaker himself as audience; the 'dramatic' audience of another person in the poem; and the vicarious audience of the reader, to whom the poem is in some sense related" (p. 15). Cf. Lowry Nelson, Jr., "The Fictive Reader and Literary Self-Reflexiveness," in *The Disciplines of Criticism: Essays in Literary Theory, Interpretation, and History*, ed. Peter Demetz, Thomas Greene, and Lowry Nelson, Jr. (New Haven, 1968), pp. 173–91.

seventeen, with the word "negotiate," and in the verbs of the past two lines before the love-dialogue: "Might thence a new concoction take [instead of "have taken"], / And part [instead of "have parted"] farre purer than he came" (lines 27–28). Whatever other reasons there may be for this tense-shift (and Donne exploits the device as far back as his first satire), it serves as a bridge to the predominant present-tense verbs of the poem's second section, facilitating reader absorption into the scene the poem recollects.[10]

2

In the first seven stanzas we are cozened in our expectations; in the last twelve stanzas of the poem we are deceived by yet-more-subtle poetic sleights of hand. This latter section also has its false start and it returns us, by masterful indirections, to the erotic situation with which the poem began. The "dialogue of one"—a transcript of the souls' conversation, though it has an unmistakably male voice and stanzas nine, ten, eleven, fifteen, and seventeen sound more like lecturing than intimate communication—consists of two parts, the first (stanzas eight through twelve) explaining the nature of the soul-union, the second (stanzas thirteen through nineteen) arguing for, then deciding upon a return to the bodies. The argument swings about a full 180 degrees, making the whole dialogue one large, and puzzling, contradiction: it first celebrates, then rejects the very notion of an ecstatic soul-union.

Though we are apt not to notice them, Donne places elements within the dialogue's first five stanzas that subvert the local context and anticipate the reformulation of the argument in stanzas thirteen and following. Here also, there are observable conflicts between tenor and vehicle. At the start of the souls' dialogue, for example, Donne deliberately seems to ignore the common Neoplatonic explanation of love's genesis; for this would have supported the context of the spiritual ecstasy:

> This Extasie doth unperplex
>   (We said) and tell us what we love,
> We see by this, it was not sexe,
>   Wee see, we saw not what did move.

(lines 29–32)

10. Cf. Richard Hughes, *The Progress of the Soul: The Interior Career of John Donne* (New York, 1968), pp. 82–84.

Instead of naming beauty as the first mover, Donne's lovers confess their ignorance. In line with the hyperbolic stanzas six and seven, which speak of a purity beyond purity, Donne outplatonizes the platonizers (his lovers so refined that their love does not even *begin* with physical appearance before it ascends the spiritual ladder). All they do say is that sex was not the mover, and, therefore, not the final cause of their relationship. Such nescience, as Rosalie Colie reminds us,[11] is a powerful instrument in the poet's hands, useful as a weapon against all dogmas and orthodoxies, including the one he seems to be propounding here.

The lovers admit to another kind of ignorance in the next stanza, which seems to confuse as much as it clarifies:

> But as all severall soules containe
> Mixture of things, they know not what,
> Love, these mixt soules, doth mix againe,
> And makes both one, each this and that.

(lines 33–36)

We do not know the composition of our own souls, or, more to the point, as the last section of the poem discovers, we do not know *how* our souls are mixed with our bodies, only *that* they are. The uncertainty of the first two lines of the stanza clashes with the self-congratulatory complacency of the latter two. Under the guise of celebrating the way the ecstasy enables the lovers both to become one and exchange identities (Ficino is eloquent on the subject),[12] Donne introduces what looks like a needless complication. "Severall soules" is a semantic pun: it means both "the souls of individual men" and "the individual souls within the single person." The latter meaning suggests the Aristotelian-Thomistic notion of the tripartite soul (vegetative, sensitive, rational), with its emphasis on the soul's inextricable involvement with and dispersal throughout the living body,[13] and this undercuts the immediate context, which assumes a neat soul-body separation. The simpler Pla-

11. *Paradoxia Epidemica: The Renaissance Tradition of Paradox* (Princeton, 1966). Cf. "The Relique," line 24 ("[we] knew not what wee lov'd, nor why. . .") and *The Second Anniversary*, lines 254–63.

12. *Marsilio Ficino's Commentary on Plato's Symposium*, ed. and trans. Sears Jayne, The University of Missouri Studies, vol. 19 (Columbia, Mo., 1944), pp. 144–45. Cf. Gardner, *Elegies and Songs and Sonnets*, p. 185.

13. Cf. "To the Countesse of Bedford" ("Honour is so sublime perfection"), lines 34–35, and Milgate's note, p. 270.

tonic version of the soul-body relationship[14] would have served his purposes better—that is, if he really wanted to encourage belief in bodiless ecstasy. Furthermore, the phrase "Mixture of things" reminds us of the world of matter or "thingness" at a time when our gaze is aimed in the opposite direction; it also suggests a blending of the material and the spiritual the stanza pretends to ignore. It may take until stanza fourteen for the Platonic and Aristotelian views of the soul-body relationship to fight openly with one another, but the battle is actually engaged here.

I would like, for the present, to postpone consideration of stanzas ten and eleven and provisionally accept them as simple metaphoric depiction of the strength and fruitfulness of that "abler soule" (line 43) composed of the separate souls of the two lovers, an entity that has self-knowledge, we are told in stanza twelve. But even at the point at which the poem most highly praises the purely spiritual union—here for its intellectual power and permanence—Donne insinuates a discordant element in the word "Atomies" (line 47), a term borrowed from Epicurean materialism,[15] a philosophical monism diametrically opposed to Platonism. He evokes in the mind of the knowledgeable reader a counterperspective, a common trick of a paradoxographer.

The whole poem pivots on the "But" of line forty-nine, which initiates the movement toward a conclusion that reverses the intellectual assumptions of the poem's first twelve stanzas, particularly the first five stanzas of the "dialogue of one." Donne very gradually leads us (by the nose) to the realization of the soul's utter dependence upon the body and the arguments and conceits he employs to achieve this end are some of the most complex and subtle in all his poetry. He begins with innocent questioning and associative thought:

> But O alas, so long, so farre
> Our bodies why doe wee forbeare?
> They'are ours, though they'are not wee, Wee are
> The'intelligences, they the spheare.

(lines 49–52)

Recalling to themselves and, therefore, to us the fact that their ecstatic experience lasts a whole day (the earlier comic realism of the introduc-

14. Donne utilizes this in a poem like "To the Countesse of Huntington" ("That unripe side of earth").

15. Austin Warren, "Donne's 'Extasie,'" SP 55 (1958): 477; cf. Graziani, pp. 132–33, who argues that the word's philosophical context implies the "omnipresence of the soul in every bodily atom" (p. 133).

tion resurfaces here), the lovers define their bodies as possessions—related to their souls, perhaps, in the manner of accidents to substance. This does not actually deny the self-sufficiency of the souls; it merely establishes that the bodies are connected with them in some way. The conceit of the intelligences and sphere, however, which supposedly illustrates the possessor-possession relationship, like so many other metaphors in this poem, over-extends itself. The rhyme-scheme and the evidence of the manuscripts support the reading "spheare," the singular form, and, therefore, the metaphor treats the souls as *two* ("intelligences") and the bodies as *one* ("spheare"), a complete inversion of the situation of the dialogue's first five stanzas. There may also be a more esoteric reason for the use of the singular form of the word. Leone Ebreo, whose *Dialoghi D'Amore* Donne apparently ransacked for this poem, has a specific discussion of the question whether each celestial sphere has one or two intelligences.[16] The context of Ebreo's argument, and of Donne's "Air and Angels," in which the same metaphor occurs, is the relation of human love to the order of the universe: Ebreo's lover, like Donne's couple, is interested in final causes; and the true end of all virtuous or rational love is God. In his argument by analogy, what Ebreo says of the intelligences, applies to lovers as well: "Thus their ultimate end and purpose is their perfection; but, since this consists in their union with the Godhead, it follows that their ultimate end lies in the Godhead and not in themselves."[17] As he does in other ways in a poem like "A Valediction: Forbidding Mourning," Donne here locates the human love-relationship in the largest possible cosmic and theological framework.[18] Perhaps if another poet had used the intelligences-sphere metaphor, we might have to refrain from drawing its implications out so far; but, recognizing here yet another example of Donne's thought-habits—particularly his desire to relate the little world of love to larger realities—these meanings are not so far-fetched. His love-metaphysic requires them. The rhetorical fact of the matter is, however, that Donne avoids presenting all this to us *directly*. The conceit pretends to be merely a casual association.

16. *The Philosophy of Love (Dialoghi d'Amore)*, trans. F. Friedeberg-Seeley and Jean H. Barnes (London, 1937), pp. 183–84; cf. Gardner, "The Argument," pp. 287–306.

17. Ebreo, p. 187.

18. Cf. John Freccero, "Donne's 'Valediction: Forbidding Mourning,'" *ELH* 30 (1963): 335–76 and Joseph Mazzeo, "Metaphysical Poetry and the Poetic of Correspondence," *JHI* 14 (1953): 221–34.

In any event, this metaphor still casts the soul in the role of the active principle (mover) and the body in the passive one (moved). Stanza fourteen departs from this formulation:

> We owe them thankes, because they thus,
>   Did us, to us, at first convay,
> Yeelded their forces, sense, to us,
>   Nor are drosse to us, but allay.

(lines 53–56)

The bodies are here more than inert matter: as vehicles of transportation they were at least circumstantially necessary for the souls to be able to meet—they moved about and the souls went along for the ride. The second two lines of the stanza lay even heavier stress on the importance of the bodies. In offering "their forces, sense," they gave the souls something *useful* (the submerged military metaphor recalls the fourth and fifth stanzas). In the dross-alloy distinction, finally, there is a dramatic shift from the Platonic to the Aristotelian version of the soul-body relationship. Instead of being an impurity that defiles the soul,[19] the body is an alloy that toughens it, and, the metaphor implies, is thoroughly blended with it. In the short space of six lines (lines 51–56), then, the argument traverses a great distance as the claims for the body become progressively stronger.

The next stanza practices a grammatical deception with its handling of verb modes:

> On man heavens influence workes not so,
>   But that it first imprints the ayre,
> So soule into the soule may flow,
>   Though it to body first repaire.

(lines 57–60)

Somehow the concealed "must" of the first two lines (astrological impulses must pass through the medium of ether) becomes the weaker "may" of the second two, disguising the real meaning of the analogy, that the souls *must* use their bodies to communicate or they cannot communicate at all. Donne, it seems, is not quite ready here to force home this conclusion, so he settles for the non-committal "may" and the misleading "though." He states his point negatively.

---

19. The earlier statement that the souls "to advance their state / Were gone out" (lines 15–16) implies the Platonic point of view of the body as an impediment to the soul.

Earlier in the poem, we move from the microcosmic to the macro-cosmic, but in stanza fifteen the direction is reversed:

> As our blood labours to beget
> Spirits, as like soules as it can,
> Because such fingers need to knit
> That subtile knot, which makes us man:
>
> So must pure lovers soules descend
> T'affections, and to faculties,
> Which sense may reach and apprehend,
> Else a great Prince in prison lies.

(lines 61–68)

The "spirits" in the body—a kind of *tertium quid* midway between the material and (what is usually regarded as) the spiritual[20]—correspond to the "ayre" (line 58) in the heavens, suggesting once again the large framing of the love experience. The argument of these two stanzas dovetails with that of the previous one and reaches an unmistakable conclusion: unless the soul descends to unite with the lower faculties—unless it uses the body—it is powerless and isolated. The crowning irony in the poem is that Donne caps his argument with a bold inversion of the conventional Platonic *soma-sema* metaphor: instead of regarding the soul as the prisoner in the body, he has it a prisoner *in itself* if it refuses to join with the body.[21] Here, as throughout the dialogue, he uses the vocabulary of Platonism to disprove it.

A combination of logical reasoning, associative thought, and poetic metaphor moves the argument to its natural conclusion. But, if we reflect critically upon what has taken place, we should be surprised to discover that the very situation the poem hypothesizes is, *by the poem's own logic*, impossible. There can be no such thing as a purely

20. See *The Poems of John Donne*, ed. Herbert J. C. Grierson (Oxford, 1912), II, 45; Gardner, *Elegies and Songs and Sonnets*, pp. 186–87; and McCanles, pp. 61–67. Just as ether serves as an intermediary element in the cosmos, the spirits produced by man's bodily organs link soul and body: the two are related, as John Freccero reminds us (pp. 357–60, 362–63), in terms of the substance "pneuma," a convenient invention to bridge the gap created by a dualistic ontology. The poem itself also mentions other half-material, half-spiritual substances: "balme" (line 6), "eye-beams" (line 7), "spheare" (line 52), "ayre" (line 58), and (possibly) "concoction" (line 27).

21. For a summary of the debate over line sixty-eight ("Else a great Prince in prison lies"), see Robert J. Bauer, "The Great Prince in Donne's 'The Extasie,'" *TSL* 14 (1969): 100. I accept the (majority) view of those who see the "great Prince" as the soul. Cf. "The Anniversarie," lines 13–15 and *Metempsychosis*, lines 333–35 (along with Milgate's note, p. 184).

spiritual love ecstasy, much less a conversation between two disembodied souls. If the lovers' souls are helpless without using their more corporeal faculties, then the experience the poem describes could never have occurred. We have been deceived by the poem's title on two counts: first, in the frustration of our expectations of an erotic ecstasy, and second, in our belief in a quasi-mystical one.

This rejection of the very idea on which the poem is based is anticipated, perhaps, by the comic spatial and temporal literalization of the ecstasy and the poem's other hyperboles, including the elaborate transcript, in heavily discursive language, of the soul-communication. Considering the attitudes Donne expresses elsewhere on the subject of ecstasy, this turnabout is understandable. He reserves the serious use of the term for those unique religious experiences of deep, loving contemplation, and he resists applying it to other situations—except, as in the case of the epistolary ecstasy, as a self-conscious metaphor.[22] He is careful to place certain limits on the experience, explicitly rejecting the inflated claims for ecstasy he associates with Catholic mysticism:

> There is a Pureness, a cleanness imagin'd (rather dream't of) in the *Romane Church*, by which (as their words are) the soul is abstracted, not only *a Passionibus*, but *a Phantasmatibus*, not onely from passions, and perturbations, but from the ordinary way of coming to know any thing; The soul (they say) of men so purified, understands no longer, *per phantasmata rerum corporalium*; not by having any thing presented by the fantasie to the senses, and so to the understanding, but altogether by a familiar conversation with God, and an immediate revelation from God. . . . This is that Pureness in the *Romane Church* by which the founder of the Last Order amongst them, *Philip Nerius*, had not onely utterly emptied his heart of the world, but had fill'd it too full of God. . . . This Pureness is not in their heart, but in their fantasie. (*Sermons*, I, 186)

Such an ecstasy, like the one in the poem, is an epistemological impossibility.[23] When he utilizes the device of the ecstatic vision in his satiric prose work, *Ignatius His Conclave*, he deliberately mocks it.[24]

22. See Grierson, II, 42; Gardner, *Elegies and Songs and Sonnets*, pp. 184–85; Evelyn Simpson, *A Study of the Prose Works of John Donne*, 2d ed. (Oxford, 1948), pp. 94–96; and Merritt Y. Hughes, "Some of Donne's 'Ecstasies,'" *PMLA* 75 (1960): 509–18.

23. McCanles, pp. 59–75, discusses the poem's epistemological issues.

24. After a fifty-page speech by Loyola, the narrator remarks: "Truely I

In "The Extasie," as in so many other poems, Donne turns his sceptical intelligence on the philosophical and literary conventions he inherits. No number of citations of Plotinus or Neoplatonic love-philosophers can obscure the basic fact that he could not take seriously the idea of amorous ecstasy as love's supreme expression. If Helen Gardner had read Leon Ebreo more carefully before offering her humorless explication of the poem, she would have discovered in this surprisingly tough-minded thinker a sceptical and comically realistic attitude similar to Donne's. Both writers knew that love-ecstasy was merely a pretty fiction, more suited to the sophisticated game of make-believe Donne could play with noble mistresses like Lady Bedford, but ill-suited to an actual, heterosexual love relationship.

The poem, then, mocks its reader's suspension of disbelief, his too-easy acceptance, as a civilized man of the Renaissance, of love conventions and their philosophical and pseudo-philosophical vocabularies. Donne left little doubt in his cynical "Love's Alchymie" of his opinion of fashionable amorous Platonism:

> . . . that loving wretch that sweares,
> 'Tis not the bodies marry, but the mindes,
> Which he in her Angelique finds,
> Would sweare as justly, that he heares,
> In that day's rude hoarse minstralsey, the spheres.
>
> (lines 18–22)

Both sphere-music and "soules language" are inaudible; what Donne calls "abstract spiritual love" ("A Valediction: of the Booke," line 30) is too delicate a commodity for the man of flesh and bone:

> Love's not so abstract, as they use
> To say, which have no Mistress, but their Muse,
> But as all else, being elemented too,
> Love sometimes would contemplate, sometimes do.[25]
>
> ("Loves Growth," lines 11–14)

Even the speaker of the eloquent "A Valediction: Forbidding Mourning" cannot pretend that he and his beloved can be content without

---

thought this Oration of *Ignatius* very long: and I began to thinke of my body which I had so long abandoned, least it should putrifie, or grow mouldy, or bee buried . . " (Coffin, p. 342).

25. The word "do," in the bawdy *double entendre*, means "copulate." "Contemplate . . . do" is exactly the order of things in "The Extasie."

physical presence. Although they "Care lesse" about missing "eyes, lips, and hands" (line 20) when they are apart than do "Dull sublunary lovers" (line 13), they do care nonetheless; hence the need for consolation. The speaker of "Air and Angels," like the lovers of "The Extasie," discovers an inescapable truth:

> But since my soule, whose child love is,
> Takes limmes of flesh, and else could nothing doe,
> More subtile than the parent is,
> Love must not be, but take a body too . . . .

> (lines 7–10)

This is precisely the conclusion reached by stanzas thirteen through seventeen in "The Extasie." What Donne calls elsewhere "firme substantiall love" ("A Valediction: of my Name in the Window," line 62) involves the whole person, physically and spiritually.[26]

Discursive reasoning permits us to approach a truth that poetic metaphor finally captures. The image of man as a "subtile knot" of matter and spirit focusses the argument's conclusion, but, in a sense, it is the insight with which Donne began.[27] Like the labyrinth and the mandala, with which it has affiliations, the knot is a far-reaching symbol.[28] In the final canto of the *Divine Comedy*, the speaker says of his vision of God's inner mystery, "La forma universal di questo nodo credo ch'io vidi" (*Paradiso*, 33.91; literally, "I believe that I saw the universal form of this knot"). All reality, material and spiritual, is a knot tied by God and, as such, is mysterious, perplexing to the mind.[29] God himself, who is mirrored in his creation, is for Dante

26. John Freccero argues, in another context, that Donne "protests, precisely in the name of incarnation, against the neo-Petrarchan and neo-platonic dehumanization of love" (p. 336). Cf. Smith, "The Metaphysic of Love," pp. 362–70; and Guss, pp. 139–70.

27. Margaret Wiley writes: "The subtle knot which makes us men [sic] represents not only an intellectual awareness of the fundamental dualism of body and spirit but a more than intellectual perception of the fact that the human entity, which is the prototype of all truth, is not simple and direct, but complex and oblique. Hence simple truths about body and spirit cannot give the sense of the knotted whole, for the knot is something other than the two strands that compose it." (*The Subtle Knot: Creative Scepticism in Seventeenth Century England* [1952; rpt. New York, 1968], p. 61)

28. See Gustav René Hocke, *Die Welt Als Labyrinth: Manier und Manie in der europäischen Kunst von 1520 bis 1650 und in der Gegenwart* (Hamburg, 1957), pp. 99 ff.; and Amanda Coomaraswamy, "The Iconography of Dürer's 'Knots' and Leonardo's 'Concatenation,'" *AQ* 7 (1944): 109–25.

29. The English word "knot," like the Latin "nodus," and the Italian "nodo,"

and for Donne, who refers to the "knottie Trinitie" in one of his *Holy Sonnets* (16.3), a knotty mystery. Symbolic gardens, with their "curious knots"[30] or labyrinths of flowers, were meant to reflect this large image of reality. Ficino called *love* "nodus perpetuus, et copula mundi" ("perpetual knot and binder of the world"),[31] an aspect of this symbolism expressed in the knot of the Graces.[32] In the little world of man, body and soul are tied in the "knot intrinsicate of life" (*Antony and Cleopatra*, 3.2.307–10)[33] which Shakespeare's Cleopatra undoes with her suicide. Donne calls this knot "subtile" both because it is delicately fragile and because it eludes our understanding. When his lovers earlier announce "This Extasie doth unperplex," the verb they use carries something of its root meaning as an untying:[34] in the hypothetical situation of ecstasy, soul and body are temporarily unbound and things made clearer to the mind. The poem has other knots. The first is figured in lines seven and eight: "Our eye-beames twisted, and did thred / Our eyes, upone one double string." Donne ties a spiritual love-knot with the substance Ficino calls the bond of the universe, light.[35] This knot is matched, at the end of the poem, by the physical love-knot the couples are to form with their own bodies.

The poem's analogical reasoning establishes the parallel between the soul-body relationship and the interpersonal one. It is an easy step, then, from the perception of man as a subtle knot of matter and spirit to the lovers' decision to join physically as well as spiritually.

---

often has this figurative meaning, as in the expression "knotty problem." This particular aspect of knot symbolism is associated with the Gordian knot: see, for example, J. E. Cirlot, *A Dictionary of Symbols*, trans. Jack Sage (New York, 1962), pp. 164–65.

30. The OED cites Peacham's *Garden of Eloquence*; Milton uses the very same words in *Paradise Lost*, 4.242 (ed. Merritt Y. Hughes [New York, 1962]).

31. Jayne, p. 152.

32. Edgar Wind, *Pagan Mysteries in the Renaissance* (New Haven, 1958), pp. 104ff., discusses this and the knot of love, but, unfortunately, apart from the general context of knot symbolism.

33. In the *Essays in Divinity*, Donne writes that man is "the *Hymen* and Matrimoniall knot of Eternal and Mortal things" (quoted in Joan Webber, *Contrary Music: The Prose Style of John Donne* [Madison, 1963], p. 17), and he says, in "Death's Duell" that it is God who "knit both natures in one" (*Sermons*, X, 231).

34. Mitchell, p. 97; cf. "To the Countesse of Bedford at New-yeares Tide," lines 3 and 38.

35. *Opera Omnia* (Basel, 1561; 2d ed. 1576), p. 981, quoted in Paul O. Kristeller, *The Philosophy of Marsilio Ficino*, trans. Virginia Conant (1943; rpt. Gloucester, Mass., 1964), p. 116.

In "An Epithalamion or Mariage Song on the Lady Elizabeth, and Count Palatine," Donne treats sexual union as this kind of symbolic knot:

> . . . when all is past,
> And that you'are one, by hearts and hands made fast,
> You two have one way left, your selves to'entwine,
> Besides this Bishops knot. . . .

(lines 53–56)

The physical consummation completes and expresses the couple's spiritual wedding. And it is this final, *marriage* knot that I see in "The Extasie." The very same poet who celebrates the incarnate love of man and wife in "A Valediction: Forbidding Mourning," here argues for wedded love, *not* Neoplatonic soul-union, as the ideal.

To demonstrate this, I realize, will take some doing, and necessarily draw us into an area scrupulously avoided by most critics of the last fifty years, one in which biography and literature intermix. Despite the risks, however, I shall follow my line of reasoning, with all its lyric leaps, for I am convinced that the tone, form, content, and circumstances surrounding this poem announce that it is much more than calm speculation about the relationship of body and soul in the love experience. I shall argue, first, from internal evidence, that "The Extasie" celebrates conjugal love; second, that it is, in effect, an artistic publicizing of Donne's own marriage; and, third, that Donne projects into it his personal experiences and conflicts in such a way that he involves his audience in the poem's emotional dynamics. The reader is drawn into the poem's world to fill various roles: he is both witness, sympathizer, critic, and convert. Through him the poet's personal struggles and convictions enter a larger world.

3

For Donne, as for poets like Spenser, Shakespeare, and Jonson, marriage was the natural fulfillment of the love-relationship, not its destruction. Truth, in Jonson's masque *Hymenaei*, states flatly: "*Marriage* LOVES object is" (line 737). Donne's own "Epithalamion made at Lincoln's Inn" addresses its refrain to the bride: "To put on perfection and a woman's name"—which becomes, in the nocturnal section of the poem, "To night put on perfection and a woman's name" (the sexual consummation, which finishes what the public ceremony begins, makes a woman out of a girl—such devirgination improves, rather than damages her). The extreme Platonist desexing of love was related to the Catholic elevation of virginity over marriage and Protestant England reacted against both. Donne himself wrote in one of his wedding sermons: "The Romane Church injures . . . the whole state of Christianity, when they oppose *mariage* and *chastity*, as though they were incompatible, and might not consist together. They may; for *mariage is honourable, and the bed undefiled*; and therefore it may be so" (*Sermons*, II, 349). In Reformation Europe, the strong tradition of defense of the married state, given popular impetus by such works as Erasmus' "Epistle to persuade a young gentleman to marriage" (reprinted in Wilson's *The Arte of Rhetorique* [1553]), seems to find its fullest expression in English literature.[36] Given the choice between cold chastity and warm chastity, virginity and marriage, most English writers praise the latter (even Sidney's *Arcadia* has a peculiarly domestic ending). In Donne's verse, the "purer" Neoplatonic tradition—characterized by "abstract spiritual love"—flowed into the verse letters and poems to noble ladies; it found a home in the fictional amorousness that bridged, and measured, the distance between members of different classes in the social hierarchy. A reciprocal, heterosexual love relationship between equals manifested itself physically and achieved its fullest expression, as in Shakespeare's plays, in conjugal union.

Any Englishman who had ever been to Church knew the three traditional ends of marriage: procreation, mutual assistance or the consolation of loneliness, and the quieting of concupiscence.[37] We can detect all three in "The Extasie." Procreation is the most explicit, almost to the point of fixation: the eyes looking babies is called a kind of propagation; "balme" (line 6) springs from the two hands; the transplanted violet increases and multiplies;[38] an "abler soule" flows from the two separate ones; the blood "begets" spirits.[39] The phrase "Defects of

36. See William Haller, "Hail Wedded Love," *ELH* 13 (1946): 79–97; and Mark Rose, *Heroic Love: Studies in Sidney and Spenser* (Cambridge, Mass., 1968), pp. 7–34.

37. Donne says in the sermon "Preached at Sir Francis Nethersole's Marriage": "The Two maine uses of *mariage*, which are propagation of *Children*, and mutuall *assistance*, were intended by God, at the present, at first; but the third, is a remedy against that, which was not then; for then there was no inordinateness, no irregularity in the affections of man" (*Sermons*, II, 339–40).

38. Cf. Gardner, "The Argument," pp. 299–300.

39. Cf. Leo Spitzer, "Three Poems on Ecstasy," in *Essays on English and American Literature*, ed. Anna Hatcher (Princeton, 1962), p. 145.

loneliness controules" (line 44) applies as well to marriage as to ecstatic soul-union; one of Donne's wedding sermons makes much of the Biblical dictum, "It is not good for man to be alone" (*Sermons*, II, 336 ff.). The end of the poem, with its open affirmation of the innocence of sexual union, anticipates the immediate satisfaction of the natural physical urges the lovers have *restrained* (this is one of the meanings of the word "forebeare" [line 50]). Earlier the word "allay" (line 56) may be a pun: the body is not only an alloy to the soul, but a source of *relief* as well. Donne's association of marriage and chastity in the above passage from his Sermons is reflected, I think, in his handling of the violet image, which, among other things, is a symbol of humble and chaste love.[40] This flower—which is placed also at the very center of the poem in stanza ten[41]—is an incongruous presence in the *locus amoenus* of the first section. Aside from the detail of its reclining position, it emphatically does *not* support the erotic atmosphere of the pleasaunce. Donne probably intended just this effect, a paradoxical juxtaposition of chastity and eroticism, which traditionally coexist *only* in the married state (Jonson's *Hymenaei* [lines 489–90] calls for violets to be strewn about the married couple's bed-chamber).

The poem's temporal structure implies that marriage is a part of the lovers' history. In an overview of the work, we can distinguish at least *six* separate, but related points in time: (1) the birth of love ("Wee see, we saw not what did move"), (2) the interval between this and, (3) the time of the ecstatic experience, (4) the time immediately following the dialogue, (5) the interval between all these past events and, (6) the temporal location of the speaker and his listener. Donne presents a man recounting the history of a relationship (and justifying it), a love that does not *end* with the experience of spiritual union (if he had wanted to write a poem about ecstasy, he would have done this).

40. See Gardner, *Elegies and Songs and Sonnets*, pp. 185–86, 262; and Spitzer, p. 146 n. Laertes says of the dead Ophelia in *Hamlet*: "Lay her i' th' earth, / And for her fair and unpolluted flesh / May violets spring" (5.1.261–63).

41. Alastair Fowler explains the poem's 7–5–7 stanzaic structure and the central position of the violet image in terms of number symbolism, providing numerological evidence for my interpretation of "The Extasie" as a poem about conjugal love: "It is appropriate that the central part dealing with the union of the two souls into one should consist of five stanzas; since not only was five a 'nuptial number' combining the first masculine and the first feminine numbers, but also denoted the fifth, purer, quintessential element. . . . The centre stanza of all, Stanza X, develops a condensed image of union: the five-petaled 'single violet transplant.'" *Triumphal Forms: Structural Patterns in Elizabethan Poetry* (Cambridge, 1970), p. 74.

It develops from innocent beginnings (temporal locus 1), through a growth in intimacy, grounded in virtuous, rational commitment (2 and 3), to physical consummation (4) and, the third stanza indicates, the procreation of children (5). This time scheme and the poem's argument make the same point Leone Ebreo takes 500 pages to elaborate, that the sexual union of lovers is legitimate and good provided that it springs from a pre-existent spiritual bond (sex cannot, then, be an end in itself). Donne pushes Ebreo's argument a step further, however, in making fruitful conjugal love the ideal.

The final stanzas of the poem conclude the work with an emblem of marital union. "The Extasie," like most epithalamia, makes sexual intercourse into a profound symbol:

> To'our bodies turne wee then, that so
> Weake men on love reveal'd may looke;
> Loves mysteries in soules doe grow,
> But yet the body is his booke.
>
> And if some lover, such as wee,
> Have heard this dialogue of one,
> Let him still marke us, he shall see
> Small change, when we'are to bodies gone.
>
> (lines 69–76)

These lines imply that the couple will make love. No lesser physical contact will do, for the poem's structure and logic both demand that the corporeal joining to be as close and entire as the spiritual one, and sexual intercourse alone can serve here as the incarnation and concrete symbol of love's deepest realities. Earlier in the poem, the soul-union is presented as a wondrous mystery in which two become one and, paradoxically, more than two ("Love . . . makes both one, each this and that"). If the coupling of bodies is to reveal this mystery, it must be more than a simple act of intercourse. In these circumstances, only the nuptial mystery of *two in one flesh* [42] and the procreation of children can properly match Donne's description of the spiritual relationship and its effects: in marriage two become one in body and (usually) more than two. The poetically blasphemous suggestion that the image of

42. Jay Levine implies that this idea is behind "the involuted conceit of The Dissolution" ("'The Dissolution': Donne's Twofold Elegy," *ELH* 28 [1961]: 304–5). In "The Canonization," Donne expresses the couple's corporeal (and spiritual) oneness in the figure of the hermaphrodite, the "one neutrall thing" to which both sexes fit" (line 25)—see below, n. 67.

sexual union is a sacred symbol, like God's revelation in the Book of Scripture, or in the Book of Nature, or in Christ himself,[43] make a serious point (as do similar religious hyperboles in the rest of Donne's poetry), marriage is only one of many incarnations of Love, part of God's natural scheme. In "The Canonization," the lovers' relationship expresses a "pattern" (line 45) that originates in heaven.

What is particularly unusual about the end of "The Extasie" is the disappearance of the customary secretiveness we find in so many of Donne's *Songs and Sonets*. Ordinarily—either out of shame or a desire to guard a precious mystery from public "prophanation" ("A Valediction: Forbidding Mourning," line 7)—Donne's poems maintain a clear separation between lovers and world: they are their own world— "Each hath one and is one" ("The Good-morrow," line 14). In this poem, the lovers open up their relationship to the world's inspection. In one sense, this is simply a way of saying "we have nothing to hide." In "A Lecture upon the Shadow" Donne writes "That love hath not attain'd the high'st degree, / Which is still diligent lest others see" (lines 12–13). Yet, the poetic gesture at the end of "The Extasie" also seems to *publicize* the love-union (the whole poem, in fact, does this). To understand this act in its proper perspective we need to be conscious, as Donne's original audience undoubtedly was, of its biographical context.

To state my critical hunch directly, I believe "The Extasie" is Donne's way of compensating, in the world of art, for what was missing from his own secret wedding, a public declaration of love and fidelity. I raise this issue not as an historical or a psychoanalytic curiosity, but because it is a part of the poem's basic frame of reference. Like "The Canonization," with its autobiographical allusion to the poet's "ruin'd fortune" (line 3), "The Extasie" has, for its coterie audience, an unmistakable biographical clue in its third stanza:

> So to'entergraft our hands as yet
>   Was all our meanes to make us one,
> And pictures on our eyes to get
>   Was all our propagation.

(lines 9–12)

Aside from the possible significance of joined hands as a symbol of marital fidelity,[44] this stanza tells us something we are apt either to miss

43. Cf. Miner, p. 79.
44. Edward Westermarck, *The History of Human Marriage*, 5th ed. (New York,

or to forget: the phrase "as yet," which qualifies the first two lines, also applies to the second two, and thus indicates that "looking babies" gives way, at some future time, to having them. John Carey offhandedly makes the inevitable connection with Donne's life, while at the same time sweeping the biographical data under his clean critical carpet: "A critic determined to read 'The Extasie' as autobiography would, I suppose, date it after the birth of Donne's first child."[45] Or his first few children, for they came yearly.

The story of Donne's marriage is well known. In December, 1601, at the age of twenty-nine, he married the seventeen-year-old Ann More in a clandestine ceremony performed by the newly-ordained brother of his close friend Christopher Brooke. After breaking the news to the girl's father, Sir George More, he was thrown into prison, lost his position as secretary to Sir Thomas Egerton, and was forced to fight a court battle to have the marriage validated. Once out of jail and the legal matters settled, he lived in straitened financial circumstances, with Ann and a rapidly growing family, surviving through the charity of friends and patrons, a continually frustrated seeker of new employment.[46] John Manningham of Middle Temple entered the following in his diary under December, 1602, suggesting the notoriousness of Donne's situation: "Donne is undonne; he was lately secretary to the Lord Keeper, and cast of [sic] because he would match himself to a gentlewoman against his Lord's pleasure."[47] Sir Isaac Walton wrote:

> His marriage was the remarkable error of his life; an error which, though he had a wit able and very apt to maintain paradoxes, yet he was very far from justifying it: and though his wife's competent years, and other reasons, might be justly urged to moderate severe censures,

---

1922), II, 439 ff. This symbolism is illustrated in the visual arts by Jan van Eyck's "Wedding Portrait of Giovanni Arnolfini" and in such literary works as *Paradise Lost*, where Milton stresses Adam and Eve's hand-holding (e.g., 4.738–39) and underscores the moral significance of their separation in the ninth book with the following: "from her Husband's hand her hand / Soft she withdrew" (9.385–86). During their experience of ecstasy, Donne's lovers hold hands and lie like "sepulchrall statues." Since this is one of the standard ways of portraying *married couples* in the recumbent statuary of sepulchral monuments in the Middle Ages and Renaissance, Donne is probably alluding obliquely to the poem's theme of conjugal love. See the illustrations in Fred H. Crosley, *English Church Monuments A.D. 1150–1550* (New York, 1921), pp. 16, 18, and 34.

45. Carey, p. 53.
46. R. C. Bald, *John Donne: A Life* (Oxford, 1970), pp. 128 ff.
47. *Diary of John Manningham of the Middle Temple*, ed. John Bruce, Camden Society Publications, vol. 99 (Westminster, 1868), p. 99.

yet he would occasionally condemn himself for it: and doubtless it had been attended with an heavy repentance if God had not blessed them with so mutual and cordial affections, and in the midst of their sufferings made their bread of sorrow taste more pleasantly than the banquets of dull and low-spirited people.[48]

Walton's pious optimism cannot disguise the obvious guilt-feelings Donne himself recorded in some of his letters. This hasty wedding and its aftermath caused the largest emotional trauma of his early manhood—one that expressed itself later in the fanatical care with which he arranged his own daughters' marriages. He felt remorse because, as he said, he "transplanted [his wife] into wretched fortune"[49] and also did himself serious harm. One moment he was a clever, young man with a bright future, in the service of a major government figure, the next he was stripped of position and promise (he had earlier burned through an inheritance).

We need, perhaps, to remind ourselves that Donne regarded poetry as an extension of his social life. One of the reasons he apparently wrote so little during the early years of his marriage was that he and his family were living with Sir Francis Wooley at Pyrford, far from London and the environment in which his poems could circulate. He wrote primarily for a private audience[50] (he learned only later, in his sermons, how to address himself to a broad constituency). His was the kind of poetry Michael Drayton said was "kept in cabinets and must only pass by transcription."[51] He penned verse, first, in the spirit of Inns of Court revelling, striking the pose of a wittily cynical gallant. He composed satires and verse letters for close friends who shared his intellectual and moral assumptions—men like Christopher Brooke, to whom "Satire II" and "The Storm" and "The Calme" are addressed. Some of his amorous verse seems designed for the cultivated atmosphere of York House, which afforded a mixed audience of well-bred men and women able to appreciate, for example, the witty manipulation of Petrarchist mannerisms. Donne usually had a clear image of his readers, whether entertaining his fellow gallants or complimenting the brilliant Lady Bedford, the teenage Countess of Huntington (with

48. "The Life of Dr. John Donne," reprinted in John Donne, *Devotions Upon Emergent Occasions Together with Death's Duel* (Ann Arbor, 1959), p. xxvii.

49. "Letter to Sir Henry Goodyer," quoted in Bald, p. 156.

50. See A. Alvarez, *The School of Donne* (New York, 1961), pp. 25–52, 195–203.

51. Preface to *Poly-Olbion*, in *Works*, ed. J. William Hebel (Oxford, 1961), IV, v.

whom he could be subtly patronizing), or his other noble mistresses. What is probably of equal significance is that his readers, like the congregations to whom he later preached, also had a vivid image of him. His role-playing, therefore, *must* be seen in its biographical context. In such a literary situation—which is quite unlike that of a publishing poet in a book culture—the religious poet of the *Holy Sonnets* could refer openly to his earlier amorous verse (*Holy Sonnet 13. 9–12*) and expect both God *and the reader* to appreciate the allusion. And the author of "The Extasie" *had to* cope with (and try to exploit) his reader's knowledge of him as the man who had been, in Sir Richard Baker's words, "very neat; a great visiter of Ladies . . . a great writer of conceited Verses"[52] and who was now a husband and a father.

As I see it, "The Extasie" unquestionably belongs to the period after Donne married. When he moved his family to Mitcham and took lodgings for himself in the Strand in 1607, he re-entered his beloved London world to re-establish contact with old friends and make the acquaintance of new ones, such as Mrs. Magdalen Herbert and her son Edward. Under these new conditions, his literary activity revived.[53] Helen Gardner assigns "The Extasie" to this time (1607–1610) and relates it to Donne's association with the Herberts.[54] This particular double friendship evidently served as an important stimulus to his art. In a verse letter to Mrs. Herbert, Donne mentions her literary-intellectual salon, her "Cabinet . . . Whither all noble'ambitious wits doe runne," ("To Mrs. M. H.," lines 34–35) with whose compositions his own must vie for attention. In July, 1607, he sent her "*Holy Hymns and Sonnets*,"[55] including the *La Corona* sequence.[56] We know, further, that he competed poetically with Sir Edward Herbert on at least two occasions: his 1610 verse letter responds to Herbert's "The State Progress of Ill,"[57] and, according to Jonson, Donne said he wrote his Prince Henry elegy "to match Sir Ed[ward] Herbert in obscurenesse." And it seems quite likely that "The Extasie" and Herbert's "Ode upon a Ques-

52. *A Chronicle of the Kings of England* (London, 1643), p. 391.

53. *Biathanatos, The Courtier's Library, The Pseudo-Martyr*, many of the religious sonnets, and several verse letters, as well as a significant number of love poems belong to this period (1606–1611).

54. *Elegies and Songs and Sonnets*, pp. 256–57.

55. Letter to Mrs. Herbert, July 11, 1607, quoted in Bald, p. 182.

56. Bald, p. 182; cf. Grierson, II, 47 and Gardner, *Elegies and Songs and Sonnets*, pp. 254–56.

57. See D. A. Kester, "Donne and Herbert of Cherbury: An Exchange of Verses," *MLQ* 8 (1947): 430–34.

tion Moved" are what Helen Gardner has called "rival rehandlings" of the matter of Sidney's eighth song from *Astrophel and Stella*.[58]

Both Donne and Herbert's poems describe an ecstatic experience —Herbert's, however, takes its Platonism seriously, climaxing with a soulful exchange of looks in which the lovers' "ravish'd spirits" ("An Ode Upon a Question Moved," line 140)[59] communicate with one another (a minor, and early, image in Donne's work). Herbert evidently believed, as he said in "Platonic Love," that a man could "grow a pure intelligence" (line 12) and like an angel "on contemplation feed" (line 20). His assumptions appear similar to those of the hyperbolically pure lover of stanzas six and seven of "The Extasie," a man who has "growen all minde" and can understand "soules language" (a truly angelic talent). Ezra Pound's epithet for Donne's poem, "Platonism believed,"[60] really belongs to the "Ode Upon a Question Moved," for Herbert, like the authors who contributed to the *Loves Martyr* collection (including such poets as Chapman and Jonson), celebrates the virtues of a purely spiritual love.

"The Extasie," then, appears to have been part of a literary debate; and this is not the first or the last time Donne engaged in this sport.[61] But what was for Herbert an artistic game and a dispassionate philosophical exercise (his poem is artificially pretty and remote), was for Donne, no doubt, a more serious venture. As an author who habitually thrust his personal voice and experiences into his poetry, he could not, I am sure, write a poem of this kind, *at the time he wrote it,*

58. *Elegies and Songs and Sonnets*, p. 256; cf. Grierson, II, 41–42. George Williamson, "The Convention of *The Extasie*," in *Seventeenth Century Contexts* (Chicago, 1961), pp. 63–77, compares Donne's poem to Sidney's, Fulke Greville's (*Caelica 75*), Wither's (*Fair Virtue 3*), and Herbert's.

59. In *Minor Poets of the Seventeenth Century*, ed. R. G. Howarth, 2d ed. (London, 1953). For the tradition of the ecstasy experienced through an exchange of the souls through the eyes, see Nicolas Perella, "Love's Greatest Miracle," *MLN* 86 (1971): 21–30. The other standard image is the ecstatic kiss (see Nicolas Perella, *The Kiss: Sacred and Profane* [Berkeley and Los Angeles, 1969]). Both metaphors reduce the world of matter to a kind of evanescence as they direct our gaze toward spiritual realities; Donne avoids them in the conclusion of his poem, as he insists on the solidity and inescapability of the physical world.

60. *The ABC of Reading* (New Haven, 1934), p. 128.

61. "The Baite" is Donne's answer to Marlowe's "Passionate Shepherd"; the verse letter to Wotton ("Sir, more then kisses, letters mingle Soules") is a response to Bacon's poem "The World" (H. J. C. Grierson, "Bacon's Poem 'The World': its Date and Relation to Certain other Poems," *MLR* 6 [1911]: 145–56); and "To Mr. Tilman after he had taken orders" may have been occasioned by a poem by the addressee (Bald, p. 303).

without transferring into it some of the pressures of the previous five or six years of his life—his worries, fears, guilts, and convictions. We know, by the way, that he suffered from acute depression at this time, the mood in which he composed *Biathanatos*, his paradoxical argument in favor of suicide.[62] He wrote in one of the letters from this period:

> Sometimes when I finde my selfe transported with jollity, and love of company, I hang leads at my heels; and reduce to my thoughts my fortunes, the duties of a man, of a friend, of a husband, of a Father, and all the incumbencies of a family: when sadnesse dejects me, either I countermine it with another sadnesse, or I kindle squibs about me again, and flie into sportfulnesse and company: And I finde ever after all, that I am like an exorcist, which had long laboured about one, which at last appears to have the Mother, that I still mistake my disease.[63]

It is interesting to note that in the *Holy Sonnets*, most of which date from this time, the major spiritual problem is despair.

Donne used art, wit, and social intercourse as ways of regaining mental and emotional equilibrium. If we can judge from a poem like "The Triple Foole," he was quite conscious of the therapeutic value of poetry ("Griefe brought to numbers cannot be so fierce, / For, he tames it, that fetters it in verse" [lines 10–11]). The power of so many of his poems seems to rest in our sense of his struggle, in the world of art, for the kind of clarity and resolution he found lacking in real life (most of the *Divine Poems* and the *Essays in Divinity* precede his decision to accept ordination). Many of his poems, like "Satire I," are psychomachic in character, externalizing a strong inner conflict and, thereby, involving the reader in a battle that is finally broader than the poet's own personal problems. "The Extasie" is such a work. Under the guise of a philosophical debate between the merits of Neoplatonic spiritual love and procreative conjugal union, Donne self-persuasively justifies his own marriage. His method is, however, to sublimate private tension, his own conflict between love and guilt, into an intellectually and emotionally lively reader-poem dynamic. He wins the battle with himself by defeating and converting us. Splitting himself

---

62. Simpson, pp. 160–61 mentions that Donne sent a copy of this work to Herbert.
63. Letter to Sir Henry Goodyer, quoted in Bald, p. 230.

into an observer-ego and a participant-ego, critic and actor,[64] he projects the resulting conflict of feelings and points of view onto poetry's stage and, in the evolution of the lyric action, deeply involves us in the final outcome.

Donne employs various strategies to draw us into the poem, some of which I have already discussed. The most complicated of these, however, is found in the final stanza of the work, to which I would like to return:

> And if some lover, such as wee,
>   Have heard this dialogue of one,
> Let him still marke us, he shall see
>   Small change, when we'are to bodies gone.

Donne, we know, placed great stress on endings and took care to leave us with precise, though sometimes enigmatic, final impressions. He wrote: "in all Metricall compositions . . . the force of the whole piece, is for the most part left to the shutting up; the whole frame of the Poem is a beating out of a piece of gold, but the last clause is as the impression of the stamp, and that is that makes it current" (*Sermons*, VI, 41). In "The Extasie" it is *the reader* who must complete the poem. *He* is the one who has just "heard this dialogue of one" and *he* must imagine the scene of love-making the couple are about to enact (the poem is open-ended and the events of the past are thus brought into the present for re-creation in the reader's imagination). Yet, because the poem asks the reader to supply its final image and suggests, through the presence of a hypothetical observer within the narrative that this is a voyeuristic act,[65] some critics have balked at the clear meaning of the last lines. Helen Gardner remarks (though her words sound more like self-persuasion than disinterested explanation): "The fact that an ideal lover is invited to 'marke' them when they are 'to bodies gone' surely makes the notion that the poem culminates in an 'immodest pro-

---

64. Cf. Norman Holland, *The Dynamics of Literary Response* (New York, 1968), pp. 54–55, and Elizabeth McLaughlin, " 'The Extasie'—Deceptive or Authentic?" *Bucknell Review* 18 (1970): 55–78.

65. Richard Hughes, pp. 84–85, relates this figure to the "observer" (or *Sprecher*) in Renaissance and Baroque paintings. Closer to Donne's technique, perhaps, would be those paintings, like Trintoretto's second "Susanna and the Elders" canvas, which reflect in their scene the viewer's act of aesthetic perception (mixed with a strong element of voyeurism in this example), thus involving him deeply in the work of art.

posal' absolutely impossible. . . . It is one thing for a narrative poet to describe two lovers in passionate embrace oblivious of a bystander, as Spenser does at the original ending of Book III of the *Faerie Queene;* it is quite another for lovers themselves to call for an audience at their coupling."[66] Aside from the fact that the poem itself says nothing about an "ideal" lover and it ends with a *decision,* not a "proposal," whose "immodesty" is all in Miss Gardner's head, her objection deserves to be taken seriously: Spenser and Donne seem to be doing two different things.

If I may digress to consider briefly the Spenserian analogue, I think we can begin to discover some things about the psychological method of "The Extasie." Spenser, it is true, has Britomart watch the sexual consummation of Scudamour and Amoret's marriage, but he translates what she sees into the Neoplatonic symbol of the hermaphrodite (which is also an emblem of marriage).[67] This and the dignified, aureate style convert a potentially voyeuristic situation into a poetically didactic one. Still, there is something telling about Britomart's reactions. She is caught between sympathy and jealousy, "half envying" (3.46.6) the lovers' happiness. In another section of *The Faerie Queene* (3.10.44–48), Spenser describes old Malbecco in the complete grip of jealousy he he spies his wife frolicking with the satyrs, then listens to her make love with one of them nine times during the night. This is the emotion Satan feels in the fourth book of *Paradise Lost* as he sees the innocent, but sensual affection of Adam and Eve: "aside the devil turn'd / For envy, yet with jealous leer malign / Ey'd them askance . . ." (4.503–505). The sympathy-envy conflict, in both Spenser and Milton, alerts us to the core fantasy implicit in these passages, that of the Freudian "Urszene," or primal scene, in which the subject

66. "The Argument," pp. 283–84 (she borrows the phrase "immodest proposal" from Frank Kermode, *John Donne* [London, 1957], p. 12). Cf. Legouis, p. 68 and Andreasen, p. 177.

67. The images of the hermaphrodite and the knot as symbols of conjugal union are combined in Barptolemaeus Anulus, *Picta Poesis* (1552), p. S14f, in *Emblemata: Handbuch Zur Sinnibildkunst des XVI. und XVII. Jahrhunderts,* ed. Arthur Henkel and Albricht Schöne (Stuttgart, 1967), col. 1631. Cf. Thomas Roche, Jr., *The Kindly Flame: A Study of the Third and Fourth Books of Spenser's Faerie Queene* (Princeton, 1964), pp. 135–36. In "The Extasie," Donne may or may not wish us to regard the physical union of lovers, as he does in "The Canonization," as hermaphroditic. A. R. Cirillo, "The Fair Hermaphrodite: Love-Union in the Poetry of Donne and Spenser," *SEL* 9 (1969): 81–95, stresses the Neoplatonic context of the hermaphrodite figure.

imagines or actually sees his parents having intercourse.[68] Spenser defends against its disturbing content with his poetry's symbolic and stylistic aesthetic distancing. Milton brings it uncomfortably close to us by reminding us in the passage describing Adam and Eve's natural eroticism that they are "our general Mother" (4.492) and "our first Father" (4.495), as both Satan and the reader are put into the oedipally jealous child's role.[69]

"The Extasie" also handles a primal scene fantasy. As Norman Holland observes, "[this] fantasy may be defended against in images of quietness, motionlessness, or death."[70] The poem's introductory section—with its arresting of physical movement, and the lovers' silence and death-like state—does just this. The poem's conclusion, which elicits the scene from the reader's consciousness (and unconscious) removes these defenses. The reasons Spenser, Milton, and Donne all employ this particular fantasy seem basically the same. In all three, the poets' and readers' confrontation with the primal scene fantasy is an essential prelude to the intellectual and emotional acceptance of marriage. The episode of Satan's peeping-tomism, for example, precedes the famous "Hail wedded love" passage in *Paradise Lost* (4.750 ff.) The envious (or potentially envious) observer, real or imagined, establishes the superiority of the lovers and the preciousness of the experience they share.

The hypothetical observer in "The Extasie," then, has two, interrelated functions: first, he points inward toward the lovers and the poet who created them, and, second, he reflects the reader and some of the ways the poem uses him. In the first place, he manifests part of the lovers' and the poet's self-consciousness, demonstrating their ability to accept the adult nature of the love-relationship. Consider the difference between the situation in "The Extasie" and that of "The Sunne Rising," which also employs a primal scene fantasy and an outside viewer. In the earlier poem, the speaker resents the intrusion of the observer-figure for more than the conventional aubade reasons.

---

68. See "The Occurrence in Dreams of Material From Fairy Tales" in *The Standard Edition of the Complete Psychological Works of Sigmund Freud*, trans. James Strachey, Anna Freud, Alex Strachey, and Alan Tyson (London, 1955), XVII, 29–47, where Freud first uses the term in his published writings.

69. Stanley Fish, *Surprised by Sin: The Reader in Paradise Lost* (New York, 1967), pp. 104–06, comments on the reader's response to the erotically stimulating elements in 3.492–504.

70. Holland, p. 46.

"Busie old foole, unruly Sunne" (line 1) he lashes out; but the grammar imperfectly disguises the fact that the libertine lover himself plays the "unruly" *son* to an angry father-figure, as in Donne's elegy, "The Perfume." He takes the morally inferior role of the child in the parent-child conflict and, because of his guilt, he interprets observation as accusation. The love-relationship is, consequently, an immature one. "The Extasie," reverses this situation to place the hypothetical viewer (and the reader) in the child's role: the lovers, in this poem, are finally self-assured and patronizing (like the couple at the end of "The Canonization"), able to accept their love as a mature relationship.

They use the observer, then, as a way of testing themselves. If they do not see him as a judge who views them from a morally superior position, they have proven the authenticity and goodness of their love. Considering the poem from a biographical perspective, we can understand Donne's method of coming to terms with the world's scrutinizing gaze, which is a potential threat to a conjugal relationship that began in secrecy (and guilt). He, first, deprives the observer-figure of the judgmental role (the whole poem works to accomplish this), then overcomes the fear of discovery by inviting inspection.

The fact that the end of "The Extasie," however, has an almost exhibitionistic character—missing certainly from the passages in Spenser and Milton—suggests the presence of an aggressive thrust originating, ultimately, in the poet's inner tensions. It looks as if Donne wishes to cause some discomfort in the reader. Whereas Spenser and Milton ease us into their scenes, Donne gives us a shove. C. S. Lewis was responding to something real in the tone and method of "The Extasie" when he called it "a much nastier poem than the nineteenth elegy"[71] (which is overtly exhibitionistic). Despite the fact that the reader is treated, at first, like a confidante, granted access to the lovers' world and invited to share vicariously in the ennobling reality of their love, despite the fact that he follows their thought-processes (which literally take place in his own head), and *he* is the one, at the crucial moment of decision, who must complete the action of the poem in his mind—despite all this, the reader is also handled like a potential antagonist. The pointed wit of the last stanza makes him the ultimate butt

71. "Donne and the Love Poetry of the Seventeenth Century," rpt. in *Seventeenth-Century English Poetry: Modern Essays in Criticism*, ed. William R. Keast (New York, 1962), p. 103. Legouis detects in the poem "an unscrupulous and selfish scheme veiled behind transcendental pretense" (pp. 63–64).

of the humor. Earlier, of course, he is deceived and frustrated in his expectations, intellectually assaulted by an aggressively dialectical argument (who else is the target of the poem's reasoning?), and made to experience his own intellectual weakness—what Donne calls in the preface to *Biathanatos* the "nakednesse and deformity of [his] own reason." He becomes, at last, the instrument and victim of the poet's wit. He is admitted into the inner sanctum of the love relationship so that his critical distance can be lost, then presented with his mirror image in the figure of the hypothetical observer, who is a docile convert by the end of the piece—a man who is, in the lovers' words, "such as we," who accepts *their* definition of love and must abandon his own.

If the poem's rhetoric works hard to *convince* the reader[72] (and the poet himself, for in this psychomachic poem persuasion is also self-persuasion), he must be assumed to hold a point of view, in some way, hostile to that of the lovers. Given the arguments the poem provides for his benefit and the nature of his fictional counterpart, the hypothetical auditor-observer, he must be a man who, like Sir Edward Herbert, regards natural sexual urges as "lustful and corrupt desires," ("An Ode upon a Question Moved," line 67)[73] and marriage, therefore, as a lower form of love. He must, like Ficino, make a distinction between intellectual and bestial love, the first involving spiritual propagation alone, the second springing from a desire for merely physical procreation. To such a way of thinking, marriage is the pedestrianization, if not the utter destruction of a love that should, ideally, move constantly away from the world of the flesh until it is consumed in "heavenly fires" ("An Ode upon a Question Moved," line 66) and enjoys the experience of spiritual ecstasy. Whether or not the reader of "The Extasie" actually holds this view, the poem assumes that he, at least, seriously entertains it, if only as a part of a fashionable love-vocabulary. Such a reader, who, by definition, is an antagonist to Donne's lovers, must be defeated philosophically and emotionally; and this is exactly what the poem accomplishes as it puts him on the psy-

72. Helen Gardner, "The Argument," p. 304, remarks: "The poem *sounds* as if someone is persuading someone. The defect of 'The Ecstasy' is that it is not sufficiently ecstatic. It is rather too much of 'an argument about ecstasy.' It suffers from a surfeit of ideas." Instead of attempting to adjust her interpretation of the poem to this insight, she condemns the work for failing to live up to her expectations.

73. Ficino states: "The lust to touch the body is not a part of love, nor is it the desire of the lover, but rather a kind of wantonness and derangement of servile man" (Jayne, pp. 146–47).

chological defensive, only to welcome him, finally, like the antagonist of "The Canonization," as a convert to the religion of love.

Treating us, paradoxically, both as sympathizers and critics, Donne *uses* us in "The Extasie"; we are his audience of "weake men." Put through a process of humiliation and enlightenment, our minds are tied in knots by a dazzling display of logical and pseudo-logical reasoning and sophisticated rhetoric. As one of Donne's elegists said to the poet, "What was thy recreation turnes our braine, / Our rack and palenesse, is thy weakest straine."[74] But Donne makes of our intellectual exhaustion an object lesson: we discover the inadequacy of our narrow conception of love *and* the feebleness of our discursive reason as we are brought to a truth only intuitive understanding, poetic symbolism, and intellectual paradox can reach. In the end, the poem offers us a valuable gift, a vision of incarnate, conjugal love set in a rich frame of reference that extends from the bloodstream to the heavenly spheres, from atoms to their Creator, from Plato to the seventeenth century, a love that can be treated comically as well as seriously because it is both profoundly human and wittily self-aware. "The Extasie" may be one of the "squibs" Donne kindled in his melancholy, or, in Walton's terms, a "paradox" in which he justified his marriage in the face of the world's "severe censures." It may be the gesture of an extraordinarily learned and gifted love poet proving he still deserved the title in his domesticated state. But, finally, the mystery of "love revealed" in the Book of Nature and in that small volume that is the human body, is a reality that transcends the narrow worlds of literary philosophical traditions, the poet's personal experiences, and the reader's awareness. Donne's genius, here, as in the best of his poems (and sermons) is his ability to let us share in the experience of discovering a large truth, and, in such a transaction, the conventional distinctions between life and art, poet and persona, reader and poem begin to dissolve.[75]

74. "On Dr. Donne's death: By Mr. Mayne of Christ-Church in Oxford" (Grierson, I, 383).

75. This essay was completed with the help of a postdoctoral fellowship from the Humanities Center of The Johns Hopkins University in 1970–71.

8. Catechizing the Reader: Herbert's Socratean Rhetoric

STANLEY E. FISH
UNIVERSITY OF CALIFORNIA, BERKELEY

1

THE DISTANCE TRAVELLED by Herbert criticism in the past thirty-five years can be measured if we juxtapose two statements by Helen White and Helen Vendler. In 1936, Professor White wrote that "there is less of surprise in [Herbert] than in most of the metaphysicals, more of inevitability."[1] In 1970, Mrs. Vendler opened her essay "The Re-invented Poem" by declaring flatly that "one of the particular virtues of Herbert's poetry is its extremely provisional quality; his poems are ready at any moment to change direction or to modify attitudes."[2] A survey of the current scene suggests that Mrs. Vendler's view now prevails and that the older view of a calm and resolute Herbert (attached, more often than not, to an over-drawn contrast between Herbert and Donne) is no longer in fashion. Even Rosemond Tuve, who emphasizes what is traditional and familiar in Herbert's art, remarks that "his Jordans never stayed crossed."[3] Writing partly in response to Tuve, Robert Montgomery focuses on the establishing, in many of the poems, of a "fictional context," the effect of which is to "remove the discourse from the level of meditation to the level of drama."[4] The "symbolic images" documented and explicated by Tuve function in the action of a "fable," and what is significant is what happens "within the mind and soul of the speaker" (463). What happens, according to Valerie Carnes, is a succession of "vacillations" and "alter-

1. *The Metaphysical Poets* (New York, 1936), p. 185.
2. "The Re-invented Poem: George Herbert's Alternatives," in *Forms of Lyric*, ed. Reuben Brower (New York, 1970), p. 19.
3. *A Reading of George Herbert* (Chicago, 1952), p. 196.
4. "The Province of Allegory in George Herbert's Verse," *TSLL* I (1960): 461, 462.

nations," "psychological shiftings" which reflect the " 'double motion' of the soul that yearns simultaneously for heaven and earth."[5] The result is a poetry in which understandings are continually being revised as "the poet's symbolic consciousness is . . . turned back upon itself with highly ironic effect" (519). This is precisely what Mrs. Vendler intends by her phrase the "re-invented poem." Herbert "is constantly criticizing what he has already written down, and finding the original conception inadequate" (204); "at any moment, a poem by Herbert can repudiate itself, correct itself, rephrase itself, rethink its experience, re-invent its topic" (45), as the poet, in effect, does his revising "in public" (22). For Coburn Freer, this re-thinking or correcting is one manifestation of what he calls "tentative form," the result of a "discrepancy between the way a Herbert poem behaves and the way it says it behaves."[6] The form of a poem, Freer asserts, often argues with its "literal meaning" and the argument is reflected in an alternation between confident assertion and "bathetic falterings" (213), between "grace and fumbling" (214).

All of these critics, then, make essentially the same point, but even as it is made, they gesture (sometimes nervously) in the direction of the other Herbert, the Herbert of a mature and unshakeable faith, who writes always from a center of certainty. The usual strategy is to place this Herbert in a separate category—"orchestral form" as opposed to "tentative form," the "meditative" as opposed to the "dramatic" mode—but these artificial divisions only displace the central question that confronts the critic, a question that is precisely (if indirectly) posed by Freer when he speaks of that "uniquely Herbertian quality of order and surprise" (218). How is it that a Herbert poem can contain and communicate both? This question, when it is asked, is usually answered by suggesting that the surprise is staged; either it is a fiction designed to illustrate dramatically a truth known to the poet from the beginning, or it is a recreation, in verse, of a spiritual crisis he has successfully weathered.[7] Explanations like these, however, solve one problem by creating another; for while they exalt Herbert the craftsman, they raise questions about Herbert the man, who is either completely separated from his speakers or made to stand in

5. "The Unity of George Herbert's *The Temple*: A Reconsideration," *ELH* 35 (1968): 517.
6. *Music for a King* (Baltimore, 1972), p. 194.
7. See Carnes, "The Unity of George Herbert's *The Temple*," p. 519.

relation to them as a player of roles, a posturer. In either case he is distanced from their concerns, becoming that much less of a Christian as he is acknowledged to be that much more of a poet. We seem, then, to be at an impasse: on the one hand the order in Herbert's poetry is denied; on the other it is acknowledged, but at the price both of his sincerity and of his wish to make his art self-consuming.[8]

The problem then is to find a way of talking that neither excludes Herbert from his poems (by emphasizing their order), nor makes them crudely autobiographical (by making them all surprise). That way is provided, I believe, by Herbert himself in Chapter XXI of *A Priest To The Temple*. The title of the chapter is "The Parson Catechizing," but it is largely a praise of "the singular dexterity of Socrates," who held "that the seeds of all truth lay in everybody, and accordingly by questions well ordered he found Philosophy in silly Trades-men."[9] That position, Herbert admits, "will not hold in Christianity, because it contains things above nature," but the general method or "skill" can be adapted and imitated, for it consists "but in these three points":

> First, an aim and mark of the whole discourse, whither to drive the Answerer, which the Questionist must have in his mind before any question be propounded, upon which and to which the questions are to be chained. Secondly, a most plain and easie framing the question, even containing in vertue the answer also, especially to the more ignorant. Thirdly, when the answer sticks, an illustrating the thing by something else, which he knows, making what hee knows to serve him in that which he knows not.
>
> (256–257)

Here, I think, is a perfect formula for the order and surprise of Herbert's poetry. The order belongs to the Questionist-poet who knows from the beginning where he is going. The surprise belongs to the reader who is "driven" by "questions well ordered" to discover for himself "that which he knows not."[10] Herbert's questions are not always posed directly, in the conventional grammatical form, any more

8. On this point see Stanley Fish, "Letting Go: The Dialectic of the Self in Herbert's Poetry," in *Self-Consuming Artifacts* (Berkeley, 1972), chap. 3.

9. *The Works of George Herbert*, ed. F. E. Hutchinson (Oxford, 1941), p. 256.

10. Arnold Stein (*George Herbert's Lyrics*, Baltimore, 1968) also relates this chapter of *A Priest To The Temple* to Herbert's poetry (see pp. 182–183), but he views the prose work more as a suggestive analogue than as a source for Herbert's poetic technique, and he is not concerned, as I am, with the implications of Herbert's remarks for the role of the reader. See also Freer, *Music for a King*, pp. 235–36.

than are the questions of Socrates. Like the philosopher he strikes deliberately naive poses that are calculated to draw a critical or corrective response from an interlocutor; that is, he makes assertions which *function* as questions because they invite the reader to supply either what is missing or what is deficient. Consider, for example, the poem "Love-Joy":

> As on a window late I cast mine eye,
> I saw a vine drop grapes with J and C
> Anneal'd on every bunch. One standing by
> Ask'd what it meant. I, who am never loth
> To spend my judgement, said, It seem'd to me
> To be the bodie and the letters both
> of *Joy* and *Charitie*. Sir, you have not miss'd,
> The man reply'd; it figures *JESUS CHRIST*.

For Montgomery, "Love-Joy" is "a brief compressed narrative," "a presentation of and commentary upon the imperfection of one man's understanding of Christian truth." The imperfection is the narrator's and it is revealed by "the order of the two interpretations" which "gently contradicts his judgment" (462). But if any judgment is contradicted in this poem, it is the reader's, even though the second interpretation is the one he has all the while been ready to deliver. Even before the poem's official questioner ("One standing by") appears, a question is being asked by the hieroglyphic riddle of lines 1 and 2: what do J and C annealed on a bunch of grapes mean? The obvious answer is "Jesus Christ," and it is the answer the reader expects to hear, especially since the word "bodie" would seem to allude directly to the typological identification of the bunch of grapes in Numbers with the wine press of the Passion.[11] Thus for fully seven-eighths of the poem it is the reader who is spending his judgment, and it is with some surprise that he hears the narrator in line 7 give what is apparently the wrong answer. This, however, is only the first of three surprises. The second occurs when the Questionist appears to approve the narrator's answer, for then it seems that the reader has spent his judgment unwisely; but when the answer is expanded and completed (this is the third surprise) it turns out to be exactly what the reader has been expecting: "It figures *JESUS CHRIST*." The point is not, as Montgomery suggests, that one interpretation is superior to the other, but that prop-

11. See Tuve, *A Reading*, pp. 112–33.

erly understood they imply each other. It is a point the reader is left
to make for himself, and he *will* make it, if only because the method of
"questions well ordered" has given him a stake in the solving of the
riddle, both the riddle as initially posed, and the interpretative riddle
of the final two lines. In short, the reader is brought by means of "what
hee knows," by "a most plain and easie framing the question," to "that
which he knows not" (or at least doesn't know consciously), not merely
what J and C stand for, but what JESUS CHRIST stands for, *Joy* and
Charitie.

2

"Love-joy," then, is not "a brief compressed narrative"; rather
it is a dialogue, with the poet (in two roles) as Questionist and the
reader as (silent) respondent. Montgomery contrives to turn Herbert
into a seventeenth-century Browning, a dramatic monologist who does
not necessarily hold the opinions expressed by his first-person speakers; but the distinction between poet and persona need not be made
if Herbert is understood to be speaking in his own *pedagogical* voice;
for then it is not a question of recollecting in tranquility a previous experience, or of fictionalizing an experience he has never had, but of
sincere role-playing, that is, of straightforwardly adapting the rhetorical strategy described in *A Priest To The Temple*.

That strategy, as Herbert elaborates it, is characterized by its
flexibility. The country parson does not employ set forms, for these
create a situation in which the catechized deliver answers by rote and
perform "as parrats" (256). The better practice is one in which the
order and the method of questioning are "varyed," as the catechizer
responds to particular circumstances and to the differing capacities of
his pupils. (Here Herbert would seem to be following the counsel of
Augustine in *De catechizandis rudibus*.) In this way the Answerer is
brought not only to a knowledge of the "dark and deep points of Religion," but to a knowledge of himself; he is led, as Herbert puts it, to
"discover what he is" (257).

In *The Temple*, this flexibility of method is reflected in the varying relationships into which readers and speakers enter. In "The Hold-
fast" reader and speaker are catechized together by a third person,
and their responses, as I have argued elsewhere,[12] trace out parallel
careers. Both are "driven" to the realization that Christ is and does

12. *Self-Consuming Artifacts*, pp. 173–76.

all things when an unidentified voice refuses to allow them the things and actions (including the action of interpreting) they would reserve to themselves. As the poem ends, they have fallen silent, and that voice is summarizing the lesson that has been "the mark of the whole discourse." In "Love-Unknown" the same three-cornered situation results in a different set of relationships. Here the reader is not allied with the speaker, but runs ahead of him, answering the questions raised by his tale, supplying the typological significances to which he seems blind, solving the puzzle of the title, anticipating the responses of the "Deare Friend" before they are offered. The context is still catechistical, but it is one stage removed, a relearning of a lesson by watching and reacting to the instruction of another.[13] (Writers of catechisms regularly urge the benefits of attendance at public catechizings.) In "Love-joy" the relationship between speaker and reader is continually changing. At one point, the reader is encouraged to think himself superior, because it appears that the speaker has given the wrong answer; but then the positions are reversed when that answer is approved by the catechizer. In a final reversal, the reader learns that he was correct after all, but his understanding of his own response is now deeper because of the sequence he has negotiated.

In each of these three poems, the shape of the catechistical experience is different, but the basic pattern remains the same: the reader, in the company of a fellow pupil, is driven by the singular dexterity of a Questionist to one of the deep and dark points of religion. In another group of poems, this same pattern unfolds in the absence of a fellow pupil; the confrontation between catechized and catechizer is unmediated and direct. The mode of catechizing, however, is indirect, since the dialogue is not built into the form, but is initiated when the reader is moved to correct or complete the speaker's statements in the light of that "which he knows."

What he knows as he begins "The Bunch of Grapes" has been nicely summarized by Joseph Summers:

> That "branch with one cluster of grapes," which was so large that "they bore it betweene two upon a staffe," had represented a joy which the Israelites refused. To them the bunch of grapes substantiated the report that it was "a land that eateth up the inhabitants thereof,

13. On this point, see Ira Clark's excellent article, " 'Lord, in Thee the *Beauty* Lies in the *Discovery*': 'Love Unknown' and Reading Herbert," *ELH* 39 (1972): 576.

and all the people that we saw in it, are men of a great stature. And there we saw the giants, the sonnes of Anak, which come of the giants: and we were in our own sight as grashoppers, and so wee were in their sight" (Num. xiii.32–33). From fear they turned to the rebellion which caused God to decree the wandering of forty years. Of all the adults who saw the grapes, only Caleb and Joshua entered the Promised Land. The image of the bunch of grapes suggests, then, not only the foretastes of Canaan and heaven, but also the immeasurable difference between those foretastes under the Covenant of Works and the Covenant of Grace. . . . The bunch of grapes is a type of Christ and of the Christian's communion. "I have their fruit and more," for the grapes, of which the promise was conditional upon works, have been transformed into the wine of the New Covenant: "I" have both the foretaste and the assurance of its fulfilment.[14]

All of this is potentially contained in the title of the poem, but, paradoxically, it is brought out only because it is suppressed. As in "Love-joy" Herbert works *against* the expectations of his reader so that in the end they may be more meaningfully confirmed. He begins with a complaint: "Joy, I did lock thee up: but some bad man / Hath let thee out again." On the surface, this is simply a testimony to the unevenness of the Christian's spiritual life, but to the reader who, like Miss Tuve, has seen one of the many "vivid representations of Christ pressed in the winepress of the Passion" (116), the note sounded here will not ring true. The language is the language of enclosures and confinements ("lock up," "let out"), but the joy of Christ's inheritance is boundless and free. It is not possessed, but possesses. We do not have it, we share in it and live in it; it contains us rather than the reverse. Of course the statements I have been making in the previous sentences are more precise than anything the reader is thinking at this point. His misgivings are more inchoate, a slight and largely undefined uneasiness that springs from his unawareness of the contexts invaded by the title. In the course of the poem, that uneasiness acquires form and substance, as the poet's assertions continue to invite a critical and corrective response. The invitation is sharpened as this first stanza proceeds:

> And now, me thinks, I am where I began
> Sev'n yeares ago: one vogue and vein,
> One aire of thoughts usurps my brain.

14. *George Herbert: His Religion and Art* (London, 1954), pp. 127–28.

I did towards Canaan draw; but now I am
Brought back to the Red sea, the sea of shame.

(lines 3–7)

Again the lines assert one thing, but the reader extrapolates something else. The poet's complaint is carried by two spatial images, one linear ("I did toward Canaan draw"), the other cyclical ("I am where I began"), the first figuring forth the direction of his hopes, the second emblematic of their frustration. Yet even as this plain sense registers, it is undermined by the typological associations of its components. Canaan, of course, is a figure of salvation, while the passage way to Canaan, the river Jordan, is a type of baptism, and this is perfectly consistent with the statement Herbert is making. The Red Sea, however, is also a type, a type of the crucifixion and more specifically of the blood that flowed from Christ's side:

> For the watyr yn the fonte [Red Sea] betokeynth the red blod and watyr that ran down of the wondys of Cristis syde in the wheche the power of Pharo, that is, the veray fend, ys drowned, and all hys myght lorne, and all cristen pepull sauet.[15]

> All our waters shall run into Jordan, and thy servants passed Jordan dry foot; they shall run into the red sea (the sea of thy Son's blood), and the red sea, that red sea, drowns none of thine.[16]

The Red Sea, then, is "the sea of shame" only under the Law when it is the passageway to forty years of wandering; but typically understood, under the New Dispensation of the Spirit, this same "font" signifies a *release* from shame, a release that has been effected by Christ's blood, simultaneously the passageway and the vehicle of passage. In the light of these significances, the poet's complaint denies itself in the uttering—I did towards Canaan draw but now I am brought back toward Canaan—and the spatial metaphor which has been carrying his argument is discredited. The inadequacy of that metaphor inheres in its rigidity, its inability to accommodate a God who is everywhere and from whom one can not move away, and that limitation is in turn a reflection of the limitation of the Law (an inflexible system of rewards and punishments) and of the minds in bondage to it.

15. From Mirk's *Festival*, quoted by V. A. Kolve, *The Play Called Corpus Christi* (Stanford, 1966), p. 77.
16. John Donne, *Devotions* (Ann Arbor, 1959), p. 127.

None of this is in the poem; it is supplied by the reader who is responding to the question the stanza indirectly poses: what is wrong with these statements? What is wrong, of course, is that they betray a misreading on the speaker's part of typological significances, a misreading that becomes even more obvious when typology itself becomes the poem's explicit subject:

> For as the Jews of old by Gods command
> Travell'd, and saw no town;
> So now each Christian hath his journeys spann'd:
> Their storie pennes and sets us down.
> A single deed is small renown.
> Gods works are wide, and let in future times;
> His ancient justice overflows our crimes.
>
> (lines 8–18)

The basis for these lines is I Corinthians 10; but while the doctrine proclaimed in that espistle is liberating—release from the letter of the law—it is here confining and legalistic, confining even in its language—"spann'd," "pennes," "set ... down"—and legalistic in its assumption of a one-to-one correspondence between the careers of the Old Testament wanderers and the lives of modern Christians. In this formulation, typology becomes a veritable prison within which we are condemned to repeat the errors and idolatries of the Israelites, and the "wideness" of God's works only serves to prevent us from escaping his "ancient justice."

Such a view of the matter, however, ignores, and by ignoring calls attention to, the distinction central to this way of reading history, the distinction between the type and the antitype, the shadow and the substance, the promise and fulfillment. The very point of bringing together the events of the Old Testament and the New is to assert the superiority of the dispensation under which the latter occur. (Noah's ark, for example, is a type of baptism, but its antitype is better because by it more are saved.[17]) Rather than penning us down, the stories of the Israelites provide a counterpoint to our happier situation.

It is this gracious difference that is denied by Herbert's determined literalism, but it is that same literalism which pressures the reader-

---

17. "The longsuffering of God waited in the days of Noah while the ark was a preparing, wherein few, that is, eight souls were saved by the water. The like figure whereunto even baptism doth also now save us ... by the resurrection of Jesus Christ." (I Peter 3:20-21)

Answerer to recall it; and the pressure becomes irresistible in the final two lines of the stanza: "Gods works are wide and let in future times; / His ancient justice overflows our crimes." The plain sense of this couplet is negative and constricting, but its experience is liberating. In place of "lock," "pennes," and "set down," the vocabulary of confinement, we are now given "wide," "let in," and "overflows," the vocabulary of release. The language is pointing us away from what it literally asserts and toward a recognition of the freedom we now enjoy as a result of the greatest of God's works, the work of self-sacrifice. (This "linguistic release" is an analogue, in the reading experience, of the release from the Law effected for us by the New Covenant of the Spirit.) This is particularly true of the word "overflows" which reaches back to the water imagery of the first stanza, and, more importantly, to the typological significance of the Red Sea, "the red blod and watyr that ran down of the wondys of Cristis syde in the wheche ... all cristen pepull [are] sauet." It is this that overflows all our crimes, inundating and submerging them in endless waters of forgiveness and redemption, and this interpretation of the word is made inescapable by what is so obviously *missing* from the line: "His ancient justice overflows our crimes." In any seventeenth-century discussion of the attributes of God, when "justice" is mentioned, "mercy" cannot be far behind. They are, as Milton declares, "colleague," and by citing the one, Herbert invites us to supply the other, and to attach it to the image which, even though it is absent, is slowly taking possession of the poem, the image of the bleeding (mercy-showering) Christ. In other words, we are provoked to remember mercy because Herbert so ostentatiously forgets it, and, as the poem continues, every detail points unmistakably in the direction he refuses (overtly) to take:

> Then have we too our guardian fires and clouds;
> Our Scripture-dew drops fast:
> We have our sands and serpents, tents and shrowds;
> Alas! our murmurings come not last.
> But where's the cluster? where's the taste
> Of mine inheritance? Lord, if I must borrow,
> Let me as well take up their joy, as sorrow.

(lines 15–21)

The "guardian clouds and fire" are evidences of God's providence; they hover over the Tabernacle (Numbers 9:15–23), which is a type both of the church and of the believer as a temple of the living God. The "brazen serpent" and manna ("Our Scripture-dew drops") are alike types of eternal life that is the reward (the "fruit") of those who believe in Christ.[18] The questions—"But where's the cluster? where's the taste / Of mine inheritance"—carry an implied accusation—it isn't fair—but the answers they draw from us deny the accusation by validating it. It *isn't* fair, but the disproportion is all in our favour: God does not treat us exactly as he did the "Jewes of old," he treats us better; we do not receive their portion of joy; we receive more, and receive it not as a reward nor upon conditions (as they did), but as a gift, freely given at great cost to him and in gracious (merciful) *disregard* of our deserts; we do not borrow *their* inheritance, *their* cluster, we share in our own, in the fruit of the "true vine" planted and nourished by God (John 15.1). This, then, is the "immeasurable difference" between the two foretastes, one under the Covenant of Works, the other under the Covenant of Grace, but it is a difference that is realized not in the poem (where it is resolutely ignored), but in the response of the reader to the poet's deliberately narrow assertions.

If we turn once again to the account in *A Priest To The Temple* of the parson catechizing, we can see how closely it corresponds to the experience of this poem. By means of a progressively "plain and easie framing" of the question ("what is missing here?") the reader has been "driven" to discover for himself the "aim and mark of the whole discourse," that is, the full significance of the bunch of grapes. The function of catechizing is, in Herbert's words, "to infuse a competent knowledge of salvation in every one of [the parson's] flock" (255). In this case, we are his flock, made competent in exactly that knowledge by a poetic variation of "the singular dexterity of *Socrates*"; and like Socrates, Herbert abandons his deliberately naive pose when it has done its work:

> But can he want the grape, who hath the wine?
> I have their fruit and more.
> Blessed be God, who prosper'd *Noahs* vine,
> And made it bring forth grapes good store.

18. "And as Moses lifted up the serpent in the wilderness, even so must the Son of man be lifted up, That whosoever believeth in him shall not perish, but have eternal life." (John 3:14–15) "Your fathers did eat manna in the wilderness, and are dead . . . I am the living bread that came down from heaven; if any man eat of this bread, he shall live forever." (John 6:49, 51)

But much more him I must adore,
Who of the Laws sowre juice sweet wine did make,
Ev'n God himself being pressed for my sake.

(lines 22–28)

At this point Mrs. Vendler might say that the poem is re-invented, while Montgomery is forced to conclude that "structurally . . . the fable of 'The Bunch of Grapes' is uncertain" (464) since it equivocates between the fictional and meditative modes. But there is no equivocation or re-inventing if the mode of the poem is acknowledged to be rhetorical; for then the change in tone and direction one feels here marks the moment when the catechism has ended and Questionist and Answerer share a level of understanding, an understanding one has earned and the other has laboured to give. Indeed, line 22 functions here much as "Sir, you have not missed" functions in "Love-joy"; for by voicing precisely the counterarguments that he has drawn from the reader, the poet implicitly approves them, and from this point on the participants in the poem's dialogue proceed in unanimity, openly proclaiming the truth they now share. The vocabulary which was the vehicle of their temporary divergence remains, but it is transformed by the single perspective that now rules the poem and its experience. For a moment, the first half of line 23—"I have their fruit"—suggests the narrow literalism of the opening lines, but the phrase "and more" is liberating for it literally overflows the spatial boundaries suggested by the verb of possession. This "having" is finally very different from the "locking up" of line 1; it is the result of realizing that such a locking up is at once impossible and unnecessary. The sense of liberation is also communicated by the rhythms of the verse. The questions and exclamations of the previous stanzas had resulted in a choppy reading experience with mandatory breaks and pauses (pauses which were to be filled by the answers of the reader); here we move smoothly and without interruption through what is essentially one long flowing sentence. The climax of that sentence and indeed of the entire poem is the verb "pressed" which, while nominally of the same class as "lock" and "pennes" and "set down," is not constricting at all; for in this context, the action of pressing is equivalent to an *out*pouring, an outpouring of red wine, red sea, red blood, mercy, love; and it is this that the poet and reader see, feel, taste, as all the significances which have been accruing to the title emblem, in the tradition and in the poem, are compressed into this sublimated image of the crucifixion.

185

3

It might seem that all I have done in this essay is substitute one set of terms for another, Questionist for persona, Answerer for reader, and dialogue for narrative. The new terms, however, are I think qualitatively superior to the old, not only because they are Herbert's but because by bringing the reader into the center of the poem's action, they make it possible to account for the "Herbertian quality of order and surprise." If the reader is not considered a party to the transaction, the critic, as we saw, has only one of two choices: if he wishes to keep Herbert the man at the center of his poetry, he must deemphasize order and design; and if he accommodates order and design by positing a succession of personae, he removes Herbert the man from the center of his poetry. Acknowledging the role of the reader cuts across these choices and dissolves the dilemma. The poet is granted "the singular dexterity" and skill of a Christian pedagogic design, and that design is realized in the series of surprises experienced by the reader. This solution also has the advantage of being true to Herbert's own hopes for his verse, hopes that are, in the best sense of the word, rhetorical. Even if Walton is writing hagiography, his report of Herbert's direction to Ferrar at the very least reflects an accepted view of the poet's intention: "desire him [Ferrar] to read it, and then if he can think it may turn to the advantage of any dejected poor Soul, let it be made publick; if not, let him burn it."[19] This concern for the soul of the reader is voiced in the poems themselves. In "The Dedication" God is petitioned to "Turn their eyes hither, who shall make a gain"; in "Praise III" the poet cries "Oh that I might some other hearts convert" (39); and in "Obedience" this wish is given its strongest expression:

> How happie were my part,
> If some kinde man would thrust his heart
> Into these lines; till in Heav'ns Court of Roll
> They were by winged souls
> Entred for both, farre above their desert.

(lines 41–45)

19. Izaak Walton, *The Life of Mr. George Herbert* (London, 1670), p. 74. The authenticity of this report has recently been challenged by J. Max Patrick, "Critical Problems in Editing George Herbert's *The Temple*," in *The Editor As Critic and The Critic as Editor*, ed. Murray Krieger, William Andrews Clark Memorial Library Seminar (Los Angeles, 1973), pp. 3–40.

In Herbert's own century, this invitation was accepted by "many pious converts" (the phrase is Vaughan's).[20] Crashaw not only thrusts his own heart in, but would extend the benefits by sending "Mr. Herbert's book" to another; she, in turn, is warned that the reading of these poems is no passive experience: "Know you faire, on what you looke; / Divinest love lyes in this booke: / Expecting fire from your eyes, / To kindle this his sacrifice."[21] Christopher Harvey is moved to build a synagogue in imitation of *The Temple* and is rewarded when Walton groups him with Herbert: "These holy hymns had an ethereal birth; / For they can raise sad souls above the earth, / And fix them there, / Free from the world's anxieties and fear. / Herbert and you have pow'r / To do this; ev'ry hour / I read you, kills a sin / Or lets a virtue in."[22] The most eloquent testimony comes from Henry Vaughan who speaks for others as well as himself when he bears witness to the effect of Herbert's "holy, ever-living lines":

> Dear friend! whose holy, ever-living lines
> Have done much good
> To many, and have chect my blood,
> My fierce, wild blood that still heaves, and inclines,
> But is still tam'd
> By those bright fires which thee inflam'd;
> Here I joyn hands, and thrust my stubborn heart
> Into thy *Deed*.
>
> ("The Match," lines 1–8)

It is more than likely that Vaughan alludes here not only to "Obedience" but to the opening stanza of "The Church-porch" where the reader is promised verses that will rhyme him to good:

> Thou whose sweet youth and early hopes inhance
> Thy rate and price, and mark thee for a treasure;
> Hearken unto a Verser, who may chance
> Ryme thee to good, and make a bait of pleasure.
> A verse may finde him, who a sermon flies,
> And turn delight into a sacrifice.

20. *The Works of Henry Vaughan*, ed. L. C. Martin (Oxford, 1957), p. 391.

21. "*On Mr. G. Herberts booke intituled the Temple of Sacred Poems, sent to a Gentlewoman*." The text is from L. C. Martin's edition (Oxford, 1927), p. 130.

22. "To My Reverend Friend The Author Of The Synagogue," in *The Complete Poems of Christopher Harvey*, ed. A. B. Grosart (Lancashire, 1874), p. 86.

Surely it is no accident that the terms in which poetry is praised here are the terms in which catechizing is praised in *A Priest To The Temple*: "at sermons . . . men may sleep or wander; but when one is asked a question, he must discover that he is" (257). It is not simply that in both texts a comparison is made at the expense of sermons, but that the virtues of poetry and catechizing are the same: they do not allow the reader-auditor to escape; he is found, he is discovered, he is drawn in, and once in he is remade into the "spirituall Temple" which both catechism and poems "build up" (255).

I am not arguing, as others have,[23] that Herbert's remarks on catechizing provide an interesting analogue to his poetical practice. I believe that the connection is much firmer, and that Herbert consciously composed *The Temple* on a catechistical model. That however will be the argument of a longer work[24] and within the limits of the present essay it is enough to point out that the experience of the poetry is in every way answerable to the description of catechizing: its questions are "chained" so that they lead inexorably to the "aim and mark of the whole discourse"; the leading—the order—is the poet-Questionist's, while the discovery—the surprise—belongs to the reader-Answerer; and the whole is "an admirable way of teaching, wherein the Catechized will at length finde delight, and by which the Catechizer, if he once get the skill of it, will draw out of ignorant and silly souls, even the dark and deep points of Religion" (256). Herbert has got the skill of it.

23. In addition to Stein and Freer (cited in note 10), see John R. Mulder's *The Temple of the Mind* (New York, 1969), pp. 106–29. Mulder discusses the echoes in Herbert's poems of Nowell's catechism, but he specifically disclaims any assertion of direct influence (p. 127).

24. *The Living Temple: Herbert and Catechizing*, forthcoming.

9. The Rhetoric of the Sublime in Crashaw's Poetry

MICHAEL McCANLES

MARQUETTE UNIVERSITY

W HEN CONFRONTED WITH the imagery of "The Weeper," "The Teare," "The Divine Epigrams," as well as stronger poems such as the "Hymn to . . . Sainte Teresa" and "The Flaming Heart," the usual reaction critics have had to contend with is quite simply embarrassment. How they justify pushing beyond this embarrassment, if they are favorable to the poetry at all, determines their interpretations of the poems themselves. The imagery seems to be deliberate. But, as John Peter remarks, "though we agree that the imagery is what it is by design, not accident, we still have little to adduce as to the spirit in which it is presented or the effect for which it was designated."[1] The imagery's hyperbole, and the overheated expression of whole poems, stand squarely against any attempt to discount them in the name of purely conceptual content, and will not budged.[2] On the contrary, perhaps the best way to get beyond initial embarrassment is not to ignore it, but to begin with it. Such is Robert Martin Adams's solution, when he says, commenting on "The Weeper,"

1. John Peter, "Crashaw and 'The Weeper,'" *Scrutiny* 19 (1953): 261.

2. Ruth C. Wallerstein, in *Richard Crashaw: A Study in Style and Poetic Development* (Madison, 1959), offers the most thorough defense of the decorum of Crashaw's imagery on the basis of its purely conceptual content: [Having discussed the traditional meanings of the lily image:] "Crashaw . . . chooses, like the maker of the lily symbol, to embody his idea in an object of sharp sensuous color and emotive power. This emotive power, or complex of suggestions, he uses as a sign, or metaphor, of his concept. Thereby he makes that single object the abstract *name* for the spiritual or intellectual concept he would express. But, it cannot be too often stressed, this sense image which he uses in his metaphor is to represent an idea, and not primarily a sense impression; it is the symbol of an idea. And the basic emotion that Crashaw seeks to create in us is to spring not from the image, but directly from the idea" (p. 85; italics in orig.).

The feeling is to be colored by a radical sense of absurdity—even to be derived, by a queer kind of negative emphasis, from the absurdity, as if the absurdity were somehow a guarantee of the point of view from which alone a grief so ghastly could seem absurd. A Christian poet, at least, can scarcely be blamed for assuming, and asking his readers to assume for the moment, a definition of reality which includes more than the humanly demonstrable; and how to suggest such a reality if not through the feelings imagined as appropriate to it.[3]

Just how far one is willing to go when asked to incorporate a sense of a poem's "absurdity" into an aesthetic response is a matter of personal preference. Nevertheless, Professor Adams has perhaps given us a correct emphasis to start from, when he recognizes that Crashaw undoubtedly intended the reader to apprehend his imagery's failure totally to render its tenor. The result of this failure, in John Peter's words, is "an effect of the inexpressible forcing its way into language and of distortion accordingly."[4]

This mention of the "inexpressible" in Crashaw's poetry points up both the strengths and limitations of a purely rhetorical analysis of Crashaw's tropes and figures. The topoi of "inexpressibility" and "outdoing" have a long history in the rhetoric of classical and medieval literature, as Ernst Robert Curtius has shown. These two figures express "the inability to cope with the subject" and "the superiority, even the uniqueness, of the person or thing to be praised" respectively.[5] In the rhetorical handbooks of the English Renaissance these topoi are classified under the term *hyperbole,* and are sometimes linked with the figures *auxesis* and *meiosis,* or intensive praise and dispraise. Henry Peacham and George Puttenham both hold that hyperbole is, in Puttenham's words, "when we speake in the superlatiue and beyond the limites of credit," and both indicate in their examples that this figure clearly communicates itself to the reader as an exaggeration of the truth.[6] Similarly, Thomas Wilson describes *hyperbole* as "mounting

---

3. Robert Martin Adams, "Taste and Bad Taste in Metaphysical Poetry: Richard Cranshaw and Dylan Thomas," in *Seventeenth-Century English Poetry: Modern Essays in Criticism,* ed. William R. Keast (New York, 1962), p. 272.

4. Peter, p. 269.

5. *European Literature and the Latin Middle Ages,* trans. Willard R. Trask (New York, 1963), pp. 159, 162.

6. George Puttenham, *The Arte of English Poesie,* ed. Gladys D. Willcock and Alice Walker (Cambridge, Eng. 1936), p. 191; in *The Garden of Eloquence* (London, 1577), Henry Peacham says *hyperbole* occurs "when a saying doth surmounte and reach aboue the truth" (Diii^v).

aboue the trueth," and it occurs "when wee doe set foorth things ex-
ceedingly and aboue all mens expectation, meaning only that they are
very great."[7] John Hoskins, in his *Directions for Speech and Style*,
only partly agrees with these descriptions, when he describes *hyperbole* as a figure which "expresseth a thing in the highest degree of
possibility, beyond the truth, and that it descending thence may find
the truth; sometimes in flat impossibility, that rather you may conceive
the unspeakableness than the untruth of the relation."[8] Hoskins adds
to the definitions of Puttenham and the rest a quite opposite effect of
hyperbole: the communication of the fact that the reality is beyond
the powers of language to express. Finally, Richard Sherry's *A Treatise
of Schemes and Tropes* (London, 1550) discusses *amplification* and
hyperbole as interchangeable types of figures, and describes one mode
of "amplyfienge that is by comparison contrary to increase":

> For as in increase the thynges that go before beyng exaggerat, we go
> from them to the hyest, so comparison taketh increase of the lesser,
> whych if they be greater in all mens opinions, that must nedes ap-
> peare verie greate that we wyll haue amplified. . . .
>
> (Eiiii[r-v])

This notion of hyperbole by comparison, whereby something appears
great when called larger even than something already granted as great,
comes closest to naming a dominant device in Crashaw's poetry.

It is clear from Hoskins and Sherry that *hyperbole* is rhetorically
ambiguous. In Hoskins' case, a hyperbolic statement may direct the
reader to discount itself for either one of quite opposite reasons: in
the one case the reader discounts it because it goes beyond the reality,
and in the other because it falls short. In both cases, it is assumed
that the reader will decide which is operative according to his prior
knowledge of the reality referred to. The rhetoricians assume this notion, first, because the very ideas of "exaggeration" and "inadequacy"
imply such a comparison, and, second, because they are not concerned
with what makes certain referents of *hyperbole* capable or incapable
of being so described. And they are not concerned with this matter for
the very good reason that it does not fall within the province of
rhetoric itself.

That part of rhetoric concerned with the available figures of which

---

7. *The Arte of Rhetorique*, ed. G. H. Mair (Oxford, 1909), p. 183.
8. Ed. Hoyt H. Hudson (Princeton, 1935), p. 29.

hyperbole is one can describe the verbal means of communicating to a reader the fact that, e.g., the mystery of the Incarnation is ultimately inexpressible. Beyond that, rhetorical analysis cannot go unless joined with terms that articulate the particular structures of human thought and of the mystery itself which, when confronted with each other, create the "inexpressibility." And it is the intelligible grounds of this inexpressibility that Crashaw explores. If we do not take these grounds into consideration, even examining the rhetorical devices in his poetry will not take us very far.

Crashaw's religious poetry expresses the confrontation between limited, finite human language and conceptualization, and the transcendence of divine mystery. For this reason, we must view his poetry's purely rhetorical means as themselves part of the poetry's subject. This poetry inhabits a middle ground between the speaker's straining resources of articulation, and a transcendent God; consequently, both meanings of *hyperbole* are brought into play. This possibility, described by Sherry, may appear paradoxical in theory, but it can and does succeed in varying degrees in the poetry itself. The hyperboles in Crashaw's poems actually refer to two realities: transcendent divine mysteries, and the items of natural human experience which metaphor, symbol, and paradox draw on to express these mysteries. In order to express (inadequately) the first, Crashaw uses hyperboles that present themselves as exaggerations of the second. Thus these hyperboles strike the reader as at once exaggerations of finite realities and as "not exaggerated enough" to express the divine. Crashaw's poetry reaches its highest point of expressivity when both kinds of hyperbole are fused, and the reader becomes aware that exaggerated violations of finite, natural images are nevertheless inadequate to transcendent divine mystery. At these moments, Crashaw's poetry achieves, within the limits of a verbal medium, the destruction of language by language, and propels the reader into an experience analogous (but only such) to mystical vision.

To account for the total rhetorical effect of Crashaw's hyperbolic tropes and figures, we need a description that includes the realities these hyperboles seek to communicate. And since his poetry assumes that the reader has prior knowledge of the mysteries it deals with, we must also take account of how the reader cooperates with the poetry in being affected by its rhetorical gambits. Immanuel Kant gives us such a description when discussing the "sublime" in *The Critique of*

Judgment. I of course pretend no influence here, since as Samuel Holt Monk has shown, Longinus' treatise on the subject exerted no influence on seventeenth-century English literature.[9] I use Kant's account of the "sublime" only to illuminate certain aspects of conceiving the inconceivable in Crashaw's poetry, and thereby to supplement a strictly rhetorical analysis of how these effects are achieved verbally.

Several points in Kant's discussion make the "sublime" relevant to Crashaw. He says at one point, "the sublime is that in comparison with which everything else is small"; and again, "the sublime is that, the mere ability to think which shows a faculty of the mind surpassing every standard of sense."[10] No matter how far we may advance in imagining the magnitude of an object given to the senses, the reason can conceive a still greater magnitude:

> But now the mind listens to the voice of reason which, for every given magnitude—even for those that can never be entirely apprehended, although (in sensible representation) they are judged as entirely given—requires totality. Reason consequently desires comprehension in *one* intuition, and so the (joint) *presentation* of all these members of a progressively increasing series. It does not even exempt the infinite (space and past time) from this requirement; it rather renders it unavoidable to think the infinite (in the judgment of common reason) as *entirely given* (according to its totality).[11]

When the reason conceives, the imagination seeks to represent:

> But our imagination, even in its greatest efforts, in respect of that comprehension which we expect from it of a given object in a whole of intuition (and thus with reference to the presentation of the idea of reason) exhibits its own limits and inadequacy, although at the same time it shows that its destination is to make itself adequate to this idea regarded as a law.[12]

From this conflict between the reason's and the imagination's attempt to represent the infinite whole of things, arises the recognition of reason's superiority, which superiority "can be made intuitively evident only by the inadequacy of that faculty [imagination]."[13] This

9. Samuel H. Monk, *The Sublime: A Study of Critical Theories in XVIII-Century England* (Ann Arbor, 1960), p. 18.

10. Immanuel Kant, *Critique of Judgment*, trans. J. H. Bernard (New York, 1951), pp. 88, 89.

11. Kant, p. 93; italics in orig.

12. Kant, p. 96.

13. Kant, p. 97 .

awareness of imagination's inadequacy for representing what the reason conceives is the emotion of the sublime.

Crashaw's religious poetry attempts to arouse this emotion in the
reader, through hyperbole and paradox in which image and statement
mediate a trans-human reality primarily by manifesting their own
inadequacy for doing so. The traditional Christian doctrines of the
infinity and unknowability of God correspond to Kant's "reason";
and to "imagination" correspond all the psychological and verbal means
through which the human mind strives to "represent" this infinity.

Relevant to this aspect of Crashaw's rhetoric is John Floyd's *The
Overthrow of the Protestants Pulpit-Bables* (1612), a defense against a
pamphlet by Crashaw's own father accusing the Jesuits of idolatry
in their poetry:

> . . . Such imaginations, conceipts and discourse are neyther false nor
> vaine; nor false, because as the Logicians teach . . . that there is
> neyther falsity nor untruth in our thoughts, or imaginations, when
> we stay in the first act of the understanding, which is to apprehend a
> thing without judging that it is so, as wee apprehend; as when we ap-
> prehend . . . God as an infinite light, or sea of glory, without bound,
> in which the world like a sponge floateth, though God be not indeed
> as we apprehend; yet are not such apprehensions erroneous or false,
> because we only apprehend, as such an infinite materiall light, not
> judging him to be so: nay we judg the contrary; yet we so apprehend
> him, because our thoughts can reach no higher conceipt of him.[14]

This distinction between apprehension and judgment was a traditional
scholastic doctrine, corresponding to that between the concept of an
object of an essence, and the judgment made on the existential validity
of some proposition about this essence.[15] Crashaw's metaphors call
both acts of the mind into play, in that they invite the reader to realize
at once their positive significance, and to discount them as falling infinitely short of reflecting the divine ineffable. Floyd's point that human minds must apprehend God through material images because
"our thoughts can reach no higher conceipt of him" was of course a
truism when he wrote it.[16] His immediate juxtaposition of two acts of

14. Quoted by Anthony Raspa, "Crashaw and the Jesuit Poetic," *Univ. of
Toronto Quarterly* 36 (1966): 41.
15. Cf. Aquinas, *Summa theologica*, I.85.1.
16. Cf. this passage from the *Christian Morals* of that indefatigable collector

the mind, one which names God through material symbol, and one which discounts this symbol, gives an unusual twist to this ancient topos. In Crashaw's poetry the sublime emotion occurs when images and statements cause these two acts to follow as closely upon each other as possible.

Three poems in *Carmen Deo Nostro* (1652) are prime examples of this technique: "In the Holy Nativity of Our Lord God," "New Year's Day," and "In The Glorious Epiphanie of Our Lord God." All three use the image of the sun to praise Christ, primarily through amplifying its inadequacy for doing so. Crashaw places natural images and their divine referents together as if they were comparable and one could move univocally from one to the other. Then this comparability is pushed to such hyperbolic extremes as to call it into question.

"The Holy Nativity" opens by explicitly identifying the two competing regions of being:

> Come we shepheards whose blest Sight
> Hath mett loue's Noon in Nature's night;
> Come lift we vp our loftyer Song
> And wake the Svn that lyes too long.[17]

(lines 1–4)

The only language available for announcing the arrival of the new dispensation of divine light amid the old law's darkness is the language of the very dispensation that is to be replaced. Therefore, the gulf between "love" and "nature" is simultaneously enforced and bridged by "Noon," which now stands poised, in juxtaposition with "Nature's night," between the realms of nature and grace.

The fourth stanza exhibits a strategy whereby the reader must distinguish sharply between the two different contexts from which clashing components of meaning have been drawn, in order simply to make sense out of the overt statement:

---

and refurbisher of truisms, Sir Thomas Browne: "Created Natures allow of swelling Hyperboles; nothing can be said Hyperbolically of God, nor will his Attributes admit of expressions above their own Exuperances." Norman J. Endicott, ed., *The Prose of Sir Thomas Browne* (Garden City, N. Y., 1967), p. 402.

17. This and all further quotations of Crashaw's poetry are from *The Poems English, Latin and Greek of Richard Crashaw*, ed. L. C. Martin, 2d ed. (Oxford, 1957). The texts of all the poems discussed here are from the *Carmen Deo Nostro* of 1652.

> *Tityrus.* Gloomy night embrac't the Place
> Where The Noble Infant lay.
> The BABE look't vp & shew'd his Face;
> In spite of Darknes, it was DAY.
> It was THY day, SWEET! & did rise
> Not from the EAST, but from thine EYES.
>
> (lines 17–22)

Supernatural referents for "day," "light," "darkness," etc. so totally transcend their ordinary meanings that the speaker must discount these words at the very moment he understands them. Thus the line "In spite of Darknes, it was DAY" enforces the overwhelming victory of Christ's grace over nature by calling for its own self-transcendence as a verbal assertion. The language in which we apprehend nature without grace, and nature with it, remains the same language, with all its limited capacity for articulating references for itself. Consequently, the reader is forced to distinguish the different senses in which the words are used, because the statements imply that both "Darkness" and "Day" belong to the same order of being and statement. In short, Christ's abrogating nature requires a statement in "natural" human language that abrogates itself in an analogous fashion. On the other hand, when the "new" light breaks not from the East, "but from thine EYES," the language of natural phenomena no longer discounts itself, having been replaced by a metaphor that overtly sets grace incarnate over against the natural sun.

Crashaw was sometimes not finicky in distinguishing metaphysical realms, as the first stanza of the "FULL CHORVS" shows:

> Wellcome, all WONDERS in one sight!
> Aeternity shutt in a span.
> Sommer in Winter. Day in Night.
> Heauen in earth, & GOD in MAN.
> Great little one! whose all-embracing birth
> Lifts earth to heauen, stoopes heau'n to earth.
>
> (lines 79–84)

"Sommer in Winter" and "Day in Night" are not the same kind of paradox as "Heauen in earth, & GOD in MAN," nor do they derive from the same dialectic. The first two, like the day/night paradox, set parts of the same paradigm against each other, and consequently set vehicle against tenor. The reader's recognition of the various solecisms forced upon him by these paradoxes, forces him likewise to re-evaluate the grammar wherein these are solecisms, and see that solecism becomes the norm and correctness the aberration. We have a metaphorical summer in a real winter, and a metaphorical day in a real night; except that the reality which "summer" and "day" refer to is more "real" than the other. With "Heauen in earth, & God in Man," however, the situation is reversed. The force of the paradox derives from joining two distinct realms of being, not, as the previous case, from setting against each other items from the same realm.

This poem, along with "New Year's Day" and "The Glorious Epiphanie," develop their themes primarily by hyperbole and diminution, *auxesis* and *meiosis*, and as long as the argument allows the same words to be instruments of both, the tension of the sublime remains.[18] For example, "New Year's Day" predicates the same "adjuncts" of the sun and of the circumcision, thereby placing them on the same level of comparability:

> Rise, thou best & brightest morning!
>   Rosy with a double Red;
> With thine own blush thy cheeks adorning
>   And the dear drops this day were shed.

> (lines 1–4)

By carrying out this comparison to hyperbolic lengths, the poem generates the realization that the two are not really comparable at all. The dignity of Christ's first shedding of blood increases with each insistence on the comparable triviality of the sun:

> Bid thy golden God, the Sun,
>   Burnisht in his best beames rise,
> Put all his red-ey'd Rubies on;
>   These Rubies shall putt out their eyes.

> Let him make poor the purple east,
>   Search what the world's close cabinets keep,
> Rob the rich births of each bright nest
>   That flaming in their fair beds sleep,

18. Rosemond Tuve has noticed that these figures are often peculiar to religious poetry of Crashaw's time, in *Elizabethan and Metaphysical Imagery* (Chicago, 1961), p. 224. In *The Garden of Eloquence*, Henry Peacham describes *auxesis* as "when we use a greater word for a lesse, or thus, when the word is greater then the thing is in deede, which it doeth signify," and *meiosis* as "contrary to that before, when we use a lesse word for a greater, to make the matter much lesse then it is" (Niiii^(r-v)).

Let him embraue his own bright tresses
    With a new morning made of gemmes;
And wear, in those his wealthy dresses,
    Another Day of Diadems.

When he hath done all he may
    To make himselfe rich in his rise,
All will be darknes to the Day
    That breakes from one of these bright eyes.

                            (lines 13–28)

    Auxesis and *meiosis* proceed simultaneously, the one reciprocally enforcing the other, and thereby achieving the effect of reversed perspective. In order to communicate a brightness beyond any seen in the natural world, the poet says that the brightness of Christ's blood will so completely transcend the sun that the latter "will be darknes to the Day," that is, to itself. We are asked to view the sun and the light of day from the viewpoint of divine light; but we can do so only as a "projection" from the one perspective we in fact know: one wherein the sun is the brightest thing we are familiar with. We can realize the transcendent brightness of Christ only by moving both through and away from the image of the sun.

    Crashaw states most completely the epistemology grounding the rhetoric of his religious poetry in "The Glorious Epiphanie of Our Lord God." Not surprisingly, this epistemology is based on the negative theology of the Pseudo-Dionysius. The poem opens by amplifying the day/Christ antinomy seen in the previous two poems (the three magi are singing):

(Chor.)   Look vp, sweet BABE, look vp & see
            For loue of Thee
            Thus farr from home
            The EAST is come
            To seek her self in thy sweet Eyes
(1)   We, who strangely went astray,
            Lost in a bright
            Meridian night,
(2)   A Darkenes made of too much day,
            Becken'd from farr
            By thy fair starr.
            Lo at last haue found our way.
(Chor.)   To THEE, thou DAY of night! thou east of west!

> Lo we at last haue found the way.
> To thee, the world's great vniuersal east.
>
> (lines 10–24)

The poem then generates an *auxesis* in which the language of the natural context of daylight and sun is both used and continually violated:

> The Generall & indifferent DAY.
> (1). All-circling point. All centring sphere,
> The world's one, round, Aeternall year.
> (2.) Whose full & all-vnwrinkled face
> Nor sinks nor swells with time or place;
> (3.) But euery where & euery while
> Is One Consistent solid smile;
>   (1.) Not vext & tost
>   (2.) 'Twixt spring & frost,
> (4.) Nor by alternate shredds of light
> Sordidly shifting hands with shades & night.
>
> (lines 25–35)

If day suffers the vicissitudes of alternating light and dark, then Christ is not "by alternate shredds of light / Sordidly shifting hands with shades & night." The "One Consistent solid smile" and the "full & all-vnwrinkled face" appear somewhat ludicrous, as if the poet were too intent on keeping his assertions and discontinuings symmetrical. This symmetry, in any case, reverses the reader's perspective, for now he sees daylight and the sun from within the perspective of Christ's transcendence over nature:

> (1.) Farewell, the world's false light.
>   Farewell, the white
>   Ægypt! a long farewell to thee
>   Bright IDOL: black IDOLATRY.
> The dire face of inferior DARKNES, kis't
> And courted in the pompous mask of a more specious mist.
>   (2.) Farewell, farewell
>   The proud & misplac't gates of hell,
>   Pertch't, in the morning's way
> And double-guilded as the doores of DAY.
> The deep hypocrisy of DEATH & NIGHT
> More desperately dark, Because more bright.
>
> (lines 48–59)

Within this perspective natural light, and by extension, human modes of seeing and understanding become dark. These modes are all the more "black" (an additional irony) to the degree that men locked up within them refuse to allow any perspectives beyond them. This irony creates the paradox of "Bright IDOL: black IDOLATRY," where we supply the causal connection that finds natural light "black" because "bright." This section of the poem parallels a *meiosis* of natural light to the *auxesis* of Christ's supernatural light.

The poem next proceeds through banishing various sun-cults, toward the darkness of the crucifixion, which will "Decide & settle the Great cause / Of controuerted light" (lines 147–148). The speaker ranges through various paradoxes, the burden of which is that the Sun's "new prodigious night" will become "Their new & admirable light; / The supernatural DAWN of Thy pure day" (lines 173–175). Reference is made to the methods of medieval negative theology, the main source of which, the Pseudo-Dionysius, becomes himself a subject of the poem. Negative theology began by asserting that finite language and conception fall infinitely short of mirroring the perfection of God. Such negative theologians as Meister Eckhart, Nicholas of Cusa, as well as theologians like St. Bonaventura who gave a large place to the *via negativa*, insisted that negative propositions alone come as close as human minds can reach to affirming God as He truly is: "Because most perfect and immense, therefore within all, though not included in them; beyond all, but not excluded from them; above all, but not transported beyond them; below all, and yet not cast down beneath them."[19]

Crashaw draws on this tradition in asserting that the "darkness" of human knowledge can become an instrument for reaching beyond itself; and in the following lines he gives a clear example of "sublime" discounting of poetic language and metaphor:

> (2.) By the oblique ambush of this close night
> Couch't in that conscious shade
> The right ey'd Areopagite

19. The passage in parenthesis is quoted from Bonaventure's *The Mind's Road to God*, trans. George Boas (New York, 1953), p. 38. For Meister Eckhart, cf. Vladimir Lossky, *Théologie Négative et Connaissance de Dieu chez Maître Eckhart* (Paris, 1960); for Cusa see Nicholas Cusanus, *Of Learned Ignorance*, trans. Germain Heron (New Haven, 1954); on the Pseudo-Dionysius, see *Dionysius, the Areopagite, on the Divine Names and the Mystical Theology*, trans. C. E. Rolt (London, 1920).

Shall with a vigorous guesse inuade
And catche thy quick reflex; and sharply see
  On this dark Ground
  To descant THEE.
(3.) O prize of the rich SPIRIT! with what feirce chase
  Of his strong soul, shall he
  Leap at thy lofty FACE,
And seize the swift Flash, in rebound
From this obsequious cloud;
  Once call'd a sun. . . .

(lines 190–202)

From here to the end, the poet states overtly the epistemology ground-ing his poetic rhetoric, by developing the essential points of negative theology:

(1) Thus shall that reuerend child of light,
(2) By being scholler first of that new night,
Come forth Great master of the mystick day;
(3) And teach obscure MANKIND a more close way
By the frugall negatiue light
Of a mos† wise & well-abused Night
To read more legible thine originall Ray,
(*Cho.*) And make our Darknes serue THY day;
Maintaining t'wixt thy world & ours
A commerce of contrary powres,
  A mutuall trade
  'Twixt sun & SHADE,
By confederat BLACK & WHITE
Borrowing day & lending night.

(lines 206–219)

The notions of the last lines can be found in the Pseudo-Dionysius, Meister Eckhart, and Nicholas of Cusa—as, for instance, in this pas-sage from the *Mystical Theology* of the first:

> We pray that we may come unto this Darkness which is beyond light, and, without seeing and without knowing, to see and to know that which is above vision and knowledge through the realization that by not-seeing and by unknowing we attain to true vision and knowl-edge; and thus praise, superessentially, Him Who is superessential, by the abstraction of the essence of all things. . . .[20]

20. *The Mystical Theology and the Celestial Hierarchies of Dionysius the Areopagite* (Nr. Godalming, Surrey, 1949), p. 13.

Though these last lines of Crashaw's poem contrast with other poems in seeming to sum up their technique of "hyperbolic discounting," we must recognize their partial failure in formulating with apparent and univocal completeness the finite/infinite tension. The critic's difficulty in talking about this aspect of Crashaw's poetry parallels the poet's difficulty in speaking about the divine: both must continually signal the need for discounting affirmations and affirming discountings. The process is open-ended, because this open-endedness is what makes it possible. When, for instance, the speaker affirms the new-found power to reach God, it is "in rebound / From this obsequious cloud [i.e., the sun]." Not only must we transcend finite concepts and images in reaching the divine, we can only use equally finite concepts in defining this transcendence. The sun remains the anchor of the vision, no matter how strenuously the speaker attempts to go beyond it. To define the goal as the negation of the starting place is equally to define it as a function of the starting place. Thus this poem requires us to discount not only affirmations but the discountings themselves. Having communicated this ultimate negation to the reader, Crashaw achieves also the apparent goal of his religious poetry; the communication of "something like" the blanking out of both sensation and thought at the moment of mystical union with God.

I believe that those poems that counterpoint "eros" and "agape" achieve a similar negation, by enforcing their simultaneous fusion and separation. These include the two poems on St. Teresa of Avila, "A Hymn to The Name and Honor of the Admirable Sainte Teresa" and "The Flaming Heart," and also the two poems addressed to an anonymous "Mrs. M. R.," "Prayer. An Ode, Which was Praefixed to a little Prayer-book" and "To the Same Party Covncel Concerning Her Choise." The difficulties found in interpreting the role of sexual symbols and allusions in these poems are real, and increase the more one looks at them. William Empson is frankly puzzled by them, because the poems do not make clear the exact point where sexual vehicle and divine tenor meet and divide:

> Crashaw's poetry often has two interpretations, religious and sexual; two situations on which he draws for imagery and detail. But are these *both* the context which is to define the opposites, or is he using one as a metaphor of the other . . . or each as the metaphor of each . . . ?

> Is he generalizing from two sorts of experiences, or finding a narrow
> border of experience that both hold in common?[21]

Empson's point is a valid one as far as it goes. Sexual experience and
religious experience, eros and agape, are different and distinguishable.
Indeed, this difference makes poetic fusions of them possible, according to whatever common ground there may exist between them. As he
runs through Empson's list of possibilities, a reader of Crashaw's
poetry will recognize all of them as to some extent relevant. The main
question then becomes which of them is the controlling one, the end
and purpose of the rest. Though agape often becomes a metaphor for
eros, and vice-versa, yet given Crashaw's overtly presented religious
intentions, it makes all the difference in the world whether or not
agape is "finally" to be seen only as an extension of eros. My own
view is that Crashaw's final purpose (distinguished from short-term
metaphorical transferences) is to sunder agape and eros completely and
totally.[22]

Robert Ellrodt notes that the "vocabulaire religieux de Crashaw
ignore même le terme" lust.[23] He does not think this suggests that Crashaw took an amoral view of fleshly appetite; in fact, just the opposite.
Rather, when Crashaw argues "chastity" in these poems he does not
oppose it overtly to lust or sexuality, but in reverse, he uses sexual
allusions as part of the means of argument. "An Ode . . . Praefixed to
a little Prayer-book," is a possible exception; but even here the lines
are not drawn as sharply as Mr. Empson would desire. It is certain,
however, that Crashaw's final statements about love, human and
divine, can be decided neither by Freudian reductionism nor puritanical
Manicheanism (which are versions of each other), two viewpoints that
reduce agape to eros, or eliminate eros in agape.

Of these four poems, "An Ode" states the problem most overtly.
The poem argues that the young lady should suspend her desire for
sexual love, and instead take God for her "lover." The poem's language,
however, involves a countermovement, whereby agape is described in
erotic terms. The poem does not "reduce" agape to eros, for this possi-

---

21. William Empson, *Seven Types of Ambiguity* (New York, 1957), p. 246.

22. Cf. M. C. D'Arcy, S.J., *The Mind and Heart of Love* (New York, 1956),
for an exhaustive account of the interrelations between eros and agape.

23. Robert Ellrodt, *Les Poètes Métaphysiques Anglais*, première partie, tome 1
(Paris, 1960), p. 396.

bility the poem deliberately abrogates by beginning with such a fusion, in order then to move the young lady (and the reader) in the opposite direction. The central section, in which this dialectic is worked out, begins here:

> WORDS which are not heard with EARES
> (Those tumultuous shops of noise)
> Effectuall wispers, whose still voice
> The soul it selfe more feeles then heares;
> Amorous languishments; luminous trances;
> SIGHTS which are not seen with eyes;
> Spirituall & soul-peircing glances
> Whose pure & subtil lightning flyes
> Home to the heart, & setts the house on fire
> And melts it down in sweet desire
>   Yet does not stay
> To ask the windows leaue to passe that way;
> Delicious DEATHS; soft exalations
> Of soul; dear & diuine annihilations;
>   A thousand vnknown rites
> Of ioyes & rarefy'd delights;
> A hundred thousand goods, glories, & graces,
>   And many a mystick thing
>   Which the diuine embraces
> Of the deare spouse of spirits with them will bring
>   For which it is no shame
> That dull mortality must not know a name.

(lines 65–86)

One does not get very far in describing the effect of these lines by first distinguishing between vehicle and tenor. "Amorous languishments," "luminous trances," and "subtil lightning" do not carry the reader down a one-way street toward agape and deposit him there. On the contrary, all of Empson's alternatives are appropriate; and I would suggest that it is the genius of these lines that they leave the reader only with a very sharp sense that the lines blur two different kinds of experiences. For every negation of the senses—"WORDS which are not heard with EARES," "SIGHTS which are not seen with eyes"—the language of this negation brings back what it denies: "setts the house on fire / And melts it down in sweet desire." Obviously, Crashaw asks the reader to take note of the fusion of spiritual and sensual; and in asking so much, he asks him further to be aware that this is a fusion of some very sharp distinctions. Through the constant juxtaposition between assertions that distinguish agape and eros, and assertions that intermingle the two, the reader becomes aware that this intermingling is specifically of two distinct realms of experience.

The paradoxes in this poem depend for their power on the *a priori* assumption of such distinctions. As in those poems where the sun and daylight are simultaneously employed and discounted as a means of envisioning a supernatural light totally beyond them, so likewise here, but also with a difference. Mystics of whom Crashaw certainly was aware, such as St. Teresa and St. John of the Cross, habitually employed erotic imagery to describe the experience of mystical union with God, while at the same time emphasizing that this experience is wholly non-erotic.[24] Obviously, these poems arouse in the reader not a mystical experience, but a sort of aesthetic analogue to this experience. To the degree that the reader realizes agape by means of erotic imagery, he is required at once to acquiesce provisionally in the fusions of agape with eros, and to distinguish them. The mental dialectic between fusion and distinction, union and separation, generates a species of the "sublime," because the reader must continually negate the meanings of these at the moment he grasps them:

> Happy indeed, who neuer misses
> To improue that pretious hour,
> And euery day
> Seize her sweet prey
> All fresh & fragrant as he rises
> Dropping with a baulmy Showr
> A delicious dew of spices;
> O let the blissfull heart hold fast
> Her heaunly arm-full, she shall tast
> At once ten thousand paradises;
> She shall haue power
> To rifle & deflour

24. Cf. Denis de Rougemont, *Love in the Western World*, trans. Montgomery Belgion (Greenwich, Conn., 1966), pp. 168–73; here de Rougemont points out how the Renaissance Spanish mystics came to employ the language and rhetoric of courtly love poetry, but for rendering experiences which totally transcended courtly love. Cf. also Leo Spitzer, "Three Poems on Ecstasy (John Donne, St. John of the Cross, Richard Wagner)," in *Essays on English and American Literature*, ed. Anna Hatcher (Princeton, 1962), pp. 139–79, for an analysis of a poem of mystical experience by St. John of the Cross similar in its viewpoint on this question to my own.

The rich & roseall spring of those rare sweets
Which with a swelling bosom there she meets
   Boundles & infinite
   Bottomles treasures
Of pure inebriating pleasures.
Happy proof! she shal discouer
   What joy, what blisse,
How many Heau'ns at once it is
To haue her GOD become her LOUER.

(lines 104–124)

The companion poem, "To the Same Party Covncel Concerning Her Choise," even more explicitly sets off agape from eros, taking as its subject the notion that the young lady's disappointment in human love was God's device for turning her to Him:

Let not my lord, the Mighty louer
Of soules, disdain that I discouer
   The hidden art
Of his high strategem to win your heart,
   It was his heaunly art
   Kindly to crosse you
   In your mistaken loue,
   That, at the next remoue
   Thence he might tosse you
   And strike your troubled heart
Home to himself; to hide it in his brest
   The bright ambrosiall nest,
Of loue, of life, & euerlasting rest.
   Happy Mystake!

(lines 41–54)

God's contriving that He "might tosse" her to Him "at the next remoue" recalls the negative theology of "Epiphanie," where the Pseudo-Dionysius is seen to "Leap at thy lofty Face, . . . in rebound / From this obsequious cloud; / Once call'd a sun. . . ." The ideas of rebounding from the earthly to the divine, from eros to agape, and from human conception to mystical vision parallel one another, and summarize the rhetorical techniques I have been describing.

    The famous lines in "A Hymn to . . . Sainte Teresa" describing the mystical death, derived from an English translation of her autobiography published in 1642, are perhaps Crashaw's most extreme attempt to mediate a spiritual experience through sexual allusions:

> O how oft shalt thou complain
> Of a sweet & subtle PAIN.
> Of intolerable IOYES;
> Of a DEATH, in which who dyes
> Loues his death, and dyes again.
> And would for euer so be slain.
> And liues, & dyes; and knows not why
> To liue, But that he thus may neuer leaue to DY.
>
> (lines 97–104)

A comparison of these lines with St. Teresa's own words is instructive:

> I saw, that he [the angel] had a long Dart of gold in his hand; and at
> the end of the iron below, me thought, there was a little fire; and I
> conceaued, that he thrust it, some seuerall times, through my verie
> Hart, after such a manner, as that it passed the verie inwards, of my
> Bowells; and when he drew it back, me thought, it carried away, as
> much as it had touched within me; and left all that, which remained,
> wholy inflamed with a great loue of Almightye God. The paine of it,
> was so excessiue, that it forced me to utter those groanes; and the
> suauitie, which that extremitie of paine gaue, was also so very exces-
> siue, that there was no desiring at all, to be ridd of it; nor can the
> Soule then, receaue anie contentment at all, in lesse, then God Al-
> mightie himself.[25]

What St. Teresa describes as an experience both of great pain and great
"suauitie," Crashaw renders in sequential form. He enhances the contradiction between them by swift alternation: St. Teresa "loues" her
death, "would" forever be slain, does not "know" why "to liue" except
that she "may never leaue" dying. Crashaw adds these expressions of
wish and purpose to express the pain/pleasure of St. Teresa's account
in overtly paradoxical form. In fastening his attention on each of these
terms in succession, the reader experiences a state beyond either
pleasure or pain, for which there is literally no single name. This
inexpressibility becomes overt when the speaker tells of St. Teresa's
final death and union with God:

> When These thy DEATHS, so numerous,
> Shall all at last dy into one,
> And melt thy Soul's sweet mansion;
> Like a soft lump of incense, hasted

25. English translation of 1641, quoted in Martin, ed., *Poems of Richard Crashaw*, p. 437.

By too hott a fire, & wasted
Into perfuming clouds, so fast
Shalt thou exhale to Heaun at last
In a resoluing SIGH, and then
O what? Ask not the Tongues of men.
Angells cannot tell, suffice,
Thy selfe shall feel thine own full ioyes
And hold them fast for euer.

(lines 110–121)

So overtly redolent of sexuality as necessarily to focus the reader's attention on that fact, the lives and deaths, and pleasures and pains of St. Teresa's love of God negate their sexual overtones through the very force with which they are rendered as conceptual contradictions. If we grant Crashaw's identifying the inexpressible with the supra-human experience, we can only conclude that sexuality in the poem communicates the mystical death by requiring of the reader an analogous death of mental conceiving. Rhetorically, sexual allusions and images are used here in exactly the hyperbolic way described by Hoskins and Sherry. The sexual element defines the upper limits of purely human eroticism, and thereby strains toward expressing a transcendent, divine experience, for the grasping of which sexuality likewise presents itself as clearly inadequate. The notion that Crashaw is talking about a pseudo-religious experience blown up out of sexual fantasy might be feasible if sexuality were more clandestinely smuggled into the poem; whereas such a notion is obviated by the fact of its so palpable presence.

"The Flaming Heart vpon the Book and Picture of the seraphicall saint TERESA (As SHE Is VSVALLY expressed with a SERAPHIM biside her)" opens with an extensive apostrophe to the painter. The speaker castigates him for giving the masculine role wholly to the Seraphim (sic), and relegating the passive, feminine role to the saint. Later, St. Teresa coalesces these two functions (lines 69ff.), and these lines reorient the mock attack on the painter as a criticism of the faulty conceptualizing that separates the male and female functions in divine love. The sexual divisions implicit in erotic love are thus dislocated to make them fit the exigencies of agape, thereby demonstrating their own inadequacy for doing so.

St. Teresa in her masculine role wounds others with the dart of God's love, because (presumably in her feminine role) she has herself first been wounded:

For in loue's feild was neuer found
A nobler weapon then a Wovnd.
Loue's passiues are his actiu'st part.
The wounded is the wounding heart.
O Heart! the æquall poise of lou'se both parts
Bigge alike with wounds & darts.
Liue in these conquering leaues; liue all the same;
And walk through all tongues one triumphant Flame
Liue here, great Heart; & loue and dy & kill;
And bleed & wound; and yeild & conquer still.

(lines 71–80)

The concluding lines, though added in the 1652 edition, develop the
direction already hinted at in the last two lines of the original 1648
version: "Let mystick Deaths wait on't [immortal life]; & wise soules
be / The loue-slain wittnesses of this life of thee" (lines 83–84):

O thou vndanted daughter of desires!
By all thy dowr of Lights & Fires;
By all the eagle in thee, all the doue;
By all thy liues & deaths of loue;
By thy larg draughts of intellectuall day,
And by thy thirsts of loue more large then they;
By all thy brim-fill'd Bowles of feirce desire
By thy last Morning's draught of liquid fire;
By the full kingdome of that finall kisse
That seiz'd thy parting Soul, & seal'd thee his;
By all the heauen's thou hast in him
(Fair sister of the Seraphim!
By all of Him we haue in Thee;
Leaue nothing of my Self in me.
Let me so read thy life, that I
Vnto all life of mine may dy.

(lines 93–108)

The poem's teleology in its final form ends with a prayer that the
speaker be allowed to give over self wholly to God in a way analogous
to the mystical deaths of the saint herself. That this passage does not
express a mystical experience has been acutely noted by Helen C.
White:

> . . . It is not mystical in the sense that in itself it involves or expresses
> the poet's achievement of the purpose he shares with Teresa. Indeed,

far from being absorbed in his own contemplation of God, the poet is quite aware of something in his own consciousness, apart from the object of that consciousness, and that he is expressing with singular passion and beauty.[26]

This emptying of self is similar to that described at length by St. John of the Cross in *Ascent of Mount Carmel*.[27] All desires of the individual soul attaching it to the world and itself must be systematically purged, leaving it wholly "dark" for the entrance of God. The specifically spiritual significance of these lines thus become one with the pattern of verbal action that has led up to them. The poem's invitation to the reader to acquiesce in an analogous "emptying of conception" *vis à vis* the masculine/feminine paradoxes enacts this significance on the rhetorical level. Indeed, all the poems discussed here operate on the assumption that the aesthetic experience of a "sublime" transcendence of conceptualization is analogous to a trans-human religious or mystical experience.

Clearly then, Crashaw's poetry takes its rhetoric as one of its own subjects. *Hyperbole, auxesis,* and *meiosis* refer to those arts of language through which the resources of humanly made syntax can render a reality that the writer (and, hopefully, the reader) understand as beyond such syntax in its "greatness." These are names, in other words, of specific ways of naming. As all five of the Renaissance rhetoricians previously cited agree, such names depend for their rhetorical efficacy on the reader's prior awareness of the discrepancy between word and thing. That such is the case with these figures they all take for granted. But as I have tried to indicate, such observations do not exhaust a rhetorical situation wherein the strengths and weaknesses of rhetorical devices are an overt part of the content. Crashaw's poetry requires the reader to become a rhetorical critic, and to incorporate his recognition of the "exaggerations" and "inadequacies" of *hyperbole*

26. Helen C. White, *The Metaphysical Poets: A Study in Religious Experience* (New York, 1962), p. 223.

27. Cf. E. Allison Peers, ed., *Ascent of Mount Carmel by Saint John of the Cross* (Garden City, N. Y., 1958), p. 27: "The reason for which it is necessary for the soul, in order to attain to Divine union with God, to pass through this dark night of mortification of the desires and denial of pleasures in all things, is because all the affections which it has for creatures are pure darkness in the eyes of God, and, when the soul is clothed in these affections, it has no capacity for being enlightened and possessed by the pure and simple light of God, if it first cast them not from it; for light cannot agree with darkness; since, as Saint John says: *Tenebrae enim non comprehenderunt*. That is: The darkness could not receive the light."

into his understanding of the poetry itself. But the poetry expresses the possibilities and limits of its own rhetoric by mediating realities that are non-rhetorical—the limits of human concepts and names as they confront divine mysteries. These realities are not only mediated by the rhetoric; they likewise comment in turn on the rhetoric itself.

Crashaw's poems continually treat two widely separate realities as if they existed on the same existential plane. Their hyperbolic rhetoric thus becomes apparent to the reader only after he sees that such hyperboles are treated *as if* they were adequate to divine mysteries. This presentation of infinitely separated realities as if they belonged to an unbroken, graded and connected scale of being corresponds to Kant's notion that reason desires to comprehend the totality of an infinite series "in *one* intuition," thereby achieving a joint "*presentation* of all these members of a progressively increasing series." Imagination, in attempting to represent adequately such a reality "in a whole of intuition," only succeeds in exhibiting "its own limits and inadequacy." This realization in turn corresponds to the reader's discovery that the poetry's presentation of finite symbols and divine realities as if they corresponded presents just the opposite: the fact that they do not.

But as Kant points out, the emotion of the "sublime" depends on the clash between two modes of knowing: the "reason" which grasps independently of the imagination (and of the poetry's rhetoric) the transcendence of divine mystery; and the imagination that seeks to comprehend and express this mystery. Consequently, a purely rhetorical analysis of *hyperbole* in Crashaw's poetry cannot fully explain the tensions it creates. Such an analysis deals with exaggeration as a function of verbal dislocation and paradox only, while necessarily ignoring the fact that the reader's prior awareness of these mysteries is a precondition of his recognizing verbal dislocation and paradox. This discussion calls attention to the necessity of including "extra-rhetorical" information in order to explain the full effect of *hyperbole, auxesis,* and *meiosis* in general. As such, this type of rhetorical analysis makes us more fully aware that Crashaw's poetic practice reaches beyond mere verbal juggling, to incorporate the already established categories of the reader's intellectual acceptances into the poetry's rhetorical address.

10. The Crossing of Rhetoric and Poetry in the English Renaissance

THOMAS O. SLOAN
UNIVERSITY OF CALIFORNIA, BERKELEY

L ATE IN THE fifteenth century a painter in Valladolid interpreted
the Annunciation in a retable, in which Mary is kneeling, book
in hand, eyes averted, with her head tilted gracefully toward the door.
Standing in the doorway is the angel Gabriel, speaking the first words
of the *Ave Maria*. Outside the open door and majestic in the heavens
visible over Gabriel's head is God the Father, and proceeding from His
mouth on beams of light which crown Mary's head are the Son, as an
infant carrying His cross, and the Holy Spirit, as a Dove encircled by
light. The painting might be interpreted didactically as a depiction of
orthodox teachings on divine eloquence. Angels, Aquinas had taught,
are pure thought and, assuming a form not unlike man's, express that
thought in ways not unlike human, verbal eloquence; whereas God's
eloquence, St. Augustine had most forcefully argued, inheres in
images, natural and supernatural things, which mysteriously penetrate
the soul. On the other hand, the painting may also be seen as allego-
rizing certain ideas about *secular* rhetoric as well. For one thing, it
shows speech and images as separable instruments of thought in an
act of persuasion; Gabriel's speech and God's images are discrete
elements of rhetoric. Both, moreover are sensuous; speech, like any
act resembling human eloquence, must appeal to the senses, most notably to the ear, but God's images have even greater sensory appeal and
are thus more efficacious. In fact, St. Thomas had argued that all
images, including those presented verbally, make a longer-lasting
impression on the soul than non-imagistic, virtually non-sensuous "intellectual" arguments.[1] And when we note that Mary is not facing

---

1. See *Summa theologica*, I.1.9; I.84.7, 8; II–II.49.1.

those addressing her, but is rather receiving these messages in contemplation, with Gabriel's words ringing in her ears but with God's images penetrating her understanding, we have before us a painting that, for all its religious import, can serve as a starting point for an essay on the character of rhetorical theory throughout the English Renaissance, at least for the period encompassed by this book. At the first of that period, the truths about sensuousness emblematized in the retable hold; toward the end of that period they were challenged as the Englishman became more and more puzzled by the extent to which sensuousness was the proper means of apprehending God. This change had immeasurable significance for the character of rhetorical theory.

Probably no single feature of the Renaissance has received such extensive attention in the last twenty years as rhetoric. Intellectual historians and literary critics, in particular, have found in rhetoric a useful way of approaching the unique qualities of their subjects, the former taking rhetoric as the embodiment of an attitude toward experience,[2] the latter taking rhetoric to mean the major theory and practice of the arts of language including above all poetry.[3] What has not been attempted yet is an approach that is at once historical *and* critical—one within which this admittedly relevant concept, rhetoric, is experienced historically, as a definite body of theory evolving within Renaissance culture, and critically, as an art whose very nature both illuminates and is illuminated by changes in the poetry of the time.

I shall concentrate on that segment of this broad subject which

2. The work of historians most relevant to students of rhetoric is, of course, in their studies of communication. See, for example, the two excellent articles by Elizabeth L. Eisenstein, "The Advent of Printing and the Problem of the Renaissance," *Past and Present* 45 (Nov. 1969): 19–89; and "Some Conjectures about the Impact of Printing on Western Society and Thought: A Preliminary Report," *Journal of Modern History* 49 (1968): 1–56. Another relevant and incisive work is Nancy S. Struever's *The Language of History in the Renaissance: Rhetoric and Historical Consciousness in Florentine Humanism* (Princeton, 1970). The forthcoming volume from MIT Press, *Communication and Propaganda in World History*, will contain an essay by William J. Bouwsma, to be entitled "The Renaissance and the Broadening of Communication."

3. Twenty years have passed since C. S. Lewis wrote that "Rhetoric is the greatest barrier between us and our ancestors. . . . Probably all our literary histories, certainly that on which I am engaged, are vitiated by our lack of sympathy on this point. If ever the passion for formal rhetoric returns, the whole story will have to be rewritten and many judgments may be reversed" (*English Literature in the Sixteenth Century Excluding Drama* [New York, 1954], p. 61). Although we may still lack sympathy for "formal" rhetoric, students of literature should now be in a better position than Lewis was to understand what rhetoric is and what it was.

pertains to the scope of this book, namely English rhetoric and poetry between Wyatt and Milton. In turn, the part of rhetoric which shall concern me most is not style, or *elocutio*, but the very heart of the creative process, that part which is usually listed first in theory, *inventio*, or finding the thought. It is important to keep in mind that, regardless of how linear or sequential the five parts of rhetoric (*inventio*, *dispositio* or arranging the thought, *elecutio*, *pronuntiatio* or delivering orally the thought so found, arranged, and adorned, and *memoria*) became from Cicero on, the traditional rhetorician continued to regard these parts as offices in (or, loosely, aspects of) the speaker's performance either in his preparation or before an audience, offices which in theory had become only nominally detached from each other, for each simply served to describe aspects of a speaker-audience relationship (a "field of energy" we might call it today) out of which discourse is created. *Inventio* is crucial to the identity of rhetoric. Without it rhetoric has little to offer which one may not learn in logic or grammar, the other two traditional *artes sermocinales*. Centering on *inventio* allows us to see some of the reasons why traditional rhetoricians insisted on the interconnectedness of the five offices; it should also let us see the extent to which those reasons became outdated in the latter part of the sixteenth century. Through centering on *inventio* I will explore two radical transformations in English rhetorical theory between Wyatt and Milton: the first occurred when the Ramists revised rhetorical theory in such a way that they made the orator's creative process totally unlike the poet's; the second occurred when rhetorical theory converged with devotional theory and once more established common ground, for a while at least, between orators and poets.

Central to these two transformations is a matter which, again, may be emblematized by the panel from the Valladolid retable. Both God and Gabriel are rhetors appealing not to reason exclusively—for neither is simply arguing, using enthymemes or syllogisms—but to the will through the imagination, the senses, and the passions. If this is divine persuasion, the human analogue necessarily makes rhetoric an "imaginative" art encompassing not only poetry but virtually all means whereby passions are aroused. For if we follow these implications to their farthest reaches and take rhetoric broadly to mean whatever moves the soul, we begin to understand not merely the difficulties of considering it solely an art of *language* but the religious, moral, ethical, and existential problems of making so complex a matter an art at all. Nonetheless, from antiquity rhetoric was regarded as essentially a linguistic art, specifically an art of public speaking. As medieval society became more literate and frequently less open to free public discussion than Roman society had been, rhetoric increasingly resembled a kind of grammar of style. Its potentially great scope grew narrower. The early sixteenth-century Englishman thought of rhetoric mainly as a rigid discipline suitable for teaching Latin to little boys. Deep within the art, perhaps concealed by its rigidity, were unresolved questions concerning the rhetor's appeals to other men's reason, the highest faculty of their immortal soul, and appeals to their passions, which were aroused through inciting their senses, faculties of their animal soul. Language, of course, could be used to appeal to both. How much it should be used to appeal to either was a question beyond the ken of most rhetoricians, who were in effect stuck with the widely held belief that *spoken* language entered the intellect through man's least trustworthy, most seductive sense. When the art was loosened up, expanded, and adapted to the practical uses of English, including printed English, all unresolved questions concerning appeals to reason and the passions had become timely and crucial. The first transformation noted above completely disrupted all possibilities for achieving a balance between the two. The second achieved something of a balance temporarily, but went even farther than the first in totally subverting the traditional character of rhetorical theory.

1

English adaptation of traditional rhetoric—the conservative standard which made the Ramists seem radicals—is best represented by Thomas Wilson's *The Arte of Rhetorike* (1553). Paradoxically, Wilson's work was both one of the first major traditional rhetorics in English and one of the last, for its spectacular success was eventually overwhelmed by revisionists. The book, written in an amiably perscriptive manner, epitomizes Ciceronian doctrines. Significantly, the differences between Wilson and Cicero, even considering the superficiality of the former, are far less noticeable than those between Wilson and Fraunce—or, better, between Wilson and Obadiah Walker in the middle of the seventeenth century.

Wilson's definition of *inventio* reveals two features of traditional rhetoric as adapted by the English:

The findyng out of apte mater, called otherwise Inuencion, is a searchyng out of thynges true, or thynges likely, the whiche maie reasonably sette furth a matter, and make it appere probable. The places of Logique geue good occasion to finde out plentifull matter. And therefore thei that will proue any cause and seke onely to teache thereby the truthe, muste search out the places of Logique, and no doubte thei shall finde much plentie. (Fol. 3^v)

As always, invention is a means of "analysis" as well as "genesis"— to use the terms later insisted upon by the Ramists. It is useful both for examining a case, issue, or document and for generating ideas. But, as this is a central principle of traditional rhetoric, *idea and utterance were not conceptually or even theoretically distinct*. In fact, this very principle of overlapping, or fusion of elements that were later to become discontinuous, is the first and most important traditional feature of Wilson's *inventio*. The idea or thought, which might proceed from a "searchyng out of thynges true, or thynges likely," is not itself separable from the process of reasonably setting "furth a matter" and making it appear "probable"; that is, thought is not separable from speech, or image (for that matter) from utterance, or invention from disposition and elocution. Indeed, the structure of Wilson's book is a concrete demonstration of the fusion of traditional rhetorical offices, those aimed at finding the thought as well as those aimed at expressing it. At the first of his book Wilson lists the five offices and indicates that he plans to take up each one in turn, but in discussing any one he refers to the other four so frequently and so casually that it becomes obvious to the reader that the naming of rhetorical offices is merely academic, a convenience for theoretical discussion.

Secondly, although Wilson does acknowledge a distinction between the demonstrable ("thynges true") and the probable ("thynges likely"), he places both within the purview of rhetoric. For Wilson is not bothered by the overlapping of logic (an art of the demonstrable) and rhetoric (an art of the probable). Nor, as his companion volume *The Arte of Logike* (1551) makes even clearer, is he concerned about the differences between logic and dialectic (like rhetoric, a probable art). The orator in his search for probability must occasionally consider features of his argument in abstraction from the specific nature of his audience, or he must sometimes have as his intent teaching the truth rather than persuasion—and in these cases he needs the assistance of "logike." Wilson places a brief abstraction of logic within his book on rhetoric, and is not at all bothered that when the orator uses the "places of Logique" he might be stepping outside the bounds of rhetoric—for these bounds were not narrowly defined in the tradition which Wilson inherited and sought to perpetuate.

However, it was precisely the construction of narrow definitions for all the language arts in the name of pedagogical efficiency that became the task of the Ramists, who appeared on the English scene in the final quarter of the sixteenth century. Much has been written of late about the English followers of Petrus Ramus, and many extreme charges have been hurled at their ghosts, ranging from insignificance to epoch-making. Early in the controversy, one scholar branded the fight a "New Petromachia."[4] My own position in the controversy is that the Ramists were indeed significant not as innovators of new trends but rather as reflectors—even at times comic reflectors—of ongoing intellectual developments whose momentum and complexity often exceeded the grasp of the Ramist mind. The Ramists were educational reformers, an identification that must continually be stressed. While it is true that they appeared on the scene just as the printing press was beginning to take strong hold on the imagination and just as the call for a "new science" was becoming most vociferous, it is also true that in an earlier time their theories, in spite of how revisionist the Ramists themselves considered their work, might have seemed merely like vapid epitomes of Aristotelianism bent to the exigencies of teaching little boys a new and rapid way to acquire what Cicero had called "eloquence." Indeed, had not their simple-minded method of achieving pedagogical efficiency made vital connections with other intellectual developments, had not the Ramists appeared on the scene with something that *looked* like a new rhetoric at the time the call was out for a new rhetoric, it is unlikely that we should ever have heard of them except in a few mouldering footnotes.

Father Walter J. Ong, who of all modern scholars has studied the Ramists most extensively and intensively, places them in an almost direct line of influence extending from Peter of Spain into the age of Gutenberg.[5] But if its intellectual milieu sheds much light on Ramism, the reverse may also be demonstrable. In that respect, there are at least

4. George Watson, "Ramus, Miss Tuve, and the New Petromachia," *MP* 55 (1958): 259–62.

5. *Ramus, Method, and the Decay of Dialogue* (Cambridge, Mass., 1958) and *Ramus and Talon Inventory* (Cambridge, Mass., 1958), are Father Ong's two major works on Ramus.

two features of Ramism which, probably because of their connection with other intellectual developments, had a lasting effect on rhetorical theory.

First, motivated primarily by a desire for pedagogical efficiency, the Ramists solved one major problem only in a manner that created another, one that continues to plague the educational scene: they stringently departmentalized the arts. The Ramists knew that any overlapping between the arts is potentially inefficient; a rhetorician, for example, should not also have to teach logic. The easiest way to solve the problem was to divide knowledge into departments and insist that what belongs to one department shall not be found in another; rhetoric and logic were to be housed in different parts of the building. Then, like college registrars making room assignments, the Ramists compartmentalized the sections of each department. And to accomplish this they used the simplest of all principles of division, the dichotomy. Ramist logic taught *only* invention and disposition, Ramist rhetoric *only* style and delivery; and these parts became the concern of these arts exclusively, that is doctrines of invention and disposition were to be found only in "logic," of style and delivery only in "rhetoric."

But, secondly, this impulse toward compartmentalization paradoxically collapsed the continually maintained though increasingly vague distinction between rhetoric, logic, and dialectic. Aristotle had insisted that a rhetor thinks about a problem differently than a logician does, each having his own methods of invention that in turn resemble while differing from the dialectician's method. Traditionalists continued to teach that whereas rhetoric and dialectic were arts of disputation the major difference between them lay in the audiences for each—the rhetor had a heterogeneous audience, the dialectician an audience of experts; on the other hand, traditional logic was not an art of disputation at all but an art of "scientific" reasoning which involved no audience considerations whatsoever. But by the sixteenth century the arts of logic and dialectic had gradually become conflated; and though ancient distinctions were occasionally paid lip-service, the conflated logic/dialectic increasingly resembled rhetoric. Another way of putting this matter is that "philosophy" had, somewhat in the Ciceronian manner, become by the sixteenth century *rhetoricized*, its conceptual structure dependent upon the duad "invention" and "judgment." It was the Ramists' folly to attempt a de-rhetoricization of philosophy without any profound change in its conceptual structure. Before the Ramists, logic in the sixteenth century consisted mainly of two parts, both of which were taken from dialectic: invention, which was based largely on the ten topics (or "commonplaces," as they were called both in logic/dialectic and in rhetoric), and disposition, which was usually called "judgment" for it was seen mainly as a process whereby arguments drawn from the commonplaces were cast into the form of valid statement. But when the Ramists arrived upon this scene, they totally dispelled all distinctions, however vague, between various modes of thought, including an insistence that the rhetor's "inventive" process does not differ from the logician's—all for the purpose of establishing discrete arts. There was to be only one system of thought, of invention, and it was to be housed in "logic." And, for that matter, there was to be only one system of disposition or judgment (the two names were to become as interchangeable as logic and dialectic), and it, too, was to be housed in "logic." In short, because *all* matters pertaining to invention and disposition/judgment were to be found only in "logic" (whose synonym was now "dialectic"), these procedures were meant to be useful alike to logicians, orators, scientists, poets, and historians.

Although it is true that this ostensibly new re-arrangement only carried to an extreme certain pervasive conceptions, what is significant in it is that its assignment of all forms of reasoning to "logic" forces into rhetorical theory a linear separation of thought from speech. The distinction is a strange one to rhetoricians, regardless of how familiar it had been for centuries to logicians. It is present in St. Augustine, as it is present not only in St. Thomas but in the theories of all those late-medieval logicians who laid the basis for the quantification of thought in symbolic logic. It is suggested, as we noted earlier, in the Valladolid retable in its representation of images penetrating the understanding without any verbal interposition. Fundamental to the Ramist re-arrangement of the language arts is the notion that thinking does not need to be vocalized—in fact, it does not need to be done verbally at all; it may be done for example with geometric figures, just as persuasion may be achieved with non-verbal images. By contrast, if ever a traditional rhetorician detached a thought from its verbal expression he did so only to reword it, as he might in searching out an idea from a collection of other men's inventions (these collections were usually called "commonplace books," the name echoing rhetorical and dialectical instruments of invention) and then working that idea into his own speech. Moreover, if it is true that the rhetor's creative process from the time of Cicero on had become increasingly linear, it is also true that this is a feature in which literacy itself must have played some role. Using a commonplace book, for example, would make the inventive process a little more discrete and even a little more silent than using formulas in an act of oral composition. But the Ramists gave vastly more linearity to the creative act by actually placing "thought" in one art, "speech" in another. As the English Ramist Abraham Fraunce states in *The Lawiers Logike* (1588) "reasoning may be without talking," and he defines "logike" as an art of reasoning (fol. 1). Though the procedures of Ramist *inventio* remained fundamentally verbal and fundamentally silent, Ramist *dispositio* emphasized a silent but non-verbal and basically visual technique of arrangement lovingly called "natural method," which consisted of disposing the parts of a discourse in space, like objects on a bracketed grid dividing a general thought into its most particular and most indivisible components. At the very least, the difference between *silent thought* and *spoken language* is for the Ramists a radical distinction between "logic" and "rhetoric." Grouped together within "rhetoric" were all considerations of vocalized discourse or oral performance. Style, for example, the first part of Ramist rhetoric, encompassed all arrangements of sound patterns, a feature which resolves such confusing differences as those between the "rhetorical" figure *metaphor* and its "logical" counterpart *comparatives*: the former was a device for impressing one's auditors, the latter for thought itself. Delivery (*pronuntiatio*), the other part of Ramist rhetoric, encompassed voice and gesture, giving added emphasis to the identity of "rhetoric" as a uniquely spoken art. The poet and the preacher might have need of "rhetoric," but the essayist and historian probably would not. The writer of a scientific or educational treatise certainly would not. In short, there were forms of printed discourse that in theory were becoming regarded as less and less oral in nature, and the Ramists go much farther than the medieval *artes dictaminis* in marking the ultimate demise in theory of anything like ancient modes of oral composition.

It is possible to recast these two features I have described—compartmentalization and the separation of thought from language, particularly from speech—in a way that is less likely to impute to the Ramists an undue amount of sophistication. To do this, we must review briefly the Ramist procedure for creating discourse. One invented by processing a thought—drawn itself from traditional knowledge or perhaps from observation—through the commonplaces, casting it ultimately into the shape of an axiom, and then fitting that axiom into a discourse in which the movement was from the general to the specific by dichotomies. The first part of this process, all of which was now encompassed by "logic," was known as invention, the second part disposition, which now included (as in casting thought into axioms) judgment. This process, the Ramists believed, preserved the thought in its natural state. A thought so "invented" and given shape had been subjected to "natural method," the most efficient way of completing the thought, of teaching it to others, or of retaining it in the memory. Considering people or audiences always introduced an "unnatural" element, causing a thought to be methodized "prudentially" by following or disrupting a chronological order or by placing one's relatively strongest arguments in his case first and last. Such other personal considerations as the sound of one's voice, if it was not to be hushed altogether, was relegated to minor matters of style and delivery in "rhetoric." One important feature, therefore, is *systematization*, a linear arrangement of the creative process into steps—in this case, from shaping the thought to vocalizing it. And a second feature is *impersonality*, a quality which was, confusedly, seen as most natural to the conditions of thought.

Turning to poetic practice and poetic theory extant in prefaces, letters, and apologies written during the time of the Ramists, one would find that these two features are exactly the ones which show the gap between poetry and the kind of theory the Ramists propounded. True, insofar as the Ramists were concerned with how the "mind in general" associates and orders, Ramist theory echoed themes of poetic theory and practice. But insofar as the Ramists insisted upon impersonality— or what was later to be called "objectivity"—and systematization, they were worlds away from the poets. Or perhaps it was the poets who were worlds away from the dawning "scientific" spirit of their age which was as hostile to traditional poetry as it was to traditional rhetoric. In the Ramists, this hostility to poetry was only crudely expressed, as a kind of vague insistence that poetry was really no more than metered discourse, any metered discourse; and as if to insist upon its similarities with other forms of discourse the Ramists used poetry as examples of arguments and ornaments in their theory. But poets themselves *seemed* to make the more egregious error; at a time when man was apparently seeking the kind of anti-traditional rhetoric

221

the Ramists offered, poets, particularly the humanist poets, of the late sixteenth and throughout the seventeenth century spoke of their art as resembling traditional rhetoric.[6]

Because "invention" and "disposition" or "judgment" seemed to name processes that fundamentally resembled their major creative tasks, poets felt no compunction in speaking of their art in these terms. And poets applied them in such a way that the terms appeared to signify—not a profoundly rhetoricized philosophy and certainly not the then-current Ramist efforts to systematize the means of conceptualization—but the traditional rhetorician's unsystematic and to Ramist eyes unmethodical conflation of thought with verbal expression. In general, the poets were simply allowing their audiences to interpret their art in terms of another art which was being so drastically revised that its identity was in jeopardy. John Rainolds in his youthful oration on poetry as the supreme persuader,[7] or any of the great humanist poets, such as Sidney in his insistence that poetry combines the best of logic and rhetoric,[8] or Ben Jonson in his reversal of Cicero's patronizing attitude toward poets[9]—these strategies in effect argued that not only is poetry a species of traditional rhetoric but it is indeed a superior rhetoric. And these strategies, to repeat, were particularly disruptive at this point in time. For regardless of how indicative of their milieu the Ramists are, their revised rhetoric and their ignorance of poetry more than simply bespeaks a radical and growing suspicion of traditional rhetoric—including not only its lack of method but also, as we shall examine below, its usual trappings, such as ornaments, images, and all sensory and emotional appeals, those features which the Ramists disposed of simply by divorcing them theoretically from the proper processes of "thought." Among the scientific vanguard, a new idea about Truth was emerging, and it was best suited to plain, objective, systematized discourse—preferably prose. In the earlier century Wilsonian poets like Gascoigne had deplored "rhyme without reason." But part of the emerging temper of the new times could ex-

6. See O. B. Hardison, Jr., "The Orator and the Poet: The Dilemma of Humanist Literature," *Journal of Medieval and Renaissance Studies* 1 (1971): 33–44.

7. John Rainolds, *Oratio in Laudem Artis Poeticae*, intro. William Ringler and trans. Walter Allen, Jr. (Princeton, 1940), p. 39.

8. Sir Phillip Sidney, *An Apologie for Poetrie*; see reprint in *Elizabethan Critical Essays*, ed. G. Gregory Smith (London, 1904), I, esp. pp. 158–72.

9. Ben Jonson, *Timber, or Discoveries*; see reprint in O. B. Hardison, Jr., *English Literary Criticism: The Renaissance* (New York, 1963), p. 284.

press its motto in the cliché that praises a discourse for containing "more truth than poetry." Surely it is this very temper which fuels Francis Bacon's fire, into which he tosses all poetry before entering at last "the judicial palace of the mind."[10]

But certain poets, who were undoubtedly aware of important differences between what was happening in contemporary rhetorical theory and how they understood their own poetic practice, continued to speak of their creative processes in terms clearly at odds with the new rhetoric. I shall argue that the non-innovative, even defiantly traditional character of their terms could be taken as an assertion, however disruptive, of the poets' credo—as the following example should indicate.

TO E. OF D. WITH SIX HOLY SONNETS
by John Donne (1609)

See Sir, how as the Suns hot Masculine flame
 Begets strange creatures in Niles durty slime,
 In me, your fatherly yet lusty Ryme
(For, these songs are their fruits) have wrought the same;
 But though the'ingendring force from whence they came
 Bee strong enough, and nature doe admit
 Seaven to be borne at once, I send as yet
But six, they say, the seaventh hath still some maime;
 I choose your judgement, which the same degree
 Doth with her sister, your invention, hold,
 As fire these drossie Rymes to purifie,
 Or as Elixar, to change them to gold;
You are that Alchimist which alwaies had
Wit, whose one spark could make good things of bad.[11]

At first glance, the poem would appear to be utilizing metaphorically the linearity of rhetorical "invention" and "disposition/judgment," a linearity present in traditional as well as Ramist theories. The Earl's "Ryme" had provided Donne with ideas which he later employed in creating seven sonnets; thus, the Earl's "invention" had also become Donne's. In the immoderately courteous style of the pe-

---

10. *Selected Writings of Francis Bacon*, intro. and notes by Hugh G. Dick (New York, 1955), p. 247.

11. From *The Complete Poetry of John Donne*, ed. John T. Shawcross (New York, 1967), p. 338.

riod, Donne's sonnet continually disparages his own work while praising the Earl's: the former are "strange creatures" born on "durty slime," the latter is an "ingendring force," "hot Masculine" but of pure essence like a "flame," both irresistible ("lusty") and loving ("fatherly"). In requesting the Earl's "judgement," that is his criticism of Donne's work, the poem continues the opening comparisons. If Donne's poems are "bad," they need only the "one spark" of the Earl's "Wit" to make them good. That "flame" which Donne associates with the Earl's "invention," he can associate also with the Earl's "judgement," because of their near-relation. Fire may purify, as in burning away dross from gold. Or, intensifying his image, Donne states that in this case the Earl's invention and judgment may become the quintessence, the purest of all substances, which can turn even base metal into gold —whether gold is "in" that base metal or not. The praise has been extraordinarily increased.

Actually, the poem diverges sharply from its contemporary rhetorical theory, a divergence that has little to do with the ostensible linearity of "invention" and "judgment." Above all the poem insists that the methods of poetic creativity are deeply subjective and at the same time curiously transactional, features expressed here in terms that are analogously sexual and mystical. "Invention" and "judgement" are not the creative arts, the efficient causes of creativity. They are, rather, passive elements and thus appropriately characterized as feminine, "sisters." The "ingendring force," which is masculine, must either work through these elements to "purifie" the materials of art or fuse perfectly with them (like the alchemist's "Elixar," a perfect fusion of mercury and sulfur, feminine and masculine) and so transform even the grossest matter into pure gold. The efficacy of the alchemist/poet is ultimately dependent not upon manner, means, or material but upon "Wit," characterized here as both the Elixar and the alembic's fire. The latter as it were "shuts up" the poem (like a rhetorical *epiphonema*) by echoing the "hot Masculine flame" of the opening line. Further, "invention" and "judgement," though skillful puns for the kinds of meaning we noted in the first paraphrase, also become, as "sisters," the veritable Muses of the poet. But Donne's final meaning is potentially more complex, for by making the two arts feminine Donne has implied they are but elements, the passive elements, of the creative act, whose mystery can only be accomplished through their union with the active, masculine force—an implication which is further strengthened not only by the sexual allusions but also by the ostensible purpose of the poem itself, to locate creativity conceptually not in solitary confinement but in the locus classicus of the traditional rhetorician, in transactions between people.

In contrast, the *orator's* creative act was coming to be understood quite differently in Donne's day. As we noted earlier concerning the Ramists: the creative process for all speakers was becoming theoretically systematized 'and personal. With these qualities, the creative process was becoming theoretically insulated from conceptualization in sexual, mystical, or above all transactional terms. As Ong has put it, in speaking of Ramist *inventio*, in particular the ten topics, or commonplaces:

> The different sorts of units in which thought is cast all tend to be assimilated to one another as they come to be viewed as little somethings-or-other which go into and come out of boxes, and which are, on closer inspection, themselves boxes out of which still further units may be "drawn."[12]

In their efforts to systematize the creative process, the Ramists had objectified thought itself and had viewed discourse as an arrangement of objects in space. The view is at a great, impersonal remove from the "outcries" of Aristotle's categories or the "seats" of Cicero's arguments—and from the practice of Renaissance poets. In Donne's references to the creative process there is neither impersonality nor systematization. And there *is* passion; Donne charges his ideas and images with an emotional force which by its very nature runs counter to impersonality and systematization.

If the rhetoricians were seeking to objectify the creative process, I think one might interpret the function of post-Wilsonian poets as redeeming their art from that state, an interpretation that might illuminate the traditionally rhetorical (and therefore defiant) critical language these poets employed in naming the processes of their art. Poetry—at least that poetry that we admire most from the English Renaissance—depends upon persons, voices (even "metered discourse" presupposes a voice), images (abstract thought—the word—has to have a body—must become flesh), and a growth that is as inevitable and as miraculous as human growth. Nowhere in the rhetorical theory of the time is there the slightest acknowledgement of this necessity.

12. Ong, *Ramus, Method, and the Decay of Dialogue*, p. 122.

2

A second radical transformation, which may also be approached through the Ramist revisionist attempts, concerns the traditional rhetorical subject known as *amplification*. Amplification was less precisely a separate part of traditional rhetoric than a subject which pervaded all five of the offices. The Ramists simply dropped all mention of the subject and made no issue of their inattention. Yet the loss of amplification in rhetorical theory actually points toward some of the gravest philosophical questions facing seventeenth-century man, such as those involving the arousing of passions. Of course, doctrines of passions are relevant to both of the transformations I am discussing. The first transformation amounted to an intensifying of the linearity in rhetorical theory to the extent that thought was placed at an "objective" and silent remove from speech. But the second, by eliminating a central rhetorical subject, eliminated also all instruction in the passions.

The principle of amplification is best understood through the traditional rhetorical figure *amplificatio*, usually defined as an "increasing" or "diminishing," making things seem greater than they are or less than they appear to be in order to control the audience's impression. On the most general level, amplification is related to *copia*, word-hoard, even verbosity, and in traditional rhetoric it was closely allied with the very process whereby the orator made his ideas available to his audience. But amplifying meant not simply clarity or perspicacity; invariably it pertained to the psychology of audiences. "The beautie of Amplifying," states Thomas Wilson, "standeth most in apte mouyng of affections" (fol. 71ᵛ). For Wilson's statement the history of rhetoric is rich in precedent. From antiquity the orator was taught to amplify his arguments and so impress them on the memory and understanding of his auditors through appeals to the senses and the concomitant arousing of the passions. Thus, to amplify the orator had to know the nature of human psychology. Plato had said that the rhetorician must be an expert on the soul; Aristotle's major work on human emotions, outside *De Anima*, appears in the *Rhetoric*; Cicero had discussed the passions at great length, and left the *Tusculan Disputations* for the edification of later generations. But moral questions surrounding the passions, particularly that willful arousing of the passions which was part of the rhetorician's task, had never been easy for even the greatest minds to solve. The solution which the Stoics offered simply proved untenable for most sorts and conditions of men. By the time of the Renaissance, moral questions surrounding the use of the passions had become particularly sharp, for the questions had been fused with issues central in religious controversies. In brief, amplification meant the use of what today we shall call "imagery"; any use of imagery meant a direct appeal to the senses: the senses, in Renaissance psychology, were the gateway to the passions, whose force could subvert the operations of reason; and the *unfettered* operations of reason had by the seventeenth century become as crucial to religious salvation as to scientific discovery.

Frances Yates, in her study of the art of memory, examines many of the religious issues surrounding the rhetorical doctrine of amplification but without centering on that doctrine.[13] *Memoria*, as Miss Yates shows, was as deeply involved in occult philosophies as it was traditionally the fifth office of rhetoric. As an office of rhetoric, it shared with amplification a reliance upon images and their concomitant arousing of passions. So far as religious controversies were concerned, throughout the Renaissance the Catholics continued the ancient insistence that abstract thought is best grasped when given some more or less tangible embodiment, and some argued that the passions if well directed by reason were potentially instruments of salvation. On the other hand, the Puritans, in their eagerness to be taught by the Ramists (whom they saw as disciples of a great "Protestant martyr"), appeared to exalt "logic" over "rhetoric" and to become militant iconoclasts, preferring plainness and shunning sensuousness in any form. However this iconoclasm, which leads to the substitution of geometrical diagrams for more sensuous figures or for words as aids to thought (and so looks back to the medieval symbolic logicians and forward to the great "mathematizing" of thought in the seventeenth and eighteenth centuries), was a tradition within which the Ramists were perhaps merely unwitting subsidiaries. The force of this tradition, moreover, continued much longer than the force of the Puritans' iconoclasm, regardless of how urgently they continued to rain blows upon *graven* images. Later Puritans were ultimately more attracted by the notion that man's sensuousness does allow him to perceive God's handiwork in nature, God's will at work in man's surroundings; and because these

13. Frances A. Yates, *The Art of Memory* (Chicago, 1966).

phenomena were to be interpreted rationally, the problem of at least allowing for man's sensuousness was again—for the Puritans as for the Catholics—referred to the operations of his rational soul.

The Ramists simply dropped the problem by applying two strategies. Whereas rhetorical and Hermetic traditions had used sensuous images as a memory aid, the Ramists, with their drive toward simplification, insisted that whatever is well arranged is easy to remember and that whatever follows "natural method" is well arranged—and they thereby buried amplification along with *memoria* in *dispositio*, and in consequence avoided moral issues surrounding the use of the passions. Secondly, the Ramists also silently avoided these moral issues through their overriding concern with making specialties out of the various disciplines of human knowledge—turning those disciplines into compartments. The passions themselves were being assigned to a new compartment, which today we call "psychology" and which received its first scientific treatment in 1649 by that great "methodist," Descartes. Thanks largely to the Ramists, instruction in the passions became no longer part of the rhetorician's discipline and remained excluded until the end of the eighteenth century. Right in the middle of the period encompassed, a major rhetorician overtly declined to discuss the passions, as a subject which "belonged elsewhere"[14]—a statement which in historical perspective seems strange indeed.

There are two possible exceptions to these observations, the first less important for this study than the second. Some mention of the passions was frequently made in discussions of *pronuntiatio*. Yet of all the offices *pronuntiatio* came next to *memoria* in virtually disappearing, this time through inattention, and *pronuntiatio* itself eventually became something of a compartmentalized specialty in the so-called "Elocutionary Movement" of the eighteenth century. Secondly, as we shall see, though *instruction* in the use of the passions was no longer part of the rhetorician's purview, some consideration of the passions became possible through a curious hiatus in rhetorical theory which occurred in the seventeenth century when rhetorical theory merged with a certain devotional practice.

To approach the characteristics of this hiatus, let us note that the disappearance from rhetoric of doctrines of amplification—particularly as that disappearance meant also the disappearance of doctrines on the use of the passions—illuminates the monologic, inner-dialogic

14. Bernard Lamy, *The Art of Speaking* (London, 1676), Fourth Part, p. 135.

character of Renaissance poetry, like those monologues and soliloquies which are the subject of many essays in this book. These genres, which derived more from devotional practice than rhetorical theory, may be seen not merely as fashions but as moral necessities. For the contemplative stance which the Renaissance inherited from medieval piety tended to neutralize philosophical objections to the sensuous nature of discourse presented in that stance, its use of images, its arousal of passions. The contemplative speaker, at least, had no overt designs on his audience, who were acknowledged merely to be in a kind of third-person, overhearing position while the speaker addressed himself, his soul, the obviously imagined presence of his loved one, or God. True, some early Puritans sought to smash the images even in contemplative discourse. But, as noted earlier, Puritans eventually moderated their stand on sensuousness so long as deference was made to man's faculty for rational interpretation; and, in the language arts, perhaps because the contemplative stance was such an even counterpart of that intense individuality, that "personal salvation" which the Puritans prized, or perhaps because the arousing of passions in "mental prayer" as well as in sermons was demonstrably effective in leading others to their "personal" savior, by the time of Richard Baxter's monumental work in 1650 even this foremost Puritan sanctioned the use of passions and images in discourse, if done rationally and prayerfully, and above all if done within the limits of pious contemplation.[15]

The argument concerning the moral necessity for the contemplative stance in communication is one which I have tried to advance elsewhere.[16] In the present study we are concerned with the relationship between poetry and rhetorical theory. As we shall see, in a book on the passions early in the seventeenth century, the contemplative stance

15. Richard Baxter, *The Saints Everlasting Rest* (London, 1650).
16. "Rhetoric and Meditation: Three Case Studies," *Journal of Medieval and Renaissance Studies* 1 (1971): 45–58. The present study, like this earlier one, is deeply indebted to Louis L. Martz's description of the connections between the contemplative stance in devotional manuals and that kind of poetry which he calls "meditative" (*Poetry of Meditation* [New Haven, 1954; 2d ed., 1962]), and to U. Milo Kaufmann, *The Pilgrim's Progress and Traditions in Puritan Meditation* (New Haven, 1966). Douglas L. Peterson has related the "plain style" in the English lyric to the Christian "Contemplative Ideal" inherited from the Middle Ages in *The English Lyric from Wyatt to Donne* (Princeton, 1967). The popularity of contemplation as a style of behavior and discourse in the late sixteenth century has been noted by many scholars; one of the most interesting recent discussions is to be found in Bridget Gellert Lyons' description of the relationship between contemplation and the fashion of melancholy (*Voices of Melancholy* [New York, 1971]).

was overtly acknowledged as a part of rhetorical practice, and in the middle of the seventeenth century Obadiah Walker became the first rhetorician to locate the contemplative stance at the very center of *inventio*. In this way, rhetorical theory assimilated something which is totally alien to its traditionally "public" character and in so doing moved closer to the increasingly contemplative practice of the poets. Looking from another angle, one might state that the rhetoricians found in the contemplative stance what they missed when they were deprived of doctrines of amplification. They found, that is, in the contemplative stance a new, philosophically "safe" and intellectually secure way of considering speaker-audience relationships and the vexing problem of using the passions. Nonetheless, this remains a discovery which, though it brought rhetoric closer to poetry than it had been since the time of Wyatt, utterly transformed the traditional character of rhetorical theory—even beyond anything the Ramists had done.

Contemplation (or meditation, the terms may be used interchangeably) is totally alien to the nature of traditional rhetoric. The former is an art of introspection, whereas the latter had always urged the orator to look outward, to keep his thoughts continually on his actual audience. Contemplation has as its primary aim personal, private devotion, and only secondarily the aim of moving an overhearing audience. The aims of rhetoric were quite the reverse; and the rhetor's audience never *overheard* him, except superficially during an apostrophe. It was the matter of the passions which disrupted the order of these two aims. To repeat, rhetorical theory had, until the time of the Ramists, offered instruction in how to appeal to the passions of individual members of the audience—the various psychological characters of which Aristotle wrote and with which Theophrastus created a literary genre. But by the seventeenth century, any practical instruction in the use of the passions could not be offered in rhetoric—again, there were too many unanswered questions of a pedagogical nature concerning the overlapping of disciplines or of a moral nature concerning the inciting of passions in others through sensuousness. And there were simply no rhetoricians around who were equal to the challenge posed by these questions; even Bacon had to fall back on clichés concerning the rational control over man's virtually ungovernable imagination and insist that it was the "proper" function of rhetoric to make man's imagination answerable to the dictates of reason.[17] The vast rhetorical heritage was itself notably weak on this point. Further, although great rhetoricians such as Cicero and Quintilian had insisted that the orator must experience the passion he would have his audience feel, none offered a systematic method whereby the orator could work up the intended passion within himself. However, *devotional* theory, particularly after the appearance of St. Ignatius's *Spiritual Exercises*, did offer such a method—even going so far as to catalog the various passions and making procedural the steps one took in experiencing each in his private "mental" prayers. Thus, practical instruction in the use of the passions, the imagination, images—what traditional rhetoric had called "amplification"—was not available in rhetoric but was available in devotional theory, which had the additional feature of offering systematic instruction in the private experiencing of emotions; however, devotional theory offered a means of communicating not with others but with oneself or with God. When devotional theory converged with rhetorical theory, traditional rhetoric was necessarily transformed and in a very fundamental way.

The transformation might be summarized by noting the change in audience considerations. The Ramists had virtually banished the audience by contemptuously considering them unnatural to the conditions of thought. The meditators in effect restored the audience. In devotional theory, the audience became God. In rhetorical theory as transformed by meditative practice and theory, the audience became an audience within, discoverable through introspection.

The first major English writer on the passions—Thomas Wright, in *The Passions of the Minde in Generall* (1604)—was the first theorist to force a convergence of rhetoric and contemplation. Wright himself was a recusant priest, an ex-Jesuit; though he sought to give method to his discussion of the passions, he was no specialist in psychology, but a "divine," whose discussion easily embraced religion and rhetoric. He is, consequently, the only theorist in his period to offer extensive, practical instruction in how to arouse passions in oneself as well as in others. The longest example which Wright offers of a practical method of arousing passions concerns the most important of all the passions,

17. In Bacon's words, "The duty and office of Rhetoric is to apply *Reason to Imagination* for the better moving of the will" (*Advancement of Learning*, Book II); for a discussion of this definition, see Karl R. Wallace, *Francis Bacon on Communication and Rhetoric* (Chapel Hill, 1943), p. 31.

love, and that method is contemplation. Wright begins his example with this passage:

> Giue me leaue O louing God, to vent out and euaporat the affects of the heart, and see if I can incense my soule to loue thee intirely and incessantly, and that all those motiues which stir up mine affections to loue thee, may be meanes to inflame all their hearts which read this treatise penned by me.[18]

Thus, Wright clearly indicates, here and throughout his book, that meditation has rhetorical implications, that devotional theory offers a way of communicating with others. One might be reminded of a similar passage in St. Augustine's *Confessions*, in which Augustine offers his life-story as an example to all who may "light" upon his writings.[19] But St. Augustine wrote another work on rhetoric, *De doctrina christiana*, in which, although the major system of *inventio* is the contemplative interpretation of the Scriptures or of any of God's "signs," rhetoric pertains (in Book IV) specifically to a public speaking situation, a direct confrontation of speaker and audience. Not so for Wright. Rhetoric and meditation have become conflated, a convergence virtually forced by Wright through his paradoxically traditional and at the time unfashionable insistence upon rhetoric as a nexus of logic, amplification, and practical psychology:

> Passions then must be moued with vrgent reasons, reasons vrging proceed frō solid amplifications, amplifications are gathered from common places, common places fit for oratoricall perswasion concerne a part of Rhetoricke called Inuentio. (pp. 184–185)

The commonplaces which Wright lists are Agricolan—short, pithy, easy to be remembered—but the practical method which immediately follows this list, and which is also designed as an aid to invention, even for "oratorical perswasion," is the method of meditation: one composes by passionately contemplating his subject, and his finished discourse may either directly (oratorically) or indirectly (meditatively) address his actual audience.

18. Thomas O. Sloan, ed. (Urbana, 1971), p. 193.
19. "To whom tell I this? not to Thee, my God; but before Thee to mine own kind, even to that small portion of mankind as may light upon these writings of mine. And to what purpose? that whosoever reads this, may think *out of what depths we are to cry unto Thee*." *The Confessions of St. Augustine*, tr. Edward B. Pusey, in *The Harvard Classics*, ed. Charles W. Eliot (New York, 1909), VII, 25.

I would be incorrect to regard Wright as an innovator. None of his writings show fresh, innovative thought. His contemporaries regarded him primarily as a controversialist. True, he was the first writer in his period overtly to regard contemplation, or meditation, as a rhetorical act. But surely in this matter he was only giving voice to something which was already in the wind. As we shall see, the next convergence of meditation and rhetoric in theory occurred over fifty years later—with no mention of Wright's contribution. In articulating attitudes already in motion, Wright at least makes clear two meditative emphases in rhetorical theory: one invents by looking within, and one speaks from a contemplative stance in order to reach those overhearing him.

This "rhetoric of meditation" is far closer, I would argue, to poetic practice than the Ramist theory was. Of course, there are apparent similarities between the Ramists and the meditators. The Ramists believed that one invented alone, silently even, by drawing his subject through the ten topics, or commonplaces, not turning to "commonplace books" but activating his own store of knowledge to find his thought and then using *dispositio* to shape that thought—and, if necessary, *elocutio* to clothe it. Father Ong explains,

> The Ramist felt less need to rely on the collections of material from authors in commonplace books, for he thought of himself as securing his arguments from the "nature of things," with which his mind somehow came into direct contact.[20]

But though one looks within for his materials, the Ramist system is far more impersonal and dispassionate than the meditative. The meditators, particularly the Ignatians, activated the imagination and utilized images and passions from the outset of the inventive process. Furthermore, it is true that the contemplative stance is itself not too far from the view fostered by the Ramist outlook. Again, Father Ong puts the matter:

> The Ramist arts of discourse are monologue arts. . . . In rhetoric, obviously someone had to speak, but in the characteristic outlook, fostered by the Ramist rhetoric, the speaking is directed to a world where even persons respond only as objects—that is, say nothing back.[21]

20. Walter J. Ong, S.J., "Tudor Writings on Rhetoric," *SR* 15 (1968): 63.
21. Ong, *Ramus, Method, and the Decay of Dialogue*, p. 287.

But it would be more precise to say that within the rhetoric of meditation a *dialogue* occurs. For intuitions, even passions, become participating personae—although the speaker himself may not seem to be directly addressing anyone. As in the Donne poem, the presence of the other is vital to the creative process—even though, in a meditative poem, that presence may be only imagined or not overtly acknowledged.

Some of these distinctions and characteristics may be illustrated by examining the first sonnet in Sidney's *Astrophil and Stella*:

Sonnet I. (1582)

Loving in truth, and faine in verse my love to show,
That the deare She might take some pleasure of my paine:
Pleasure might cause her reade, reading might make her know,
Knowledge might pitie winne, and pitie grace obtaine,
   I sought fit words to paint the blackest face of woe,
Studying inventions fine, her wits to entertaine:
Oft turning others' leaves, to see if thence would flow
Some fresh and fruitfull showers upon my sunne-burn'd braine.
   But words came halting forth, wanting Invention's stay,
Invention, Nature's child, fled step-dame Studie's blowes,
And others' feete still seem'd but strangers in my way.
Thus great with child to speake, and helplesse in my throwes,
   Biting my trewand pen, beating myselfe for spite,
   'Foole,' said my Muse to me, 'looke in thy heart, and write.'[22]

The poem *seems* almost thoroughly Ramistic. In considering this point, one might consider also that it may indeed have been reasons other than patronage and favor which caused one of the first major English Ramists, Abraham Fraunce, to name his treatise on rhetoric after Sidney's longest work, and so offer to the world *The Arcadian Rhetorike* (1588), illustrated with passages from Sidney's writings and dedicated to the sister of the then-deceased poet. In this first poem from *Astrophil and Stella*, the speaker insists that Invention is "Nature's child"—not nature herself, but a near-relation, a common observation that the Ramists were peculiarly fond of underscoring—as Fraunce, for example, in *The Lawiers Logike* (1588) states that the precepts of logic were "collected out of, and always must be comformable vnto those sparkes of naturall reason, not lurking in the obscure head-

22. From *The Poems of Sir Philip Sidney*, ed. William A. Ringler, Jr. (Oxford, 1962), p. 165.

peeces of one or two loytering Fryers, but manifestly appearing in the monuments and disputations of excellent authors" (fol. 2). In Sidney's poem, "step-dame Study" is not the natural mother of "invention" and seems to harbor a kind of scholastic resentment against the latter, perhaps because "Nature's child" is more ingenuous and simple than subtle and complex. Secondly, like the Ramists, Sidney's speaker presupposes a linear method of composition: one must complete invention (and disposition) first before turning to elocution. Sidney's speaker did just the opposite, and consequently "words come halting forth" because they lacked the "stay" of a true invention. In other words, the creative process depicted in this poem implies a linear divorce between thought and speech. A similar kind of divorce is implied or stated in other poems in the *Astrophil and Stella* sequence—and few sequences of the period are so rich in observations on how poetry is best created. In the "Fifth Song," for example, the speaker states, "While favor fed my hope, delight with hope was brought, / Thought waited on delight, and speech did follow thought. . . ." The speaker of Sonnet 1 made the mistake of going to "rhetoric" first, searching for words to express his thought, but his search is complicated by the fact that he lacks a genuine thought, a true invention. Thirdly, a true invention, the "Muse" insists, is to be found within (in the mind's analysis of a subject, the Ramists would argue) and not externally in the collection of material by other authors. Indeed, others' inventions, including their prosodical feet, caused the speaker to stumble in the process of his search. As we have observed, the Ramists taught that one should draw his material out of the subject itself, securing his arguments from the very "nature of things." Throughout the *Astrophil and Stella* sequence there is the constant assurance that the best words are found by turning one's thoughts within, to contemplate the object itself:

> —in *Stella's* face I reed
> What Love and Beautie be, then all my deed
> But Copying is, what in her Nature writes.
>
> (3)
>
> 'Scholler,' said Love, 'bend hitherward your wit.'
>
> (19)

But at least one feature of the poem is decidedly non-Ramistic. It is far richer in a sense of audience or presence of others, both real and imagined, than the dispassionate opening of boxes that Ramists advised for the process of invention. And it is, consequently, passionate. The speaker begins and ends in recalled "paine." At the end of the poem, the Muse tells the speaker to look in his heart, where the Petrarchan lover conventionally kept the image of his beloved; but the heart is also the "lodging" place of the passions in Renaissance psychology[23] and consequently the very last place where a Ramist speaker, Muse or otherwise, should urge the "inventor" to search. Unless one wishes to argue that Sidney uses Ramism as his "norm" to judge the folly of his speaker, as if Sidney were dramatizing how the speaker's passions misled his wit by creating a personification ("Muse") which sanctioned the intensification of his passions, one cannot call the poem strictly Ramistic.

I should insist that the poem says something about *inventio* that is not to be found in the rhetoric books of the time; above all, it is not to be found in the Ramist books. In sexual terms similar to those which will be used by Donne thirty years later in *The Second Anniversary* the male speaker is pregnant with a child conceived in union with his Muse and he must body forth and deliver this child with the only materials this *mater* can provide, words. This is hardly a dispassionate artificial insemination produced by looking at a subject through a list of the ten commonplaces or through an impersonal concept of nature. In the passage quoted earlier from *The Lawiers Logike,* Fraunce continues,

> Art, which first was but the scholler of nature, is now become the maystres of nature, and as it were a Glasse wherein shee seeing and viewing herselfe, may washe out those spottes and blemishes of naturall imperfection. For there is no one particuler nature so constant and absolute, but by examining and perusing her owne force, shee may bee bettered: no nature so weake and imperfit, which by the helpe of Art is not confirmed. (Fol. 2)

Fraunce's position, characteristic of the Ramists, is closer to the Rationalist poetic that today we term "neo-classical" than to the poetic of Sidney and Donne or of all those late Renaissance poets whose sensibility found its true art in a convergence of traditional rhetoric and meditation.

---

23. See Thomas Wright, pp. 32–36. Ringler confuses the issues by taking "heart" to mean "the mind in general" (p. 459).

In his recent book *The Veil of Allegory*, Michael Murrin argues that Sidney marked a turning in English poetry from the language of allegory to a language more appropriate to oratory.[24] But it would appear that the creative process underlying Sidney's poetry as well as the stance employed in many of his poems are less oratorical than they are contemplative in nature. In the sonnet just reviewed, the speaker employs a contemplative stance. He seems to be soliloquizing, addressing no one in particular—or, at most, reviewing an experience for the benefit of an almost casual audience. In its indirect mode of address, its resonant solitariness, the poem is imitative of the creative process which is its subject. Both in his mode of address as well as in the act of creation which he describes, the speaker, as Douglas L. Peterson has noted, seems to follow the advice which Musidorus in Sidney's *Arcadia* offers to Pyrochles: "Separate yourself a little (if it be possible) and let your owne mind look to your own proceedings."[25] Perhaps the poem itself is merely a strategy, designed to impress upon readers—and above all on "Stella"—the deep honesty and sincerity of "Astrophil's" emotion. If so, those qualities only enhance the importance of contemplation, within which one comes face to face with something in himself. And, as is usually true of poets and never true of Ramists, this contemplation is filled with voices. As evidenced by this poem, the ultimate effect of the contemplative stance is similar to the effect Morris Croll attributes to the Baroque style in prose: "to portray, not a thought, but a mind thinking, or in Pascal's words, *la peinture de la pensée*."[26] But this portrait is a visual representation of resonance as the solitary mind echoes with talk and is profoundly moved by its sense of others.

By the middle of the seventeenth century, rhetoricians began to

24. (Chicago, 1969), pp. 169–71. Moreover, Murrin notes that Sidney as well as Donne are difficult to classify, in part because they were something of transitional figures (pp. 184–95). Sidney and Donne may have been transitional figures for other reasons as well, as I have been suggesting in the present essay. In addition, both were at the center of such conflicting interests as those represented by the Ramists on the one hand and the occultists on the other. Frances Yates (p. 283) has suggested that Ramism and Brunianism may have competed for Sidney's favor. Donne's occult characteristics seem as obvious as Sidney's Ramism, and his Ramism (or at least those qualities that may be loosely called Ramistic) as subtle as Sidney's Brunist qualities.

25. Peterson, p. 191.

26. Morris W. Croll, "The Baroque Style in Prose," *Style, Rhetoric, and Rhythm*, ed. J. Max Patrick and Robert O. Evans, with John M. Wallace and R. J. Shoeck (Princeton, 1966), p. 210.

catch up with developments in poetry. If Thomas Wright was the first man in the seventeenth century overtly to encompass the art of meditation—that is, the contemplative stance—within the art of rhetoric, the second person to do so is a man whose place within the history of rhetoric has been well acknowledged: Obadiah Walker, in *Some Instructions Concerning the Art of Oratory* (1659).[27] Howell had described Walker as one of the four "chief English rhetoricians of the Neo-Ciceronian school during the seventeenth century."[28] Like a Ramist, Walker divides his art of rhetoric into two parts but these two parts are Invention and Elocution, not Elocution and Delivery. Howell calls him a Neo-Ciceronian because Walker in his discussion of these two parts manages to discuss all five of the traditional parts of rhetoric. But Walker does this in a distinctly non-traditional way. Walker's contribution to rhetorical theory does not lie in his restoration of a Ciceronian wholeness after the rampages of Ramism. Rather, it lies in his unique and wholly non-traditional discussion of Invention. Invention, for Walker, is no longer a way of analyzing a case or of finding a pre-existing thought. It is rather a genuinely creative act, an act of conceiving akin to that very process which *poets* had called "invention." And it is as humane, as personalized, and as contemplative as any to be found in the descriptions of the process in the poetic practice of the time.

We have already remarked that the Ramists combined judgment with disposition—probably with good cause, for one must judge as he arranges and arrange as he judges. But it was Walker's insight to consider judgment and disposition as offices of Invention. What Walker does is to place at the center of the creative process a discourse-maker who is at once his own speaker and his own audience, a creator who is at the same time his own critic. Thus, Walker's rhetoric is for a new age of self-awareness even among orators. Like the medieval contemplator or the Ignatian mediator, the orator is to use his own self-awareness as a guide through the woods of invention—as the guide that earlier rhetoricians had insisted was to be found in the topics and the commonplaces. To use the jargon of our day, one might say that the orator or writer was taught to create discourse through "intra-personal

27. There are two editions of Walker's book: 1659 and 1682. The second made some minor additions to the doctrines on style and pronunciation, but left the invention theory unchanged. All quotations are from the first edition.

28. Wilbur Samuel Howell, *Logic and Rhetoric in England, 1500–1700* (Princeton, 1956), p. 325.

communication." One student has come up with a much better phrase to describe the phenomenon: dialogic invention.[29]

At first Walker sounds like a traditional rhetorician reeling under the impact of Ramism and of the moral questions surrounding the arts of communication in the Elizabethan period. He advises the orator to let his imagination be guided in a solitary way by his own reason and by the standard commonplaces. But, in a movement imitative of the very practice he advocates, he then turns on that advice and urges the orator to set down his "inventions" in a haphazard fashion, which he may then later review and order:

> It is convenient there fore, often to break off the thread you are spin-
> ning; and set your imagination on work afresh, upon some other
> new circumstance, as if nothing at all had been meditated before. All
> which variety of incohering is to be joynted and set together in the
> second review. (P. 13)

I do not find in rhetorical theory before Walker anything like this reliance upon the fertility of the orator's disordered imagination. Certain-
ly order is to be applied in the ensuing critical review, the vestigial act of *dispositio*. But *inventio* no longer relies upon system, either that fatherly guidance offered by Cicero or the rigid method propounded by the Ramists. In another passage, in which Walker cautions against the early use of other men's writings in the process of *inventio*—
shades of Sidney—he urges that the mind be given free reign to follow the devices and desires of its own inherent nature:

> For, if you exercise your own Meditation, after you have read theirs,
> most-what, the wit is not so active and loving of trouble; but that,
> like other bodies in motion, it will follow a Tract and Rote made be-
> fore it, rather than its own Biass, and Force. (P. 14)

The words "mediated" and "Meditation" in these passages are important clues to Walker's conceptual model of the rhetorical situation. The model is about as far removed from the classical speaker-
audience situation as one can imagine. For one thing, the orator is essentially a writer. In this respect, Walker follows developments given strong impetus by the Ramists. No longer is the orator seen as one who composes most of his oration orally in the presence of his auditors. Rather, any oral composition is undertaken alone, unsyste-

29. Diane Keane, "Dialogic Invention: Four Enlightenment Theories," unpub. Ph.D. dissertation (Berkeley: University of California, 1971).

matically (here Walker parts company with the Ramists), giving fancy free rein; system, order, method, are applied in the act of committing these fanciful thoughts to writing—all before the discourse is offered to the "auditors," who either read it themselves or hear it read aloud by the "orator." Within these conceptions, and most likely by virtue of them, Walker can give some attention to amplification and, however fleeting, to the passions and the senses. Secondly, in Walker's theory, one learns about his audience through introspection. One does not analyze an external audience, or imagine a public situation within which he will deliver his oration. Rather, he "invents" by means of an inner, solitary dialogue within which he views, reviews, and revises—a dialogue akin to the medieval one between Self, or Body, and Soul, or the Renaissance one between the meditator and God. The contemplative stance has, for Walker, moved to the very heart of the creative process.

For example, in discussing style, Walker teaches that the invented matter is to be varied for the sake of the "auditor's" attention, memory, and passion. But he provides no means for analyzing that audience, no suggestion that they should be divided into psychological types, or characters, each with his own set of motivations that must be appealed to. Rather, one is to test out his style either by allowing a few friends to read his discourse or, more significantly, by reading it aloud to himself. Walker describes the latter process, when the orator reads his own words aloud to himself:

> The soul, receiving them more remotely, conveyed to the ear by the voice, and from this returned to her, as it were, from abroad, and that onely in a transient sound, sits now as the most disinterested Arbiter, and impartial judge of her own works, that she can be. (P. 115)

When compared with classical rhetorical theory, this passage is astounding. It reveals the extent to which the eye had replaced the ear as the immediate entry to the soul. When compared with Wilsonian rhetorical theory, the passage reveals the extent to which rhetoric had incorporated tradition-shattering elements. However, ironically, those who placed meditation at the center of their rhetorical theory and so shattered its traditional basis, were the only ones in the period who managed to keep such traditional parts of rhetoric as *inventio* and *pronuntiatio* together.

Personalized, passionate, and unsystematic—these characteristics would make any creative theory differ from the Ramists'. But when the meditators shaped these characteristics and placed them at the center of a new poetic/rhetoric, they transformed traditional doctrines of public discourse more profoundly than the crude disruptions of the Ramists. Meditation marked a point where poetry and rhetoric crossed —and where each was transformed before their subsequent divergence.

In tracing these developments, one may venture that the effects of printing may have had something of a determining role. Again, our emblem, the Valladolid retable, comes to mind: Gabriel's words are represented in script and Mary holds an opened book. But the Spanish painter, regardless of how much he obviously prized literacy and acknowledged its centrality within Christian traditions, could not have foreseen the tremendous revolution in literacy which was to occur in the following century. Even orators, preachers, and poets would be broadcast through the printing press. Print itself would become the major "amplifying" system, delivering a speaker's thoughts to his audience without relying upon effective gesture, lively voice, or in some cases the mysteries of imagery. But, more than manuscript, print not only enhanced a speaker's removal from his audience, it forced his removal from his discourse itself. A "speaker" whose discourse became printed had in effect created something which could be duplicated by a machine, something that was more like an object or an artifact than like the existential process of speech or the greatly individualized production of manuscripts. Print was surely one of the many causative factors that made the age demand a new rhetoric. When that new rhetoric appeared, contemplation became its keynote—first, the systematic solitariness of the Ramists and then the passionate, personalized, resonant contemplation of Wright and Walker; even overheard discourse became a rhetorical act—the actual audience became a third person—and these views made the rhetor's creative process resemble the poet's more than it had after Wilson. When Shaftesbury in the first years of the eighteenth century advised the "author" to create his discourse through a process of solitary dialogue and advised all men to vanquish the allurements of appetite through "inward rhetoric,"[30] one must think of the theories of Walker and the art of meditation— and behind those of the systematization and impersonality which at first marked the major rhetorical theories in the English Renaissance

30. Anthony, Earl of Shaftesbury, *Characteristics of Men, Manners, Opinions, Times*, ed. John M. Robertson and intro. by Stanley Grean (Indianapolis, 1964), I–II, see esp. pp. 111–12, 123.

and removed them from their contemporary poetic practice. But in rhetorical theory the unifying contemplative strain was broken after Shaftesbury and lost among the tones and stances of the ensuing age of reason.

Index